WITHDRAWN

SCHOOLCRAFT COLLEGE

W9-BSU-701

Fresh Water

WITHDRAWN

Fresh Water

WOMEN WRITING ON THE GREAT LAKES

Alison Swan, *Editor*

Michigan State University Press • *East Lansing*

PS
562
.F74
2006
c. 2

Copyright © 2006 by Alison Swan

♾ The paper used in this publication meets the minimum requirements
of ANSI/NISO Z39.48-1992 (R 1997) (Permanence of Paper).

 Michigan State University Press
East Lansing, Michigan 48823-5245
www.msupress.msu.edu

Printed and bound in the United States of America.

12 11 10 09 08 07   2 3 4 5 6 7 8 9 10

LIBRARY OF CONGRESS CATALOGING-IN-PUBLICATION DATA
Fresh water : women writing on the Great Lakes / Alison Swan, editor.
p. cm.
ISBN-13: 978-0-87013-789-1 (pbk. : alk. paper)
ISBN-10: 0-87013-789-1 (pbk. : alk. paper) 1. American prose literature—Great Lakes Region
(North America) 2. Canadian prose literature—Great Lakes Region (North America) 3. Women
authors, American—Homes and haunts—Great Lakes Region (North America) 4. Women
authors, Canadian—Homes and haunts—Great Lakes Region (North America) 5. Great Lakes
Region (North America) I. Swan, Alison.
PS562.F74 2006
810.9'97—dc22
2006017110

Cover design by Heather Truelove Aiston
Book design by Sharp Des!gns, Lansing, Michigan

Cover art is "Changes", 42" × 60" oil on canvas, ©1987 Ann Mikolowski. Used by permission of
Ken Mikolowski.

g green press Michigan State University Press is a member of the Green Press Initiative and is com-
INITIATIVE mitted to developing and encouraging ecologically responsible publishing practices.
For more information about the Green Press Initiative and the use of recycled paper in book pub-
lishing, please visit *www.greenpressinitiative.org.*

For all Great Lakes women, however near or far from the Lakes, especially Sophia Grace, who makes them new

Contents

GHOSTS

UPLAKE AND DOWN

Introduction

One quiet fall day, on the strand near Saugatuck on Lake Michigan's southeastern shore, I find a fist of tiny mollusk invaders, dozens of zebra mussels, so-called for their black-and-white-striped shells. Each is smaller than a plum pit, but there are millions of them scouring the waters of the Great Lakes, crowding out native species and allowing sunlight to penetrate so deeply that water-temperature patterns are being altered more quickly than local fish populations can adapt.

Zebra mussels were discovered in Lake St. Clair, a (very) wide spot in the river between Lakes Huron and Erie, in the late 1980s, right about the time I was admitting to the fact that South Florida's Atlantic coast could not replace the Great Lakes' shores as my home landscape. Scientists believe the mussels were probably dumped in ballast water from a cargo ship hailing from a fresh-water port near the Caspian Sea. They've since spread throughout the Great Lakes basin.

When my daughter Sophie and I play in the waves at Saugatuck, we're pelted with molecules that will flow back up the lobe of Lake Michigan, through the Straits of Mackinac, down Lake Huron and the St. Clair River to Lake St. Clair. There, some will crash against the breakwater, where my child self watched freighters cross and crisscross in the shipping channel cut through the shallow lake, uplake to the ports of Bay City, Duluth, Green Bay, Chicago, and downlake to Cleveland, Buffalo, Toronto—some all the way out through the mouth of the St. Lawrence River. Especially when the vessels were ocean-going with curved prows and foreign flags, I felt like the world was passing by.

Compared to the Great Lakes, Lake St. Clair is tiny; for me, however, it might as well have been the sea. Its opposite shore lies hidden around the curve of the earth, and somewhere over that mesmerizing water horizon was Canada. I imagined myself hundreds of nautical miles north to the headwaters of Superior, and hundreds more east to the Gulf of St. Lawrence, where fresh water from the heart of North America empties into the Atlantic.

The waters of Lakes Superior, Michigan, Huron, Erie, Ontario, and their various connecting waterways function as a single body of water. Geologists call this single body of water a river. Early French explorers, marveling at the lack of salt in apparently boundless bodies of water, called them *les mers douces*—"sweet seas"; locals often call them "the big lake" and "the big water," as did and do the local American Indians. The truth is, the Great Lakes are unique in the world. Lake Baikal effectively matches Superior in surface area and holds fully twice as much water, but it lies alone in its Siberian landscape. Perhaps this uniqueness explains why the Great Lakes are mostly bereft of their own language. *Lacustrine* ("of, relating to, formed in, or growing in lakes") nomenclature doesn't exactly apply to the Great Lakes, nor does *riverine* or *marine*.

Since the earliest incursions of Europeans, looking for passage to China about four hundred years ago, the lakes have been exploited more than they've been honored, celebrated, and until recently, studied, at least by the people who took them as their New World. The first incarnation of the city of Chicago was situated with its back to Lake Michigan. Stand on any of the lakes' shores, turn your back to the land and face the lake with its big sky and big weather, and only superlatives will come to mind. That big weather was endemic, and until recently, not so easily evaded.

It is fashionable to talk about the interconnectedness of all things; I believe this interconnection is inescapable. For me, however, the scale of the connection between, say, the subtropical verdure of the Everglades and the sometimes frozen, sometimes sweltering peninsulas of Michigan is too large to feel anything but hypothetical. The connection between Lake Superior and Lake Michigan, between Lake Michigan and Lake St. Clair, is not. From there, it is not too far of a leap to imagine my connection to the Caspian Sea.

The women whose Great Lakes words are collected here hail from as far away as Norway. Many, like Linda Nemec Foster, Gail Griffin, Judith Minty,

Anne-Marie Oomen, and Susan Power, were born in the Great Lakes basin and grew up knowing one or more of the lakes as intimately as family. Others, like Heather Sellers, Sue William Silverman, and Leigh Allison Wilson, came to the lakes in adulthood and forged with one or more of them a bond as fierce and complicated as the connections we share with kin. A few, like Anna Mills and Diane Wakoski, probably wouldn't describe themselves as intimates of any of the lakes, but their essays reveal the familiarity born of attentiveness.

Of course this book is our invitation to revel in the pleasures of reading, to help us shape a language for the Great Lakes. It is also our invitation to deepen your acquaintance with Lakes Superior, Michigan, Huron, Erie, and Ontario, the sweet seas that not so long ago were teeming with untainted fish, and drinkable, right from the shore.

I stoop to pick up the little bundle of water-slick zebra mussels from the sand where the waves have dropped it and examine it more closely. Halfheart-edly, with my fingers, I try to pry open a shell. It is locked shut, alive. To pry it open or smash it, I would need a tool. Of course I wonder about the glistening animals inside—interlopers all, but my neighbors, nonetheless. I will not disturb them further. When I lay the clump back down on the sand, I notice the incoming waves are full of thousands of empty zebra-mussel shells. Their pearly interiors and dark exteriors flicker a few inches below the surface of the blue-green water. Now some of the grains of sand that make up this Lake Michigan beach will come from mollusks native to the other side of the earth.

Fresh Water

Write what you know. And go on knowing only what
We know? And never know the lakeness of the lake?
— *Constance Merritt*

Comes

The shore of Lake Michigan at Evanston, Illinois, is lined with boulders. If you clamber around on the rocks, you'll find reject tombstones, half a name, half a date, etched into the stone. You'll see places where the stonecarver's tool slipped, places where the metal edge skritched out of control. You can touch these stones and wonder who they were meant for, wonder what stone rests upon what person now, wonder what date will be etched upon your own. Sometimes the lip of the water is dotted with dead fish, silvery, eyes pecked out, the stink mixing with the wet stone scent of the air. Sometimes you find a fish bone on the ground, a head, or a rib, something that surrounded a small thudding heart. Who could fathom how much this place will pull you after you've moved away? Who could understand how the waves still whisper "home."

—*Gayle Brandeis*

I am standing by the edge of the great lake, hauling up water, hands freezing, heart white-hot with wonder. How is it that what was once misery becomes pleasure? I'd come to look forward to the cold nights and cold mornings, to the forest noises and forest silences, to the creaking of my rough rope mattress, even to the scurrying of small critters at my feet: in short, the wigwam had become my home, and I tidied it every morning like a proud housewife.

—*Virginia Chase Sanderson*

As I walked into Room 101 that morning, I was taken aback by the stretch of blue water and sky that seemed to fill the room. It was as if my dying mother's bed was suspended in azure. These days, her mind seemed to carry her out across the Lake Michigan horizon to a land none of the rest of us could see. Her blue eyes were as deep and diaphanous as the water. Her face was gaunt, with pronounced cheek bones she once might have said would be good for sketching. I wondered what her artist's eye was seeing now.

—*Margo LaGattuta*

Mary Torsky had a lot of fishing secrets. One of them was where to get perch. Another was how to get them to bite. She reached into a gray burlap bag and pulled out a sparse handful of raw oatmeal which she casually tossed into the gentle waves lapping at the side of the craft. Anyone observing her next movement might have thought she was getting ready to start singing, because she began to lightly tap the bottom of the boat with her right foot. "That oughta make 'em come," she thought. She waited patiently.

—*Mary Ann Zink*

HOMES: Living with Lake Michigan

JUDITH MINTY

OMES: It was our third-grade lesson when we studied Michigan geography, our mnemonic device, a way to remember the names of those five Great Lakes that surround the peninsula where we lived: Huron, Ontario, Michigan, Erie, Superior. For me, I thought, they really were home—where I had originated, where I belonged.

"Look," I still say, even after having lived in states as remote from the lakes as California and Alaska, my right hand now raised in greeting, palm out, life line, heart line, fate line, the mounts of Venus, Mars, and Jupiter exposed for any stranger to study. "Homes," I say. "Mine." I wave my left hand around its partner, pointing to where each inland sea might be as if the hand was actually Michigan and surrounded by water.

I must have been nine when I first fell in love with one of those lakes. Each summer, my parents packed clothes and dishes, blankets, and pots and pans into the Blue Moon trailer that had languished all winter in our Detroit backyard. Then they hauled it and my younger brother and me a couple of hundred miles up Highway 27 and across the state to the shore of Lake Michigan for a glorious month of camping in the "wild."

How filled with joy I was to escape vacant-lot play and scrub baseball in the street, to exchange my predictable city life for the chance to encounter deer and raccoon and fox without a zoo fence separating us. "I'm headed for the center of HOMES," I boasted to those I was leaving behind, "right to its heart."

It never took long to settle into our trailer space at Ludington State Park, to string the cord for electricity and set up an awning over the picnic table. The camping area was, and still is, nestled in woods so dense that all human sound seems to be muted. Here, the rustle of a chipmunk scampering through the brush or the call of the white-throated sparrow are what the trees listen to. The park itself is a world of forest, sand dunes, and freshwater enchantment. As fast as we could, my brother and I changed into swimming suits, gathered shovels and pails and minnow nets, and made our way to the "big beach."

No sooner had I tested the water that first summer and inched from shore to stand knee-deep in its chill, no sooner had I felt those waves slapping at my skinny body, than I understood, even at nine years of age, that this expanse of churning, frothy lake, which spread as far as I could see, was alive, and too magnificent to be owned by anyone. It belonged only to itself. That summer I learned, too, how quickly Lake Michigan's mood could change from calm and serene to jolly and wavy to thunderingly violent. But it was already too late. I had given my heart away forever.

In 1960, after I'd married, and after my husband Ed and I lived briefly in Upper New York State, we returned to Michigan. We settled in Muskegon on the shore of Lake Michigan, where he had been born and where his family owned a manufacturing business. I was overjoyed to be near this water again. So was Ed, and we soon bought a small runabout that we motored around Muskegon Lake and, on calm days, out to Lake Michigan. As our family grew, so did the size of our boats. When we reached the point where we actually had a cruiser with bunks and galley as well as a head, we began to take trips to harbors further from home.

It was at about this time that I came to comprehend the magnetism of these sister lakes that encircle the hand of Michigan. I was struck dumb by northern lights as they rolled over me in monstrous abandon like twisted rainbows run amok. I followed stars on a compass course during midnight sails and suffered hallucinations of the land closing in around our boat. I turned my face to wind, rain, sleet, snow—the constancy of blue lake beyond, waves often reaching up and toward me in crashing whitecaps, sometimes in tremulous ripples. I saw waterspouts on the lake's surface, upside-down tornadoes spinning and dancing on a watery ballroom floor. And I felt the ghost-like shift and pull on our lines as a seiche crept into a northern harbor to lift us, then slowly drop us, at our slip.

I've been rocked in a cradle on these lakes, and I've been pulled by undertows and tossed by breakers. And yes—like many sailors—I've even survived a few of those frightening storms that seemingly appear from nowhere, unannounced.

Lake Michigan is 300 miles long, but extremely narrow in comparison—only 118 miles from Michigan to Wisconsin at its widest—so as storms build, wind moves off the lake's western shore and waves quickly grow to disproportionate heights, occurring in quick succession. In no time, sailors can find themselves in raging gales, tossed about, one wave after another threatening to capsize their boats, with no safe harbor in sight.

One August, nearly thirty years ago, Ed and I were returning to Lake Michigan with our twelve-year-old daughter Ann and her best friend Ellen in our thirty-three-foot shoal-draft sailboat after two weeks in Lake Huron's North Channel. We'd spent the night at Mackinac Island, and had risen early and set sail. The weather forecast was "sunny and warm." Summer was in its glory and so were we, carefree and young, tanned and full of vitality after having followed the wind to deserted islands and remote dockages of the north for so many days.

About 10 A.M., we passed under the Mackinac Bridge, a towering suspension bridge which stretches five miles across the Straits of Mackinac, connecting Michigan's upper and lower peninsulas. We were having a nearly perfect sail, moving along at six to ten knots, about as close to flying as you can get on a sailboat. The four of us were relaxed in the cockpit, lazing in our separate reveries. There was no engine sound, just an occasional flap of canvas and the swish of water being displaced by our hull. By noon, we'd headed west above Gray's Reef, keeping the lighthouse to port, and sailed into open seas.

Our destination was Beaver Island, three or four hours away, but we were planning to drop anchor for the night in a little cove off Garden Island, which is directly north of Beaver. Beaver Island is one of four large islands and a few very small, rocky islets clustered in the middle of Lake Michigan. The complex is approximately thirty-five miles northwest of Charlevoix, Michigan, and further than that from Wisconsin. Beaver, the only island with a harbor, or ferry and plane service, has the dubious distinction of being known as the sole self-proclaimed kingdom in the United States. In the 1840s, its harbor town was settled by James Strang, a renegade Mormon "prophet," who named the town St. James—which stuck—and himself God's Vice Regent and King—which did not. He was assassinated in 1856; his kingdom dissolved and his followers scattered or disappeared. In the 1970s, Beaver Island was still sparsely populated. Its one grocery store, saloon and restaurant, post office, and its combination bingo hall, church parlor, and sometimes-movie-theater were enough for travelers like us.

As we approached the island archipelago that day, the wind began to pick up and the afternoon rapidly lost its luster. Clouds were layering the sky. Our plan was to drop down, approach from the north, and enter the islands from the west. That way we could pick up a buoy that would keep us from running aground on rock shelves, that would mark safe passage to little Garden Island. I had been hoping to visit this mysterious place, nicknamed "Snake Island," for four or five years, but each time our plans had been thwarted. It either had rained or someone had gotten sick or we'd run out of time. This year, we were ready: we each had a pair of rubber boots to keep the snakes at bay. Ed and the girls wanted to visit the island's graves, and I was more eager than ever to follow its paths. I had recently read a slim and stunningly beautiful book about some of the uses of fungi among the Anishinabe. Its author, Keewaydinoquay, the highly-respected medicine woman and herbalist, had been the only resident on Miniss Kitigan, the Ojibwa name for Garden Island, for several years. This was where hundreds of her people had once lived, and where she now tended their graves. It was my hope that someday she and I might find a way to talk.

The sky continued to darken, and we were suddenly in choppy seas. The wind had been steadily increasing, and now it began to whistle around us. The chop continued to grow, and we were having difficulty locating that black buoy which would lead us through deep water. All four of us were on deck, in our life jackets now. We had dropped the sails after we'd rounded the northernmost tip of Garden Island. The wind, by that time, had reached forty knots and we had been fearful the sails would rip. Ed started the engine, but the horsepower wasn't sufficient to make any headway. Instead we hung there, facing into the wind, unable to move.

Then it began to rain. Rain isn't exactly the word. We were being stabbed by needles of water, the wind was howling, and the sea rose in spears around us. It was impossible to keep our eyes open for more than a few seconds, for the rain had turned to sleet and the sleet made a blurry wall. Ed was trying to hold the wheel steady with one hand while, with the other, he shielded his eyes from the pelting sleet.

"Go down below and hand me up your swim mask," he shouted to Annie above the wind's roar and the chatter of hail hitting the deck.

As we attempted to round Garden Island, the wind broadsided us. It threatened to blow us sideways, more off course than ever, closer to land where we might run aground or be battered against rocks. The lake began to ripple in eddies around us, and water seemed to want to leap over our gunnels. I watched, horrified, as a whirlpool began to swirl in our path. The throttle was full forward, but we were barely moving. I looked at the meter. We were going only half a knot. The whirlpool widened. Would it swallow us, I wondered, if we were washed overboard in our life jackets, if the boat sank? All four of us leaned forward, as if urging the boat along, as we searched for the buoy. Through stabbing sleet and tears, I strained my eyes. We were close to reeds and rock. Ed gripped the wheel, trying to hold us steady. He looked absurd, like a space traveler at the helm of his ship in his yellow slicker, his orange life vest, his blue knit cap, and the ridiculous swim mask shielding his eyes. In the midst of all this peril, I couldn't help laughing.

And just at that moment, as I turned again toward the bow, I saw a speck, so fragile, so small, it might have been a stick bobbing in the water. Could this be the black can we were looking for, I wondered, as I watched it bounce up and down in the gray expanse ahead? I pointed. First Ed, then Ann, then Ellen saw it. It was not an illusion, after all.

Now, at least, we knew the way. If the wind would let up, and the sleet, and the rain, we could get past that first buoy, and the next one. And then we would be in the lee of Beaver Island. We would not be going to Garden Island. We already had passed the entry to our little cove. How lucky we were not to have anchored there. We would have been stranded, with no protection, at the mercy of the wind. Instead, we headed for the cut into St. James Harbor. We would tie up at a sturdy dock that would be attached to solid land, and we would wait out the storm. We would make it. Now that we had found the buoy.

Many sailors who were on the lake that day have similar stories. A boat that left Beaver Island that morning arrived in Wisconsin in the evening with shredded sails and a wet and battered crew. There were numerous capsizings of small boats up and down the lake, and more than a dozen fishermen ran aground. But everyone eventually got safely to land. Other storms have been more murderous, before and since. The beds of the Great Lakes hold hundreds of wrecks and the bodies of countless lost sailors.

Today the lake is flat and blue, as if it had no memory of turbulence, of screeching gales or winter blizzards. I no longer sail the Great Lakes. I live in a house high on a cliff above Lake Michigan. I have come down my stairs today to walk the beach again after winter's confinement. The sand is free of its mounds of snow, and the undulating islands of ice that choked the shore are gone. My children have scattered to other parts of the country. My husband has been dead for a year, and I live alone now with a yellow dog named River. The March sun is bright, but the air still has a chill. I have pulled my knit hat over my ears and wrapped a scarf tight around my neck. Except for an occasional floating gull's shriek, I am in a soundless world.

Out of habit, I head north and take note of changes as I walk. Nothing is constant on this lake. A little more beach here by the slough, but less further south. The first sandbar has shifted closer to shore. The pine that was leaning over the cliff has toppled; perhaps there will be a slide soon. My neighbor has begun to repair his stairs.

In a grave that the wind hollowed out, I find a doe, tan coat still clinging to her white bones. Over here are gull feathers, and further on a few crow feathers lie scattered about. Once I saw a large bluish-green egg on this beach; when I looked it up later in my field guide, I discovered it belonged to a heron. There, by the water's edge, is a dead lake trout. Soon the gulls will be sharing it with their kin. Another time, I righted a turtle flipped by the breakers. Years ago, I saved a gull tangled in fishline. I couldn't save the buck though, already dead from the arrow in his side. Or the trees in the mudslide south of us. I couldn't save my neighbor's burning house. Or my father, who lived to nearly ninety. Or my grandmother, who hung herself before her time. Or my husband, though I tried.

I turn and head back the way I came, following my footprints in the sand. I pull off my hat and let the breeze lift my hair from my face. I am glad to be here on this early spring day. The trees are not yet in leaf, but soon they will be, and the trillium will spread out their white carpet in the woods. The blue-green of the sky is nearly the same color as the lake, as that heron's egg I saw here so long ago. Sand squeaks under my feet. I am home. This is my home, and this is enough.

Lake Erie as the Color of Hazel Eyes

LINDA NEMEC FOSTER

That sullen girl in the aqua bathing suit squinting in the sun of a 1964 faded photograph is me. My father, younger than I can ever remember, is on my left. My younger sister, blindly smiling into the camera, is on my right. Notice how my mother is not in this family snapshot. She took the picture, so she's absent; but hating beaches and swimming like she did, she'd be absent anyway. In the background, flat and looming, is the wide expanse of Lake Erie. From this photo's vantage point—Sandusky, Ohio—you could never tell that Lake Erie is the smallest of the Great Lakes. "Puny runt," my Uncle Joe always called it. And in the middle of a hot summer, the lake was always warm—like bath water. For as long as I can remember, every summer we spent one week in Sandusky: our bona fide vacation from the dreary suburbs of Cleveland, not that Sandusky was bucolic or picturesque. "It was something different," my mother recited like a litany chant. But the Lake Erie of my childhood always looked the same, whether it lapped the beach at Cedar Point, made a crashing statement in Toledo, or accepted, like a bored housewife, the greasy advances of the Cuyahoga River in Cleveland. Lake Erie always looked like an immense flat plain of green/blue/yellow/brown, a large and open hazel eye. As a girl, I imagined it to be the source of all hazel eyes. Hazel—that rare color—was nothing more than a combination of many colors, all vying for attention and not quite getting it. And so every year, I swam in the color of hazel eyes, never stopping to realize that I submerged myself in the color of my mother's eyes. The mother who hated water, who only took vacation photos but was never in them. The mother who was rarely present, but was always there.

Freshwater

SUE WILLIAM SILVERMAN

Where is the sea, that once solved the whole loneliness of the Midwest?

—*James Wright*

*I*n the fall of 1995, in Grand Haven, I see Lake Michigan for the first time. The water is slate gray, barely breathing in dull afternoon light. A small drizzle dampens sand. The beach is deserted. No shells or seaweed litter the berm. No salt water or saltwater taffy. No Ferris wheel, no coconut suntan lotion, no sweat. No honky-tonk boardwalk. No sailor bars. No penny arcades or games of chance.

No chance: for salty spindrifts, for the fury of hurricanes, for the scent of the exotic, the faraway. Rather, it is *this* Midwestern emptiness that feels foreign to me, a girl who once lived on tropical islands. I'm no longer a girl, but still I miss unruly liana vines, mimosa trees, fever grass, ginger flowers, vanilla pods. I crave volcanic mountains, the jungled clutter of rain forests. I want to be submerged in seawater, feel it tangle my hair. I moved here because of someone else, but now I'm only myself.

◆   ◆   ◆

The next day, seeking the scent of salt, I get in my car to drive to the Gulf of Mexico. Speeding south down interstates, I feel trapped in a massive expanse of land. I'll never reach the end of asphalt, barren fields, leafless forests. That first night on the road, lying for a few hours in a motel room, I sense the vibration of car tires still spinning as if I can travel even in sleep. I am awake before dawn. I have no choice.

It is my body that tugs me. The salt in my skin longs to return to the familiar, feel the warm dissolve of constant summer. The Gulf is not the Caribbean Sea of my childhood, but I once lived on Galveston Island, too.

It is closer to home.

◆ ◆ ◆

Barefoot, in shorts and a tank top, I wade into the Gulf down by the south jetty, as close to the Caribbean as possible. The beach is a jangle of radios, towels, teenagers, children, sandcastles. Lotioned torsos, far from shore, glisten, swirling in waves. Sand and shells scuff the soles of my feet. A slow, damp breeze thickens my hair. In the liquid sky, I imagine watercolor images of childhood—of tropical rain showering ashore, trade winds gusting a crimson blizzard of frangipani, hibiscus, bougainvillea. The *Danmark* cruised white into the harbor, anchoring in the blue tessellated sea. Wands of light shimmered off mounds of bauxite on the pier. I loved to suck tart, salt-crusted sea grapes at Magens Bay.

Now, here in Galveston, the sky drips waxy humidity, weighting the scent of salt and seaweed to my skin. I smell like "me" again.

◆ ◆ ◆

That December, one evening close to Christmas, I sit in the smallest room in my house in Michigan and stare out the winter window. There is no one with whom I can talk. No one to call. Alone, I must now find my own way. Across the streets and yards, green, red, white lights reflect on drifts of snow. My house is dark. I am empty.

I zip up my white parka, pull on my new boots, and walk outside. I pass no one as I shuffle along unshoveled sidewalks the four blocks to the lake. My footprints are the only ones to track the snowy sand. The ivory moon hangs heavy, swollen, anchoring the night. Stars dangle from the globe of sky like ornaments. In the breeze they seem to blur, humming. Water has frozen mid-wave, sculpting odd forms: waves shaped like beckoning arms—or torsos rising up from sandbars. Other frozen waves are transformed to crystal urns, sailing vessels, mounds of salt. Filaments of starlight shimmer off these apparitions. I imagine removing my boots, my wool socks, gliding across the lake, grasping translucent arms and waists, swirling from figure to figure along the coast.

I move closer to the lake. Brittle edges of frozen foam, arabesqued like spun sugar, crack beneath my feet. I scoop up a fragment and lick it. The sudden cold in my mouth startles me, seems to shock me awake. I bite off a small nugget and feel its weight on my tongue. In its denseness I sense eons of dune grass, pine and black cherry trees, magnetite sand. As the ice melts, I taste lakewater in my mouth: cool, sweet, alive.

I swallow.

Shiver Me Timbers

Sharon Dilworth

*T*hat was the summer I worked at the Crow's Nest Bar & Restaurant on the sixth floor of the Old Marquette Inn. The hotel, shaped like a ship, was situated in the lower harbor in downtown Marquette, and the owners, proud of the place they had just purchased, boasted a view of Lake Superior from every window. We, the wait staff, wore nautically decorated aprons, and visors embroidered with anchors and winking pirates. Fresh oysters and lobsters were flown in from Boston once a week, confusing the customers who had grown up on locally caught whitefish and trout. "Where in the world did this come from?" They looked to the lake, then back at their pink lobster tails. Hot butter was served in little silver bowls that tipped over easily. We walked around, licking butter from our fingertips and making grease spots on everything we touched.

It was the summer the cook, an ex-Marine, with a nasty habit for Scotch and milk—anything else bothered his ulcers—pushed his wife overboard. She held onto the side of their small fishing boat, screaming, "Help me, help me! He's finally done it." Her husband pried off her fingers one by one, and she was forced to stay afloat in the cold waters of Lake Superior. The Coast Guard cutter came to her rescue; she was only thirty feet from land and, had she not been so afraid of drowning, she could have walked the short distance to shore. The local prosecutor, a regular at the Crow's Nest (Jack and Coke, six shucked oysters, two slices of garlic bread), called him foolish, then upgraded the charge to attempted homicide. The cook was arrested. He claimed that even after twenty-two years of marriage, he did not know that his wife couldn't swim. He pleaded practical joke, but was sentenced to three years because of some mysterious prior that we speculated was the murder of his previous wife. Whether or not he really had been married before never actually presented itself to us as fact. Still, we liked our rumor. The cook's twin, another ex-Marine with a nasty habit for any kind of alcohol, took over the kitchen duties at the newly opened Crow's Nest Bar and Restaurant, with a view of Lake Superior from every window.

That was the summer we first learned about the undergraduates who were the victims of a freak spring storm while walking on the pier. Strong winds and fifteen-foot waves came crashing over the rocks, and they were instantly drowned in Lake Superior. It happened in April, and months later, the divers hired by the county morgue were still trying to recover their bodies. The tragedy of the *Edmund Fitzgerald* was only a few years past, but we knew that the Lake "never gave up her dead," and the trio became mythical in our imaginations as we walked the breakwater, always on the lookout for storms or bodies. That was the first summer we heard about the drowned coeds. We heard about them every year—a recurring accident—no one was ever sure exactly when it happened. No one ever knew them personally. No one ever knew their names. No one ever found their bodies.

That was the summer of the Elks. Much to the delight of the local merchants and hotel owners, their annual convention was held in Marquette. Friday night, they rented out the entire Crow's Nest and preordered surf 'n' turf for everyone. One hundred twenty-one men. The week before, every plane flying up from Detroit carried live lobsters and iced oysters in its cargo hold. The night began with a cocktail reception, all the Black Velvet and Southern Comfort the 121 Elks could drink. And drink they did. Two hours later, 121 surf 'n' turf dinners coming out of the kitchen, the kitchen staff proud of their travails, but not an Elk in sight. The buses had already left, in a flurry of raunchy songs and lecherous demands. The Elks were going off to explore the wilds of the strip clubs west of us in Negaunee.

We were left with 121 fresh lobsters, filet mignons, baked potatoes, tubs of hot butter, sour-cream sides, and sprigs of parsley. We looked for someone to tell us what to do next. There were trays set in the halls, along the windows sills, on the bar, in the clothes closet. The place dripped in plenty. The phone calls went out. Come. It's free. And everyone did. Friends and family—what seemed like the entire city of Marquette—ate free surf 'n' turf, donated by the fun-loving Elks in their maroon-colored fezzes.

That was the summer (or maybe the spring) that Jimmy, the night manager at the hotel, a Marquette native but a Parisian wannabe, invited the entire female wait staff to go smelt fishing with him. We met at midnight near Presque Isle, where Jimmy showed us the inlets and streams feeding into the rivers. "Best spot in the whole world to catch smelt," he assured us. In the glare of the spotlight, we saw the shimmering scales of the thousands of fish swimming upstream.

"They're here. They're here!" And then out of the woods came dozens of other fishermen, everyone with nets and buckets, pails and pots, kneeling and scooping and hooting.

There was Jimmy, yelling at us, the only females there, to reach down and grab a smelt. Then he gave us the news that we had to bite off its head. We balked at this. None of us were that drunk. But Jimmy insisted. "Tradition," he yelled, and showed us how. "You have to do it. You have to. It's bad luck for all of us if you don't." We waitresses were more than a little in love with Jimmy. We knelt and scooped our hands into the freezing water and grabbed the slippery fish with our bare hands. Did we bite the heads off like Jimmy told us to? I think we did.

That was the June when Randy, the busboy with the dreamy blue eyes, moved to his grandfather's cabin out on Big Bay Road. Trying to mend his broken heart when his girlfriend since third grade, the beautiful Cecelia, left him for ugly old George who drove the Zamboni at the ice rink. Randy was going to live off the land. Self-sufficiency was his goal. He wasn't going to need anyone ever again. He would kill or make anything he needed to live. He didn't want visitors, not yet, but promised to come into town if he got lonely. Two months later, we got news that Randy was set to marry his UPS driver, the only woman driver in the Upper Peninsula. Their wedding was on top of Sugar Loaf Mountain at sunset, and invitations went out to everyone, even Cecelia and George. The photographer, like the rest of the guests who had climbed to the top of the mountain, was drunk by the time the ceremony got started. All of the wedding photographs were missing the bride and groom. Fifty-five photographs of Sugar Loaf Mountain. Lake Superior shines in all, which actually worked out for the best. The UPS driver left Randy after three weeks, and

Randy moved back to his grandfather's cabin. He didn't make it through his first winter, one of the coldest on record. He moved into the hotel and worked night shift at the front desk. That was the summer Randy gave me the wedding rings—both his and hers, the ones I wear to this day—silver bands with arrows pointing towards a future they never shared.

. . .

That was the summer the theater kids quit the restaurant and went to New York to find acting jobs in summer stock. They wanted to be in *Chorus Line*, *Annie*, *Dames at Sea*, anything on Broadway; or, if those dreams couldn't be realized, they wanted the East Coast, something different from what they knew. All four of them were hired by an outdoor seasonal theater in Opelika, Alabama. Not exactly East Coast, but different. The theater, an open-air structure on the grounds of the Sacred Heart Campground, did one show all season: *Veronica's Veil*, a passion play that reenacted the crucifixion of Christ, focusing on the veil that Veronica used to wipe his brow. The director was a devout Catholic who made the cast pray for forgiveness before and after the show. Jesus had very few speaking lines, and the Cross was difficult to carry. They slept in tents and had to cook their own food over open-pit fires.

Disillusioned with summer stock in Opelika, Alabama, passion plays, and religious campgrounds, they drove home, twenty-four hours up Interstate 75. Too broke to stop anywhere—their contract stipulated they had to perform until Labor Day in order to get paid—they sang and danced outside a restaurant in Findley, Ohio, for burgers and made it to the Mackinac Bridge on July fourth. It was a busy summer, and what with the Elks and the National Frisbee tournament, Ted rehired all of them.

. . .

That was the summer that bartender Bonnie and I would end our shifts on the roof of the hotel. Late-night drinks in huge hurricane glasses. White Russians, up the fire escape, and across the boards set up by the pot-smoking kitchen staff, until we got to the lawn chairs we'd salvaged from a room on the fifth floor. Lake Superior would be nothing more than a huge black hole in the darkness surrounding us.

No boats travel on Superior at night, and we imagined that we could see all the way across to Canada. Our White Russians, the cold war, the dark sky

. . . we talked invasion. But the only local intruders we knew of were the wolves that have for some inexplicable reason returned to the Upper Peninsula. The Department of Natural Resources speculates that the wolves walked over from Canada. The wolves, taking advantage of the deep cold of the winter—the first time on record that Lake Superior ever froze all the way across—were able to walk across the lake. We have learned that wolves travel in packs and there are six known packs. Experts predict their numbers will increase rapidly. But on the roof, with our White Russians, Bonnie and I were not concerned with attacks of that sort.

We sipped our vodka, Kahlua, and creams. We looked at the stars. We talked about the absence of boys in our lives.

One night, as we crawled in through the window, expecting the quiet hum of the refrigerator deep freeze, we were met instead by a man wearing a black ski mask.

It was too warm for winter wool.

"Looks like trouble," Bonnie said.

We were confused. We had locked the doors and turned the key in the elevator, so that access to the sixth floor should have been denied to anyone trying to get in.

The three of us stood there staring at one another—Bonnie and I waiting for him to tell us the punch line of the joke we were sure he was pulling on us, he wondering where we had come from.

"Give me your money," he demanded, but it was difficult to understand what he was saying, all that wool in his mouth. His mumblings made us laugh, either that or the alcohol. He put his hands on his hips and yelled, "This is serious!"

And then we saw that he didn't have a gun, which was good for us since the cash box was on the roof, an oversight that we seemed to repeat more often than not. Bonnie was quick. She kicked him in the shin and he fell to the ground. We pulled off the ski mask. His spit and sweat covered his face. "Don't hurt me," he said. But Bonnie wanted to know how he had gained access to the sixth floor.

The guy squealed and blamed Randy, the night desk clerk. Their plan was to split the money. We found it hard to believe that Randy, beautiful Randy with the broken heart, was involved. He denied it, and because we thought he might one day love us, we believed him and never called the police.

. . .

This is the summer, twenty-two years later, that I go back to Marquette. The hotel, under a new name, still stands like a magnificent ship, its bow jutting out into the recently developed parks in the lower harbor. The interior of the hotel shines, and there's nothing shoddy about these renovations. All brass and glass, the color theme is warm terra cotta.

The new owner, a woman in a navy blue sweater set, asks if I would like to look around, and when I say yes, she insists on accompanying me. We tour the place together.

On the way up to the sixth floor, the elevator no longer smells of garlic potatoes or burnt applesauce. There are no butter stains on the fresh white walls. The nautical theme has been replaced by early American, but nothing is authentic. Everything is brand new. It smells like a forest, but looks more like a large walk-in closet. The bar is on the right. A small window overlooks Lake Superior. The owner explains that the rooms overlook the lake, but as I am no one special, she cannot show them to me unless I'm planning to stay and pay.

The people of that summer are gone; the ghosts have been replaced by pine wood, and gaudy wallpaper covered with violets and daisies.

"A bit claustrophobic, isn't it?" I ask, but she can't agree. They've spent too much money not to be admired. The owner takes me out to the fire escape when she senses my disappointment in the work that they've done.

There, the sapphire waters of Lake Superior open up before us. She points to the pier and tells me about the recent drowning of three coeds from the university. "A-hundred-mile-an-hour winds came out of nowhere," she tells me, as if I don't know this. "The poor things had no chance. None whatsoever." She sighs as if personally responsible for the weather. "Their bodies have never been recovered."

And they won't be, I want to tell her, but don't.

"Shiver me timbers," I say. It's too bad about the lack of view. A ship in dry dock is a terrible thing.

Lake Effect

Linda Loomis

From my Oswego office window, I look out over a campus daycare playground and the vast waters of Lake Ontario. As I watch children swing, ride tricycles, and toss colorful balls between me and the rocky shoreline, I wonder if they have learned to orient themselves and everything around them to Lake Ontario, as I did growing up mid-century on these same shores.

"Stand and face the lake," Miss McLaughlin told us in kindergarten. "Everyone lift your left arm." Pointing to someone in the front row, she showed us that our left arms were pointing west. She lifted the right arm. That was east. Behind us was south, and in front, north. We learned that another country, Canada, lay north, across the water, but the lake was so big we could not see it.

Remembering, I am carried back to the years after World War II. I am six, perhaps seven. I have slept all night with the knowledge that, if the weather is good, I will go with my family to Fair Haven State Park. Bright sunshine awakens me and, with thoughts of the sandy beach, I dress quickly. But there is no hurrying Daddy. He gets his coffee, eggs, and toast; his routine does not vary.

"You eat a good breakfast," he says. "It's going to be a long day." We swallow cereal sweetened with anticipation. The longest part of the day is now: waiting while Mumma washes dishes, mixes huge bowls of potato and macaroni salads, feeds baby Carol, packs the cooler. Waiting while she gathers towels and old woolen army blankets, scratchy even before they are dragged through the sand.

"Let's go now," says my older sister, Norma.

"Feed the dog."

"Now, let's go," beg my brothers, Harold and Jimmy.

"Help carry things to the car."

"May we go? Now? Please?" I implore.

"Pile in!"

We hustle into our huge old Packard. Toys and beach gear are stuffed at our feet. In the trunk, a folded-down baby carriage sits beside baskets of food and a carefully wrapped and cushioned chocolate cake.

The drive is interminable. We bargain everything: who claims a window for the ride home, whose feet are first in the lake, who gets the biggest piece of that cake. Warned against asking, "How far?" and "When will we get there?" we count hills, the Seven Sisters; after the seventh, the road takes us along apple and peach orchards and dairy farms.

Past a turn in the road, we watch for a cemetery on the right and await our father's question. "Why is there a fence around that cemetery, kids?" he always asks. We magnanimously let him have the punch line: "Because people are dying to get in."

We take a right turn onto the long road that leads straight between dense woods, where trees seem to hold up the sky as we look ahead for the first view of water. At last we come to the gate, where Daddy flashes a gorgeous smile to the girl collecting twenty-five cents and asks if the lifeguards are on duty. The answer is yes, and we cheer.

Beyond the gate, the view changes as dense woods give way to a panorama of sandy beach, then wide waters that stretch to the horizon. Daddy parks close to a lifeguard station, and we leave shirts and shorts in the car to plunge barefoot across the hot sand, over the line of jetsam left by last night's waves, and into the cold lake.

Swimming, I think only of the water and the motion. North, south, east, west—these directions are meaningless in the currents, where huge sandbars stretch far out into the lake, keeping it shallow for yards and yards away from shore.

Only when we are called to dinner do we crawl from the water and beg to eat with our swimsuits on so we can return immediately after the picnic. Mother gives the familiar warning: "You can't swim for an hour after we eat or you'll get cramps and drown." And so we wait, again, for the water.

◆ ◆ ◆

Memories of idyllic summer days on Lake Ontario are balanced by the realities of geography. Once the trees have dropped their leaves and autumn fades, Oswegonians brace themselves for the inevitable fury that follows. Our city is buffeted by prevailing northwest winds and buried annually beneath an average thirteen-foot snowfall.

Meteorologists can explain it all now—how the arctic air sweeps down from Canada and absorbs moisture from the warmer, open waters of Lake Ontario; how it arrives at shore saturated, shudders at the cold land mass, and drops the crystals of snow that have formed. There are other scientific details, but what local residents know is the effect of the phenomenon. They see heavy snow-bearing clouds approaching and hurry out for extra bread and milk, set shovels near the door, and check the fuel in the snow blower.

Every Oswegonian has a weather story to tell. Old timers recall the blizzard of 1946, when snow reached second-floor windows and drifts plugged country roads for weeks. Too young to remember the details of that storm, I claim bragging rights to the blizzard of 1958. The storm began midday, December 7, with gorgeous fat flakes drifting in a gentle breeze. We went to bed that Sunday anticipating our weekly routine, but awoke instead to a muffled silence inside and out. The first sound of Monday was Jimmy's calling, "Holy cow! Everybody come and look at this."

Gathered at his upstairs bedroom window, we marveled at the unfamiliar landscape. There was no distinction between sidewalk, street, or garden. Bushes were gigantic mushrooms, and houses looked like rolling, snow-covered hills. We knew immediately we would not be leaving home that day. Harold, Jimmy, Carol, and I pulled out our tattered Monopoly game, assorted books, and 45-rpm records, and prepared for fun.

The ringing telephone startled us. Our older sister, a switchboard operator for the New York Telephone Company, was being called into work. The mayor had declared a state of emergency, but the phone lines had to be kept open.

Norma trudged several blocks through hip-high drifts to Bridge Street, where city plows made regular sweeps to clear the main road. Half a century later, she still shivers when she recalls her brush with death. Walking in the street with her head bent against the wind, she lifted her eyes just in time to see a plow approaching. She looked around for an escape route, and as she dove into a snow bank, expecting to be buried alive, the driver spotted her and slammed on his brakes. She brushed herself off and hurried to work, staying on duty for three days straight.

Tales of brave and generous deeds spread from neighbor to neighbor. Some, no doubt, were exaggerated, but children really did take their sleds down long unplowed roads to the highway to meet the trucks coming from Syracuse with food and supplies, then hauled boxes to Matteson's Oak Hill Superette, my best friend's family's store. The mayor toured the business district on a dogsled pulled by a team of Alaskan huskies, but most people were stuck at home, shoveling driveways and roofs, trying to stay ahead of the snowfall. Schools and factories closed, and undeliverable mail accumulated at the post office.

Life magazine gave us our moment in the national spotlight when it ran several pages of photos of the Lake Ontario city that had received six feet of snow in five days. Two weeks passed before our lives returned to normal.

Finding My Way Home

BETH ANN FENNELLY

The rich are different. They're better looking, for starters. The people in the other cars following the curve of Lake Michigan north out of Chicago to the suburbs do not have buck teeth or pigeon toes or huge noses or moles. Things have been pulled back or turned out or shaved off in their childhoods. These people have good haircuts. They've been color-analyzed, and they don't wear autumn if they're summer. I'm reminded of how in other parts of the country I'm considered pretty—in fact, when my fiancé brought me to his hometown in Alabama, I was pronounced "gorgeous." But I'm not gorgeous; I just had the advantages of growing up on the North Shore. My teeth are straight from two years in braces, and my nails are strong thanks to vitamins laid beside my breakfast napkin, and my posture is good from years of ballet. If you had lived here, you would have the same.

What my fiancé notices is the cars. The rust-spotted Datsuns chuff off the highway, leaving only the forest green Jaguars, pale gray Mercedes, or this year's fashion, the high-powered, all-terrain sport-utility vehicle, which must be bored, I think, purring along these streets smooth as the show-room floor.

. . .

Tommy and I used to listen to Books on Tape on long drives, but last year his father, a mechanic, took the CD player out of a totaled Chevy (it was smashed like a beer can, and hanging from the cracked and bloodied windshield were long blond hairs) and he put it in Tommy's Nissan where the tape player used to be. So instead, driving from Arkansas where we met and live, I've been reading aloud *The Collected Stories of John Cheever*. I read, "We are a family that have been very close in spirit," and I try to make my voice hit all the different notes like an actor does on tape.

It's strange to be reading these stories as we drive to my hometown, because Cheever's world and the one I escaped are so similar. In Cheever's stories, the people are always milling about cocktail parties at the same houses on the same streets. This static feeling also governs Lake Forest, as if it's a book you could put down and come back to. Maybe because the people never move away. The Schweppes of the seltzer, the Wrigleys of the gum, the Armours and Swifts of meat packing, these are the names in the cemeteries and these were the names of my classmates. No upward mobility can be gained by moving, so people don't. You might shuttle between Lake Forest and Grosse Pointe, Michigan, or Greenwich, Connecticut, but otherwise you're slumming. I don't often talk about this place I come from. When I'm asked, I say I'm from Chicago.

.   .   .

Thirty miles north of the city, we pull off at the Lake Forest exit and the transition is complete—the only car that looks like ours is ours. We drive down Deerpath Road, and although Tommy says it all looks familiar because he has seen the movie *Ordinary People* a half-dozen times, I can tell he's unprepared for the beauty. Sometimes I forget that part of it, but for most people, this town is like one of those rare women who shouldn't be evaluated on any matter without taking beauty into consideration. Great elms planted on either side of the road by the women's league of 1904 arch and interlock. We drive through a tunnel of crystal, sun glinting off the ice-covered branches. I point out the Frank Lloyd Wrights, houses so magnificent Wright hid the front doors so visitors had time for admiration before going inside. They are decorated for Christmas with tiny white lights in Frazier firs—no rooftop Santas or neon-nimbused Christs. In fact, no neon at all—the city passed an ordinance against it, as well as fast-food chains and buildings higher than the clock tower. And ever since the actor Mr. T moved in ("Our one black," the real-estate agents assure, *sotto voce*) and took a chain saw to the hundred-year-old oaks on his lawn, they've outlawed unsupervised landscaping, too.

We drive by the mapled entrance to Woodlands Academy of the Sacred

Heart, the Catholic boarding school I had to pass an interview to get into. Although the school was all-girl, it was no breeding ground for nascent feminists; the juniors' service project is a fashion show, proceeds for the needy. The irony of this is unappreciated. We were encouraged to take our responsibility as torchbearers of high culture seriously, and each girl had to volunteer twenty hours a year to a project of her choice. Every other Saturday I'd take the train into the city with my mother to the Terra Museum of American Art, where she volunteered as a tour guide, and I'd pass out pamphlets for a lecture on colonial portraiture or an exhibit of Marsden Hartley oils.

Tommy knows me as someone who makes friends easily, so I have trouble explaining why I was so unpopular here at Woodlands. Yes, I made a 4.0, but I didn't even fit in with the other brains who wouldn't skip Biology to get facials. And while my parents were at the lower end of the Woodlands financial spectrum, not owning a yacht or villa, there were others equally impoverished. True, I had chubby thighs at a school where popularity rose in proportion to your number of eating disorders. But it was more than this that made me different.

And from the start, I knew I was getting out. I would not stay and breed. I saved the money I made waitressing at the Deerpath Inn, filleting Dover sole tableside for guests who never tipped less than 20 percent. I picked a Catholic college—the only kind my father would pay for—and I left. I found my first real friends, and I was happy and came home less and less, which made me happier.

I started traveling. I gave away all my clothes that wouldn't fit in a backpack. I had my hair hacked off, almost two feet of it, at a beauty school in London. I threw the rings that had colonized my fingers as belonging to high school, parents, or boyfriend into the Irish Sea. I slept under a fruit stand in Seville when I ran out of money, and it rained in the night, so I woke with pomegranate smeared across my belly. In a letter waiting for me at the American Express in Morocco, my boyfriend Hamilton told me that (a) he was worried about me, and (b) he was going "to ask my parents' permission for my hand in marriage." I dumped him. I got a tattoo at 3 A.M. in Berlin from a man who didn't speak English but somehow divined that I wanted a small green lizard on my butt. I had sex with an Italian at the top of Mount Tiberio. I did stupid things, I knew that even then, but I was becoming more myself and leaving Lake Forest behind.

Back home my parents sensed I was changing, but figured all I needed was a job selling jewelry at Tiffany's to get me shaving under my arms again. "I *wish*

you'd take more *pains* with your *appearance*, Beth Ann," my mother would say, although pain was what I was trying to avoid. I didn't tell them that I was going
to teach English in the Czech Republic after graduation until my university's
commencement mass. I waited until President Bush (the first) stood up for his
address, figuring they'd find it hard to make a scene then, but my father's "I'll
cut you off!" interrupted Bush anyway. We had gone out to brunch, so he was
drunk. Men with dark suits and little wires curling into their ears started edg-
ing towards us between the bleachers.

"Fine," I said.

And so I said goodbye. I said goodbye to my childhood and the half-
friends of my childhood. I said goodbye to Lake Forest and financial security.
While I was away my father's benign alcoholism turned malignant, and he took
up with a stewardess. I said goodbye to him, and soon after to his side of the
family. I left the Catholic Church and said goodbye to my other patriarch.

So I think about this Cheever story, "Goodbye, My Brother," about four
grown children reuniting at their summer home. One of the siblings,
Lawrence, is fiercely disliked by the others. He's the outsider. He grew up dis-
gusted with the wealth and waste of his family, and he has learned who he is
by defining himself against that lifestyle. During the visit Lawrence realizes
that he can no longer be part of his family; he says goodbye forever. I'm pretty
sure Cheever wants us to dislike Lawrence for his strict practicality and unwill-
ingness to ignore flaws in beautiful people or things, his calm ability to say
goodbye. But somehow I find myself thinking Lawrence had the right idea.

◆　◆　◆

Now, like Lawrence, I return after a long absence. My mother, the one person
in Lake Forest I give a damn about, wants to meet my fiancé. And I want her
to get to know Tommy, who, in his childhood, had a single pair of jeans, cut
into shorts for summer; who ruined his back heaving bags at a sandblasting
factory all day in order to pay for his community college at night. He appre-
ciates simple pleasures, and he is happiest watching *Seinfeld* and stroking my
hair, or drinking Bud Lights on the steps of our tiny house lined with paper-
backs and love.

Now he turns left from Deerpath onto Lake Road and stops the car to
stare as a house is hoisted twelve feet into the air. It's a remodeled carriage
house where the oleomargarine magnate used to store his four carriages, and it

sat at a ninety-degree angle beside the mansion on Lake Michigan. Now a valuable home, it's made more so when the cranes and pulleys turn it around so the water shows in the arching windows and doors. The lawn has been torn up by machinery, so the owner stands on a dolly to avoid muddying his cuffs. He holds four Gucci leashes with four lunging white Lhasa apsos, which gives the absurd impression that he's on a miniature dog sled. He carries a pooper scooper embossed with "Groomingdales" in the other hand—dog shit is illegal here too. "This about-face will cost 2.3 million," he tells us when he sees we've stopped to watch, "but it's worth it for the view." We nod, then drive away giggling to my mother's house.

◆ ◆ ◆

That evening Mom asks us, "Please, for a Christmas present," to go with her to a cocktail party at Birdie and Brent Fulton's, so we do. Their house is a grand Victorian on the lake, and the sport-utility vehicles parked outside clash, like a woman dressed in furs and wearing sneakers. Birdie, who has a British accent although she's from Cincinnati, greets us at the door, where the maid takes our coats. Birdie recommends that we pop into her greenhouse later to see the rare midnight-blooming black tulip flown here from Oude Niedorp. Tommy squeezes my hand—he knows the greenhouse is a sore spot with my mother because ever since Brent had it built for Birdie for their twenty-fifth anniversary, she wins the flower show. As we walk to the bar, Mom whispers, "I think her gardener arranges the flowers. It's against the rules."

They don't have Bud Light, but the bartender indicates they have Heineken by holding up a bottle. When Tommy reaches for it, the bartender yanks it back and pours it into a glass with a prissy shake of his head. I squeeze Tommy's hand. The invitation read "casual," so all the men wear wool sweaters with a Christmas tree and presents, or a Santa with real bells on his reins, or a Rudolf with a red-bulb nose that lights up. Tommy looks at the tanned men debating this year's snow in Breckenridge. "They only wear these sweaters once a year?" he whispers. I nod. At the buffet he picks up a shrimp longer than his pinkie and dunks it in cocktail sauce. He chews sadly. He says, "I want a Christmas sweater." Tommy is wearing an Atlanta Braves sweatshirt. I nod. We eat more shrimp.

Birdie glides over to where we're leaning against the piano and deftly slips coasters under our Heinekens. She hands us presents. For Tommy, a cigar clipper, and for me, a silver holder for Sweet'N Low packets. We thank her and she glides away. Tommy recently gave me an engagement ring, and this makes him notice other women's diamonds for the first time. Birdie's is the size of an ice cube.

"Is everyone in this room a millionaire?" Tommy asks.

"No," I say. "Some are billionaires."

We sip our Heinekens. The ceiling is vaulted and mistletoe hangs from the Waterford chandelier. There are perhaps fifty people in this room with the buffet, fifty more next door in the library with the bar. On the recamier to our left, Hildegard Mendenhall-Palmer, called Honey, tells Tinkie Porter of her daughter's wedding: "It's a garden theme and we've ordered 700 painted lady butterflies, one for each guest to release outside of St. Mary's." Tinkie approves: "One *does* so tire of throwing birdseed." Brent Fulton is rounding up a group for a tour of the "Shaker Wing." The Fultons are the biggest private collectors of Shaker furniture in the Midwest, and once a year they open their home to enthusiasts who come in buses to see the Shaker hymnbook in the temperature-moderated display or the wooden chairs hanging from wooden pegs on the wooden walls.

I try to imagine how Tommy sees all this. When the sandblasting factory closed, Tommy and his ruined shoulders got a job in a Mobile hospital rolling fresh corpses from their rooms to the morgue. Maybe he's also thinking of this, because he says, "I resent not being rich."

◆　◆　◆

People get drunk. Cork Templey starts playing the piano and sings "O Come All Ye Faithful" and "Silent Night." That must be the extent of his Christmas carols, because he launches next into the Notre Dame fight song. Tommy goes on a shrimp-and-Heineken-gathering mission and gets stopped by my mother's friend, Marnie McMann. I decide to peek in the greenhouse, so I swing by the bar, trail a maid into the kitchen, skirt the caterer's bustle, and push open the glass door into the balmy air. Inside, there's a world of flowers with spiky green stems and plate-sized blooms in fuchsia and orange. Some smell like cinnamon and others like strawberry jam, and as I walk between the rows it occurs to me that I'll never know the names of flowers like these.

At the end of that Cheever story, Lawrence and his brother, the narrator, are walking on the beach. The narrator wants Lawrence to admit that the day is beautiful, but Lawrence won't, and they have a big fight. Lawrence tells his brother that their family is foolish, bigoted, and superficial. Then he bundles up his drab wife and peevish children and leaves the summer house on the next ferry. The narrator watches him go, musing, "Oh, what can you do with a man like that? . . . How can you teach him to respond to the inestimable greatness of the race, the harsh surface beauty of life?"

Although I'd normally be on the ferry with Lawrence, it occurs to me that there's some kind of truth to the narrator's belief in the power of beauty. How much is beauty worth? Is the creation of beauty a moral good? On one hand, there's the irresponsibility of spending 2.3 million to pivot a house to face a lake. On the other hand, I think, admiring the blue crests from the greenhouse window, it really *is* a great lake. At night, the moon shimmies on the waves kneading the shore, and the day's palette is the muted pastels of a rich man's shaving kit: the sterling silver of the handle, the mauve-tipped bristles, the fluffy white foam. With such a view, one might find it easier to be kind. For such a view, it might be worth turning a house.

At the back of the buzzing greenhouse, I see the black tulip. It's almost midnight, but Birdie has forgotten; I'm alone. I can faintly hear the piano— Cork Templey is exhausting his repertoire by singing "Happy Birthday," although it isn't anyone's. When it gets to the fill-in-the-name part, he croons "Baby Jesus," which earns him applause for resourcefulness. I lean over the terra cotta pot. The petals of the tulip are darker than the darkest black. Darker than the inside of a black-lipped South Sea oyster rolling a black pearl around and around its tongue, darker than the bottom of the sea where drowned men with satchels gather their bones, darker than the leaves of the darkest tea the ancient Albanian women use to foretell the miles you'll sail to find true love. The petals unfold deliberately. Inside are six curved black stamens, pointed and furry like the slippers of pixies, and the black pistil, moist and bulbed, naked and un-shy. It rings me like the clapper of a bell.

◆　◆　◆

The harsh surface beauty of life.

I leave the greenhouse and think about how I've said goodbye to this town. I wouldn't even update the *Woodlands Alumni Newsletter*, which reported "1989 Valedictorian MIA" Maybe for a while I needed to hate Lake Forest for the strength it gave me to get out. But at some point it became an indulgence and a matter of pride. Now, returning down the long foyer to the glass French doors of the living room, I see Preston McMann display three similar coats for his wife: "Which of these mink died for you?" Kippy O'Leary is dabbing club soda on the bodice of her Ferragamo where she's dribbled cabernet. Byrne Whistmorn waits until a woman walks by, then holds a sprig of mistletoe over his head. These are the people I've pitted as my adversaries? I look at them hard. On the piano bench, my mother and Tommy sit side by side playing "Heart and Soul," the only song either of them knows. She's enjoying her new role as mother-in-law, and she's enjoying Tommy, who sips his Heineken and puts it back on the coaster. In fact, everyone's enjoying Tommy; they're not judging him because of his working-class background, I realize—they're admiring him for it.

I think about these women I've scoffed at, women who've never worked outside the home, whose education allows them to discern fake pearls at ten yards but not balance a checkbook. But I also think about what they give to the world by their insistence on beauty. These women are room mothers and Brownie leaders. When a neighbor is sick, these women bake casseroles. These women have beautiful penmanship, and when someone needs to be thanked, these women use monogrammed stationery and fountain pens. They speak French. They set tables with linens passed down from their grandmothers, and damask roses cut from their gardens, and they never skimp for convenience or time. They give to charity and they plant trees for their children's children. They read good novels in rooms lit with pale pink bulbs, for such light is kindest to laugh lines. They always take pains with their appearances. Sometimes they meet with tragedies, and when they do, the rich are no different from us at all.

To hate your hometown is to hate yourself. I realize this as I put my hand on the door leading back to the party. I remember one time when my mother took me to her museum for a ceramist's slide show. In each slide he included an egg for perspective to show the size of his pots and vases. That's what this town is to me, I think. It's not what I've made of my life, but what I measure everything against. This town is the egg. I say something then that I have not said for many, many years. I say it aloud: "I'm Beth Ann Fennelly, and I'm from Lake Forest." I say: "Hello." I turn the handle, and I go inside.

Dunetop Dying

GAYLE BOSS

When I tell my husband I want to call a lawyer, inquire how to get it in writing, legally binding that, should he outlive me, he must take me to the Lake Michigan shore to die, he's going to think I mean to the Charlevoix Hospital in northern lower Michigan where I was born, with its rooms a hundred yards from the water and big picture windows overlooking it. So I'll spell it out to the lawyer, to him: I want to die *on* the shore, fingers in the sand. And not the sand a stone's throw from the hospital in Charlevoix. I want to die some two hundred shoreline miles south of my hometown, and on top of a dune, one particular dune, between Holland and Saugatuck.

I was there yesterday. It's what geologists call a "parabolic dune," a huge crescent-shaped mound of sand, its arms reaching toward the lake. Over two hundred feet high, it is one of the tallest in a ridge of parabolic dunes stretching along Lake Michigan's southeastern shore, the largest assemblage of freshwater coastal dunes in the world, visible from a spacecraft orbiting the earth. Roughly four thousand years ago, when swarms of slaves were finishing the pyramids in Egypt's desert as burial palaces for her pharaohs, strong westerly winds were heaping sand up into these hills, sand that retreating glaciers had left after gouging out the Great Lakes, sand washed to the coast when lake water rose—thirty, forty feet higher than levels we know today—and eroded the land.

Only in the last twenty-five years have we begun to step back and see the bigger earth story, to see the dunes as unique and precious and, for all their girth, fragile, and to enact laws to protect them. The laws on the statute books mostly try to protect the dunes against sand mining; whole dunes—like Pigeon Hill, measured at 217 feet in 1907 and named for the flocks of now extinct passenger pigeons that rested there on their north-south migration—have been leveled, nature's pyramids four thousand years in the making hauled away and fed to the automotive industry.

Climbing is not, so far as I know, a punishable crime. Still, signs at the base of the dune where I repeatedly go ask me not to. Parabolic dunes like this one exist only where vegetation anchors its arms. (Mars, for example, with all of its dune forms, has none that are parabolic.) Pioneer grasses, like marram grass and sand reed, catch blowing sand and help build up the dune. Climbing can damage these and other native plants—some of them, like pitcher's thistle, threatened species. If anchoring plants are damaged, wind erosion can cause a "blowout"; the dune, destabilized, can waste away as sand is blown inland, helter-skelter. I do want every inch of this dune to exist just as it is, to rise up out of the blue and into the blue for my own grandchildren. But I can't resist. It will feed my passion for the dunes, and my activism on their behalf, to climb— or so I justify. And so, each time I'm there, I climb.

After fifteen yards or so of upright, it's down-on-all-fours climbing, heaving upward against the press of gravity and the centrifugal pull of sand. Up, push up. I let myself breathe out loud and loudly, from the belly—like in childbirth. It helps the push. The muscles in my thighs and buttocks and calves feel like they're doing what they were made to do. Also like in childbirth. I resist the temptation to stop climbing and look up, look down, measure how far. Keep going, steady pace, feel each reach and breath, each push and pull, keep going, so that the crest comes almost by surprise—though there's the smell of it coming, summit air—it comes in a gush, a whoosh, of sweet relief. *I'm here.*

Here. On hands and knees, chest heaving, now I feel like the one birthed. Scrambling to my feet and gulping air, I see I am enveloped in blues and greens. I think of the view of earth from space, that delicate blue-green sphere, held up somehow in the void.

I am here, but *I* am lost. Vast waves of deep green—miles of tree tops— undulate out away from me to the east, as far as I can see, and to the south and north too. On a September morning this dunetop seems earth's summit, a gentle Everest of sand. Far below, the lake is a swath of variegated blue silk spread smooth to the west edge of earth's table.

The morning sun has risen just high enough to find my neck and shoulders. I want to turn slowly, a few degrees at a time, to take the panorama in. But my discipline is undone—the beauty is too much—and I crank my body around—first this view, then that, as if any part or all of it might be a mirage.

Three dead trees, pale as the sand, stand with me at the summit. Little birds—sparrows, slivers of finches—fly up and light on the bare branches. They sit and merely turn their heads, no chirping to one another. The crows seem not to bother flying this high. There's little carrion up here, and no buttons, earrings, or shiny wrappers dropped by those simply beach-going. The wind whispers; the waves two hundred feet below shush it.

After a time, sensations congeal into a dominant thought: *There's nothing I need.* Food, yes, but not particular food; the apples in my backpack will do. No music, pictures, or books—no further information, explanation, or story. Certainly not the organizations to which I belong. Nor the people I love and who love me—friends, some loyal over decades; my sister and brother, mother and father. My husband and two young sons?

Down from the dunetop, at my desk in a house on the fringe of a small city, I feel ashamed afterward to say it. Do I appreciate so little the volumes of energy and emotion—even at the expense of their own flesh—others have lavished on me to step so easily out of that shower? Have I given so little out of the reservoir of my self that turning off the flow altogether would cause others little discomfort and would feel like freedom to me?

Of course not, no, I want to insist. And here, back in my house, I'm worried about my youngest son being bullied by the big second-grade kid on the playground again today, and I'm looking forward to this late afternoon when he and his older brother and I will play with their pet rabbit on the porch. And my body is at ease, contented in its memory of this early morning when my husband pulled me to him. After which I sat in my chair and prayed. I got up and drove to a pool to swim, and came home to sloppy kisses from all three boys before they drove off for school. Breakfast included a pear ripe from the tree.

And the memory of another morning on top of the dune is indelible. I felt then that I could have stayed there and thought fondly of my loves and not returned. I felt it without shame, as simple description: at the threshold between worlds we are each alone, and finally we make our crossing, alone.

When we were young, living in a house six small-town blocks from Lake Michigan, my father would tell my brother and sister and me about how

Eskimo old ones were put—or asked to be put?—out alone on the ice to die. He said this simply, without approbation, but without condemnation either. Though we could imagine it—he was, and is, an avid ice fisherman—we tried not to, and never dared to think he was giving us actual directions for his last days. Two winters ago I watched him watch his own mother die slowly in a nursing home. Now I think about bringing up the subject with him. Maybe the frozen plain of lake is his dunetop.

Archaeologists in West Michigan have no material proof that Americans native to this place practiced dunetop dying. It's not likely they'd find any. Unlike the burial mounds along the Grand River thirty-five miles or so inland, where the bones and treasures of notable Hopewell Indians have lain still for almost two thousand years, the sandy earth of the dunes is moving. Another parabolic dune near the one I climb is known to have migrated four-and-a-half feet east last year alone—a literal picture of "the shifting sands of time." I'm reminded of Moses who, according to the book of Deuteronomy, after leading the Hebrew slaves out of Egypt's grip, climbed Mount Nebo in the desert to see the Promised Land he was not allowed to enter, and died there, where "the Lord buried him . . . but no man knows the place of his burial to this day." In the hands of the wind, sand scours bone into particles twin to itself, particles the prevailing winds then lift and take to new places.

Lack of material evidence aside, I'm sure I'm not the first or only inhabitant of West Michigan to want to die on top of a tall dune. Like their isle of Iona, a dunetop is what the Irish would call "a thin place"—where life less visible but more intense presses close. Even at a healthy forty-five, it feels like, if I sat at the summit long enough, I might simply pass over into the other, flesh no impediment. The little I've read of quantum physics tells me that matter is merely fields of force made dense by the spirit of energy. Frailer and fading, its energy ebbing, wouldn't the "matter" of the body put up even less resistance to the draw of another dimension?

Because that, in the end, is what I'm after: a frictionless passage from this life to whatever waits—whatever, without knowing. I *do* want to go gentle into that good night.

Except that it isn't night in the picture of my dunetop dying. Nor is it November, when winds from the northwest heave the lake into waves able to split and sink a 640-foot steel steamer, the *Carl Bradley*, which went down offshore from Charlevoix the night of November 18, 1958; only two of the thirty-five sailors on board survived. It is not January, when day after day of subzero cold freezes the waves into the absolute stillness of ice. No, in the death I've designed for myself, it is a September morning—an azure sky and a warm rising sun, barely a whisper of wind. Ninety-five years old, I'm still able to climb the dune myself. Though I don't need anything, I'd like a mat, maybe a pillow, so I won't have to lie in the sand. I don't expect my ninety-five-year-old husband to carry them up for me. Maybe they could be dropped on the dunetop by helicopter— before dawn, so as not to draw spectators. Note that for the lawyer, too.

And there's the problem—no, the lie—in this design. I've painted my dying scene down to the overnight temperature of the sand and the baromet-ric pressure, the number and kind of clouds in the sky (a few, cumulus; no rain, God forbid). Yet I claim the summit air in my bloodstream relaxes the clutch I keep on time, money, possessions, the ones I love—all the conditions I've thought necessary for a happy life, and death. If it's true, then I should expect the paintbrush to drop from my hand, too—the dune releasing me even from love for itself, for its literal self. After enough climbs to the top, after enough hours spent there, I should be able to die anywhere, anytime, without objec-tion. Because the dunetop would be inside of me.

That's a climbing dune protectors would be glad for, too. Until then, I climb, and beg their pardon.

Water Birds

ANNE-MARIE OOMEN

I once slept alone on the shores of Lake Michigan. I made love on the same shore with a man I met waiting tables in the breakfast bar just that morning. Before we lay down, we swam. He walked into the water with his head high, but the temperature killed his lovely erection just like that. The lake can do that even to the most eager. Put you in your place. Women have it easier with the cold. Still, my nipples were so tight, it hurt when he kissed them.

Some water plovers nest in a hollow on the cool sand, within reach of the waves—one reason they're so rare. It takes a long time to warm a hollow. Like the lake, it holds cold as a self.

I told my mother once that all her daughters were eager lovers. She ticked her Catholic guilt at me, but I saw the smirk at the corners of her lips. Though she never loved water the way we did, would only go in to squat and cool, she perceived as necessary certain lifesaving skills and got us swimming lessons. We took to the water, especially the big waters of the Great Lakes, always too far out, standing on our toes, up to our necks. *Now I can touch, now I can't.* Love of fear at the edge of the drop-off. Stand at the end of earth for as long as you can, teetering. Always in too long, coming out blue-lipped and shivering, radiating an identity of cold into the air even as we ran our fingers along our lake-softened skin, our first sensuality.

I told the man I'd served breakfast, *That's why I keep going in.* I told him as I left him, as I walked into the waves and washed. *I love the cold.* And why I'll sleep alone in reach of the waves. Bird in the hollow.

Chicago Waters

SUSAN POWER

*M*y mother used to say that by the time I was an old woman, Lake Michigan would be the size of a silver dollar. She pinched her index finger with her thumb to show me the pitiful dimensions.

"People will gather around the tiny lake, what's left of it, and cluck over a spoonful of water," she told me.

I learned to squint at the 1967 shoreline until I had carved away the structures and roads built on landfill, and could imagine the lake and its city as my mother found them in 1942 when she arrived in Chicago. I say *the lake and its city* rather than *the city and its lake* because my mother taught me another secret: the city of Chicago belongs to Lake Michigan.

But which of my mother's pronouncements to believe? That Chicago would swallow the Midwestern sea, smother it in concrete? Or that the lake wielded enough strength to out-politick even Mayor Richard J. Daley?

Mayor Daley Sr. is gone now, but the lake remains, alternately tranquil and riled, changing colors like a mood ring. I guess we know who won.

When my mother watches the water from her lakeside apartment building, she still sucks in her breath. "You have to respect the power of that lake," she tells me. And I do now. I do.

I was fifteen years old when I learned that the lake did not love me or hate me, but could claim me nevertheless. I was showing off for a boy, my best friend Tommy, who lived in the same building. He usually accompanied me when I went for a swim, but on this particular day he decided the water was too choppy. I always preferred the lake when it was agitated because its temperature warmed, transforming it into a kind of Jacuzzi.

Tommy is right, I thought, once I saw the looming swells that had looked so unimpressive from the twelfth floor. Waves crashed against the breakwater wall and the metal ladder that led into and out of the lake like the entrance to the deep end of a swimming pool.

I shouldn't do this, I told myself, but I noticed Tommy watching me from his first-floor window. "I'm not afraid," I said to him under my breath. "I bet you think that I'll chicken out just because I'm a girl."

It had been a hot summer of dares, some foolish, some benign. Sense was clearly wanting. I took a deep breath and leapt off the wall into the turmoil, since the ladder was under attack. How did I think I would get out of the water? I hadn't thought that far. I bobbed to the surface and was instantly slapped in the face. I was beaten by water, smashed under again and again, until I began choking because I couldn't catch my breath.

I'm going to die now, I realized, and my heart filled with sorrow for my mother, who had already lost a husband and would now lose a daughter. I fought the waves, struggled to reach the air and the light, the sound of breakers swelling in my ears, unnaturally loud, like the noise of Judgment Day. *Here we go*, I thought.

Then I surprised myself, becoming unusually calm. I managed a quick gasp of breath and plunged to the bottom of the lake, where the water was a little quieter. I swam to the beach next door, remaining on the lake floor until I reached shallow waters. I burst to the surface then, my lungs burning, and it took me nearly five minutes to walk fifteen feet, knocked off balance as I was by waves that sucked at my legs. This beach now belongs to my mother and the other shareholders in her building, property recently purchased and attached to their existing lot. But in 1977 it was owned by someone else, and a barbed-wire fence separated the properties. I ended my misadventure by managing to climb over the sharp wire.

I remained downstairs until I stopped shaking. Tommy no longer watched me from his window, bored by my private games, unaware of the danger. I didn't tell my mother what had happened until hours later. I was angry at myself for being so foolish, so careless with my life, but I was never for a moment angry at the lake. I didn't come to fear it either, though it is a mighty force that drops 923 feet in its deepest heart. I understand that it struck indifferently; I was neither target nor friend. My life was my own affair, to lose or to save. Once I stopped struggling with the great lake, I flowed through it, and was expelled from its hectic mouth.

◆ ◆ ◆

My mother still calls Fort Yates, North Dakota, "home," despite the fact that she has lived in Chicago for nearly fifty-five years. She has taken me to visit the Standing Rock Sioux Reservation where she was raised, and although a good portion of it was flooded during the construction of the Oahe Dam, she can point to hills and buttes and creeks of significance. The landscape there endures, outlives its inhabitants. But I am a child of the city, where landmarks are man-made, impermanent. My attachments to place are attachments to people, my love for a particular area only as strong as my local relationships. I have lived in several cities and will live in several more. I visit the country with curiosity and trepidation, a clear foreigner, out of my league, and envy the connection my mother has to a dusty town, the peace she finds on a prairie. It is a kind of religion, her devotion to Proposal Hill and the Missouri River, a sacred bond that I can only half understand. If I try to see the world through my mother's eyes, find the point where my own flesh falls to earth, I realize my home is Lake Michigan, the source of so many lessons.

As a teenager I loved to swim in the dark, to dive beneath the surface where the water was as black as the sky. The lake seemed limitless and so was I—an arm, a leg, a wrist, a face indistinguishable from the wooden boards of the sunken dock, from the sand I squeezed between my toes. I always left reluctantly, loath to become a body again and to feel more acutely the oppressive pull of gravity.

It was my father who taught me to swim, with his usual patience and clear instructions. First he helped me float, his hands beneath my back and legs, his torso shading me from the sun. Next he taught me to flutter-kick, and I tried to make as much noise as possible. I dog-paddled in circles as a little girl, but my father swam in a straight line perpendicular to shore, as if he were trying to leave this land forever. Just as he had left New York State after a lifetime spent within its borders—easily, without regret. His swim was always the longest, the farthest. Mom and I would watch him as we lounged on our beach towels, nervous that a boat might clip him. It was a great relief to see him turn around and coast in our direction.

"Here he comes," Mom would breathe. "He's coming back now."

My father also showed me how to skip a stone across the water. He was skillful, and could make a flat rock bounce like a tiny leaping frog, sometimes five or six hops before it sank to the bottom. It was the only time I could imagine this distinguished silver-haired gentleman as a boy, and I laughed at him affectionately because the difference in our years collapsed.

*   *   *

My mother collects stones in her backyard—a rough, rocky beach in South Shore. She looks for pebbles drilled with holes, not pits or mere scratches, but tiny punctures worn clear through the stone.

"I can't leave until I find at least one," she tells me.

"Why?" I ask. I've asked her more than once because I am forgetful.

"There are powerful spirits in these stones, trying to tunnel their way out."

Ah, that explains the holes. What I do not ask is why she selects them, these obviously unquiet souls, why she places them in a candy dish or a basket worn soft as flannel. What good can it do them? What good can it do her to unleash such restless forces on the quiet of her rooms?

I finger my mother's collection when I'm home for a visit. I have even pressed a smooth specimen against my cheek. The touch is cool. I believe it could draw a fever, and the object is mute and passive in my hand. At first I think there is a failing on my part, I cannot hear what my mother hears, and then I decide that the spirits caught in these stones have already escaped. I imagine them returning to the lake, to the waves that pushed them onto the beach and washed their pebble flesh, because it is such a comfort to return to water.

And then I remember my own weightless immersion, how my body becomes a fluid spirit when I pull myself underwater, where breath stops. And I remember gliding along the lake's sandy bottom as a child, awed by the orderly pattern of its dunes. Lake Michigan is cold, reliably cold, but occasionally I passed through warm pockets, abrupt cells of tepid water that always came as a surprise. I am reminded of cold spots reputedly found in haunted houses, and I wonder if these warm areas are evidence of my lost souls.

A young man drowned in these waters behind my mother's building some years ago. Mom was seated in a lawn chair, visiting with another tenant on the terrace. They sat together facing the lake so they could watch its activity, though it was calm that day, uninteresting. A young man stroked into view, swimming parallel to the shore and heading north. He was close enough for them to read his features; he was fifteen feet away from shallow depths where he could have stood with his head above water. He called to them, a reasonable question in a calm voice. He wanted to know how far south he was. The 7300 block, they told him. He moved on. A marathon swimmer, the women decided. But eventually my mother and her friend noticed his absence, scanned the horizon unable to see his bobbing head and strong arms. They alerted the doorman, who called the police. The young man was found near the spot where he'd made his cordial inquiry.

"Why didn't he cry for help? Why didn't he signal his distress?" my mother asked the response unit.

"This happens all the time with men," she was told. "They aren't taught to cry for help."

So he is there too, the swimmer, a warm presence in cold water or a spirit in stone.

◆   ◆   ◆

I have gone swimming in other places—a chlorinated pool in Hollywood, the warm waters of the Caribbean, the Heart River in North Dakota—only to be disappointed and emerge unrefreshed. I am too used to Lake Michigan and its eccentricities. I must have cold, fresh water. I must have the stinking corpses of silver alewives floating on its surface as an occasional nasty surprise, discovered dead and never alive. I must have sailboats on the horizon and steel mills on the southern shore, golf balls I can find clustered around submerged pilings (shot from the local course), and breakwater boulders heavy as tombs lining the beach. I must have sullen lifeguards who whistle to anyone bold enough to stand in three feet of water, and periodic arguments between wind and water which produce tearing waves and lake-spattered windows.

When I was little, maybe seven or eight, my parents and I went swimming in a storm. The weather was mild when we first set out, but the squall arrived quickly, without warning, as often happens in the Midwest. I remember we swam anyway, keeping an eye on the lightning not yet arrived from the north. There was no one to stop us since we were dipping into deep water between beaches, in an area that was unpatrolled. The water was warmer than usual, the same temperature as the air, and when the rain wet the sky, I leapt up and down in the growing waves, unable to feel the difference between air and water, lake and rain. The three of us played together that time; even my father remained near shore rather than striking east to swim past the white buoys. We were joined in this favorite element, splashing, ducking. I waved my arms over my head. My father pretended to be a great white whale, heavy in the surf, now and then spouting streams of water from his mouth. He chased me. My mother laughed.

Dad died in 1973 when I was eleven years old, before my mother and I moved to the apartment on the lake. We always thought it such a shame he didn't get to make that move with us. He would have enjoyed finding Lake Michigan in his backyard.

We buried him in Albany, New York, because that is where he was raised. My mother was born in North Dakota, and I was born between them, in Chicago. There is a good chance we shall not all rest together, our stories playing out in different lands. But I imagine that if a rendezvous is possible—and my mother insists it is—we will find one another in this great lake, this small sea that rocks like a cradle.

Trouble

In the half dark of early morning my mother loops our clothesline through her belt, knots the other end around my waist and leads me through the wet grass, over rocks and moss—our feet slipping as we climb the pier where she will fish until the sun becomes oppressive. I am three then, four at most—too innocent to protest a rope or whatever else would moor me to her, or to understand that, because she cannot swim, her fear of losing me gets complicated. Instead, I swirl my hand inside the bucket of minnows until I'm dizzy, and count the carp that flash and disappear like gold medallions between the rushes. When the sun casts beads of light onto the water like a rosary, I pray this time will soon be over.

—*Alinda Dickinson Wasner*

After my grandmother died, I found a letter my grandfather had written her, on the day he died, sending her two dollars. From Michigan. Lake Michigan, someone else said, was where he drowned, while he was away with his boss purchasing mining equipment. He was in a boat with his boss and his boss's friend. The friend decided to dive in for a swim, cramps or something else tugging him under. My grandfather, a good swimmer, tried to save him. When their bodies were found, my grandfather was locked in the other man's arms. I could have walked into the waves of Lake Michigan many times, forgetting how to come back, forgetting how to swim, forgetting there was time outside the moment. But I didn't. I remembered my grandfather.

—*Anita Skeen*

A year previous [to the Water Walk around Lake Superior], I was at a Sun Dance and I heard our spiritual leader, Grand Chief E. Benton-Banaise-Bawd-wayadun, speak about the water and how in thirty years it was going to cost so much, an ounce of water comparable to an ounce of gold. It was foretold how this would happen if we don't mend our ways. In most prophecy, though, there is hope. In the word "if" was the hope I rested on. Then I thought about women all across the nation, North America and South America, and the world. If all women got up and spoke on behalf of Mother Earth and the water and ourselves, how powerful it could be.

—*Josephine Mandamin with Bonnie Jo Campbell*

I lay there on the wet earth with the misty rain falling, afraid to sit up for fear the pain would return. But I was calm. I was not utterly alone. I kept looking at the trees, listening, knowing that I would be all right if I could just keep listening. After a time, I sat up. Getting my clothes off felt as significant an accomplishment as landing safely on the beach some long long time ago. I was standing naked in the wind and rain and shaking so violently I could scarcely pull on my dry long underwear. But I belonged here.

—*Ann Linnea*

The Gray Lady of Lake Huron

Laura Kasischke

*I*t might be the fog. When the wind and the water temperatures go to war, so much of that chalk-thick stuff rolls off Lake Huron that to drive through Alpena is to wander through a town populated by ghouls and the shadowy edifices of the past.

That man crossing the street in a black suit? He's stepped out of the past, right into the path of my car. But instead of the weighted bump of a body on the hood, I pass through him, or he passes through me. Out of the fog and back into it in a heartbeat.

And that church over there, all blond bricks and ghostly spires? It's only nine o'clock in the morning on a Tuesday, but can that be a bride, veiled, holding a bouquet of pale flowers, standing at the top of the steps?

No.

That's a pillar. No one is on the steps of the church this morning in the fog, which is rolling off Lake Huron in great disintegrating walls, and everything has taken on its strangeness, everything has become like it: here, and not here, substance and nothing.

. . .

So, friends of mine who lived in Alpena told me with straight faces that there was a ghost in the Old Presque Isle Lighthouse.

Oh. No kidding? Are there anymore beers in the fridge?

They settled in to tell me about it. I settled in to hear. Kaylee's eyes got damp as she talked. Her husband Kurt patted her shoulder. Outside their little tract house in the snow, there was the kind of silence you only hear when, close by, there are vast stretches of nothing over which the wind gets tired of blowing. That was Lake Huron, a few miles down the road, that big half-frozen blank where the road abruptly ended and the nothing began.

Twenty-three thousand square miles of blank. In some places that lake is seven hundred and fifty feet deep.

Suddenly, everything had changed. An ordinary evening visiting with my college friend had turned into something new and strange.

It never crossed my mind that they were right, that there was a ghost in the lighthouse up the road, that my friend Kaylee had heard it. What set my heart racing was, instead, the other supernatural thing taking place at that moment: someone I'd thought of as utterly normal was, perhaps, not. Someone I'd thought of as a bit chilly and ironic and scarily smart, someone I'd thought I'd known pretty well for many years, believed (strongly enough that there were real tears in her eyes!) in something so romantic and unlikely and Victorian that, without any conscious effort on my part, my tongue, as she told me the story, made its way to my cheek and began to make little circles on the soft inside wall there.

Kaylee had occupied a dorm room next to my own for only a year. All totaled, I suppose the amount of time we'd actually spent in one another's company wouldn't have added up to more than a few solid days, but we'd always kept in touch. Postcards. Phone calls when there were big announcements to be made. I'd been a bridesmaid at her wedding, satin shoes dyed green to match my dress and the whole nine yards. When we lived in the dorm together, we used to go to a restaurant around the corner almost every night to eat cinnamon rolls with ice cream, until one night each of us felt that it was her duty as a friend to point out to the other that she was putting on an alarming amount of weight. We were both insulted, but started exercising in the evenings instead of eating cinnamon rolls and ice cream.

I knew she liked horses, although I'd never had occasion to see her ride one. I knew she passionately hated her own sister, who had seemed truly hateable when I'd met her at Kaylee's wedding. I knew she'd had her heart broken by a hockey player in high school. If asked if my friend Kaylee believed in ghosts (or elves, or angels), I'd have been willing to bet my life that she did not, or that if she did, it would have been in only the loosest of ways. Liberal, magnanimous, at most she might have said that the world was too mysterious to rule anything completely out of the realm of possibility.

And her husband, Kurt. He listened to a lot of Bruce Springsteen and read history textbooks for pleasure. He was the one from Alpena, who brought Kaylee back there to live. One of his many, many hobbies was polishing rocks.

But here I was with a bottle of Corona between my knees on my old friend's couch, finding out that she'd heard, only eight months before, the ghost of a woman wailing in a lighthouse.

Who was she, Kaylee?

It suddenly struck me that I had no idea, that I was staying overnight in the house of someone I thought I'd known for years, but didn't know at all.

Of course, similar things had happened to me, have happened to us all. Imagine, if you can, the incredulity with which the old college pals of the members of Heaven's Gate (the cult that eventually committed mass suicide in the belief that a mother ship in the tail of the Hale-Bopp comet was waiting to bear them away) learned of their friends' new convictions. It's hard enough sometimes to look at the mates our friends choose and imagine what they're thinking, what reality looks like though their eyes. To find that a friend believes in ghosts or aliens or reincarnation is to see not only the friend but the world in a new light.

Tongue moving in circles inside my cheek, I went over the possibilities in my head as she spoke.

Maybe, in the years since we'd lived together in the same town, she'd become an entirely different person. A New Age person. Or maybe she was on some prescription drug she'd never mentioned, overmedicated. Maybe it was genetic. Had her mother believed in ghosts? Or perhaps there was simply some kind of ordinary confusion. Yes, she'd heard something, and then she'd had a dream . . .

Or maybe I'd just never known her very well. That was surprisingly likely, I supposed. After all, somebody was Ted Bundy's girlfriend for years and never noticed anything unusual about him. I'd worked with a man who'd seemed the embodiment of the word *asexual*—small, shy, fat, and honest—and found out years after the fact that the whole time I was working with him, he was having a wild love affair with the drop-dead-gorgeous wife of our macho boss.

But I thought I knew Kaylee pretty well.

Once, I'd had to pick a piece of lettuce out from between her two front teeth with my fingernail because she couldn't get it.

She was a photographer of the calendar/greeting-card sort. She'd gone to the Old Presque Isle Lighthouse to take a photograph early on a September morning when the sun was just rising. She'd parked a half-mile away, where the road met the sand, and walked with her equipment in a bag slung over her shoulder to the lighthouse.

Chilly morning, of course. The green of the beach grass and the surrounding white pine. The meandering line of grit between the water and the dry sand. The steel blue of the water. A streak of orange from the sun rising right down the middle of the lake. Gulls, gray and white, bobbing on the water.

Presque Isle means "almost an island" in French. It's a spit of land that juts from the western shore of Lake Huron. The Indians and the French used to portage across it in order to avoid the bad bigger waters around it. It's easy to see them there, dragging their boats through the white birch while the deer scattered off into the woods. The place couldn't be much different now from what it was then. The lighthouse was built in 1840, then shut down thirty-one years later when the New Presque Isle Lighthouse was built on the other side of the spit.

The last Old Presque Isle Lighthouse keeper was appointed by President Lincoln. Not much has gone on there since then. Some tourists. Some photographers. Some vandals spray-painting *Fuck You* on the outside of the tower, expressing some obscure hostility toward, perhaps, everything in general.

The tower and the keeper's quarters are built of stone and cement, which, smoothed down and painted white, have taken on the look of stucco. Or flesh. The tower looks less phallic than many lighthouse towers because of the curved waist and hips of the thing, the way it tapers into a long swan-neck at the top. It's not that tall. Thirty-nine steps inside, whereas a lot of lighthouse towers have hundreds of steps leading to the light at the top.

Kaylee had all her photographic equipment ready to go. She was looking for the perfect spot from which to aim it. Where the water slid into the sand, the sun had turned it to a pink and blue shingle.

For me, growing up a good forty miles from Lake Michigan, hours to the Upper Peninsula, on the other side of the state from Huron and Erie, the big lakes always meant vacation. Summer. Suntan. Sand in my peanut-butter sandwich. But my father, who grew up on Lake Michigan, always provided a less recreational vision of the big water. He'd nearly drowned in it. Had friends who did. A cousin who was yanked right off the end of a pier by an anomalous wave on a windless day and was never seen again. He had a memory of standing on the beach with his parents watching a hapless rescue attempt being made for a sinking freighter. On more than a few occasions, he saw bodies being dragged out.

The lakes can suggest many things. Infinity. Death. Buried secrets. Sunken desires. Lost hope. A big comma inserted into time.

Add a lighthouse. Keep it isolated. Make it September, the leaves getting ragged around the edges. A few crows screeching in the pines.

Kaylee grew up in a suburb of Detroit. Until Alpena, I'm not sure she'd had much to do with lakes or lighthouses at all.

She found the perfect shot in her viewfinder.

Of course, any woman alone on a spit of land at the end of a gravel road in the morning is afraid that she might not, really, be alone. That someone's watching from the woods. Some ax murderer driving by in a van. A woman alone is always listening. Alone outdoors, what a woman worries about is hearing something human, something male. A man by himself. Or with a dog. Or two men on their own. What you want is to stay alone or encounter, if other humans are around, a man and a woman together, or a woman and a child. She was absorbed in her view of the lighthouse through that tiny window, but also listening for the sound of motorized vehicles or a man clearing his throat. What she heard instead was the steady coming and going of Lake Huron, those few crows screeching, a bit of breeze through the pine needles, and then a low, cool shiver of moaning coming from the tower.

She let the camera dangle from the rope around her neck and stood frozen for a moment, listening.

Nothing.

She picked up the camera and aimed it again, but she was worried now. She only half believed she'd heard something, but she felt sure she was going to hear it again, and did. Louder this time, higher, no doubt about it. This wasn't a sound coming off the lake or a sound she was imagining, coming from the base of her brain. This was a woman's voice, and it was coming from the tower.

She let the camera dangle again, and then, again, it came. The same. Low, cool, rising, female. Not supernatural. Not a movie-ghost moan. But the sound of a real woman, really moaning, about twenty feet away from where Kaylee was standing, coming from either inside the tower or just behind it.

"Hello?" Kaylee called out.

No answer.

She took the camera off from around her neck and started to put it back into her bag when she heard it again.

"Hello?" This time she shouted over the moaning, and that seemed to cut it off. "Hello?" And then it started again.

"I didn't know what the fuck to do," Kaylee said. There were tears on her face now. "I mean, I thought there was some woman in there. What was I supposed to do? Just run off? It sounded like a *real woman*, and there's *no way* she'd be making a sound like that if she was *okay*."

My husband has told me that his ex-wife used to call the moment when the protagonist in a horror film decided, say, to investigate the dark attic from which the scrape of a chain being dragged around bare floorboards was coming, the "Principle of Maximal Stupidity." She hated the principle, and hated the movies.

But it's hard to think of Kaylee being just plain stupid as she headed for the lighthouse tower from which she heard a voice coming—a physical voice—of a woman in pain.

Still, it's hard to see yourself in that position, too. To imagine doing what she did. She didn't have a cell phone with her. (This was 1990; who had a cell phone?) Why didn't she drive into town and get the cops?

But the strangest thing of all to contemplate, as I sat there watching Kurt rubbing the shoulder of his wife as she stammered out this story, was why she would make it up. The thing that sent chills down my spine and forced my tongue back into its place beneath my palate was when I began to wonder if my friend was nuts.

Schizophrenic. Paranoid. Or a pathological liar.

Did she have some kind of addiction to drama? Did she believe her own story, or did she know she was making it up? What did she want from me, telling it? Or was this a way of getting some kind of attention from her husband? Was she attempting to hide something with this story? Had she done something she had to cover up? An affair? A burglary? A murder? I had, myself, told plenty of lies in my life. Whoppers. But there had always been reasons:

I'd told my college boyfriend my family was Jewish because he was Jewish and I thought if he thought I was too, he'd love me more. I told my first husband I was a virgin when nothing could have been further from the truth. But I did not recall ever having done anything like this, like telling an elaborate ghost story to an old friend, and I'd never been that good at lying (fabricated tears were way out of my league) and couldn't imagine under what circumstances I would ever consider putting on such a show. Or for what purpose. I was going back to Ann Arbor in the morning. Kaylee and I probably wouldn't see each other again for a year or more. Why she would want to impress me, or how she might think that this would, was hard to figure. Anyone I would share the story of her ghost with wouldn't even know who Kaylee was.

Kurt.

It had to be for the benefit of Kurt.

But why? Surely Kurt was no secret ghostbuster. And if you wanted to invoke, for some reason, a protective or sympathetic response from your spouse, there surely had to be easier lies to tell than this one.

And, as far as I knew, Kurt was a fine husband. Kaylee was happy. In a couple of years they'd have kids. She liked Alpena. They had a tandem bicycle which they rode long distances together on the weekends. Their cat had recently died, but they were going to get another one when the time was right.

Because there was no woman behind the lighthouse, according to the Principle of Maximal Stupidity, Kaylee had to go inside.

Well, naturally, it was very dark. Those thirty-nine stairs. You could reach out and touch both sides of the tower at once. It smelled like mold and wet stone.

"Hello?!"

Nothing.

She kept climbing the stairs.

The stairwell grew narrower.

She was in the swan-neck of the tower, climbing gradually toward the light at the top, when she heard it again, behind her.

Kaylee spun around fast while the moan was still rolling out of the space between herself and the bottom of the tower, and what she saw was a young woman dressed in a gray dress holding a candle, climbing toward her as she moaned.

Very pale.

Kaylee screamed (of course) and ran down the stairs straight through the woman (who looked, she thought, as frightened and surprised to see Kaylee as Kaylee was to see her) and out the door, back onto the beach. She ran to her camera equipment, grabbed it, took off running for the car, and never looked back.

That was the end of the story.

Kurt, apparently, offered to go there and look for the woman, but Kaylee insisted he do nothing of the sort. Winter had passed between then and now. Everything was normal. She'd never taken a photograph of the lighthouse, and wasn't going back there, of course, ever. Ever. Except for Kurt, I was the only person to whom she'd told the whole awful episode.

Had anything like this ever happened to her before?

No.

Had anything like this ever happened to Kurt?

Hell no.

Immediate family? Distant relatives? Neighbors? Had she recently read any books about, seen any movies about—

No, no, no, no, no.

We talked about other things, drank a few more beers, listened to Bruce Springsteen, and that night I slept on their couch..

In the morning, I drove out of Alpena in a fog so thick that Lake Huron did not appear to exist. Just an emptiness. An obscured swing set on the beach was the only hint that anything but fog was out there at all. The stoplight at the edge of town burned yellow, then red, then green through the fog, appearing to be attached to nothing. It crossed my mind to stop by the lighthouse, but for a great many reasons I didn't. I didn't want to see a ghost, but I also didn't think I would.

◆　◆　◆

Years passed. Normally enough. She had kids. I had one. We fell out of touch except for Christmas cards, which I never saw the point of until I turned forty and so much of my past was in the past, my old friends scattered, and so much distance between us that it was too much (like staring directly into the sun) to actually get together, and the telephone (like shouting across an abyss) not enough, so that Christmas cards became just the right way to keep, sort of, in touch.

Since I'd last seen Kaylee, the Internet had been invented, and, bored at work one day, I looked up "Old Presque Isle Lighthouse" on it.

Someone had written something on an amateurish ghosties-website about how the last lighthouse keeper (the one appointed by Lincoln) used to lock his wife in the tower of that lighthouse at night while he went to visit his girlfriend in town. One morning he came home hung over and worn out to find she'd hanged herself in there. Since then, she could be heard moaning out over Lake Huron or in that closed-down tower now and then.

In a ghost story, this would be the point where everything would come together in an *ah-HA* moment, except that the entry was anonymous, so it seemed quite possible to me that, if Kaylee was capable of making up such a story, she would also be quite likely to get on the Internet and write an anonymous entry on a website about it.

Or could this be an old story, one Kaylee had heard in Alpena, maybe a story everyone in Alpena had heard all about? Had she gone to the lighthouse with her camera that day expecting to find a ghost? Would she have been disappointed if she hadn't?

♦   ♦   ♦

Last summer, I drove with my husband through Alpena on the way home from the Upper Peninsula. We didn't stop except at that stoplight. There was, as there had been the last time I'd been through that town, a thick rolling fog coming off Lake Huron. We were waiting for the red light burning through the gray to change to green, and I was telling him Kaylee's story—the story of Kaylee telling her story—when the light changed and he stepped on the gas pedal of our Toyota just as a woman stepped into the street in front of us. My husband slammed on the brake, but it was too late; we'd already slid straight through the woman and the gray dress she was wearing, and when I turned fast to look for her in the road behind us, there was no one. But I did see, clearly, stepping up onto the curb on the other side of the street, a woman I recognized instantly from the family photograph she'd sent me the Christmas before:

Kaylee.

"What the hell?" Bill said.

I told my husband to keep going, that it had only seemed that we'd run over a woman, a woman who, I didn't tell him at that moment, was Kaylee, because I thought, at best, he'd think I was imagining things, and, at worst, he'd think I was making it up. And also because I knew it had to be one of those two things, that nothing else made any sense at all, and that I had no idea which it was.

Against the Law

ELIZABETH A. TREMBLEY

One cold November morning, while illegally walking my German shepherds off leash at a nearby state park, I found a body in the woods.

. . .

No matter what the season, I take the dogs to the Lake Michigan woods and beach—always unleashed and against the law. In winter, we celebrate free access to the lake's openness, its rule of chaos and mystery, sometimes foaming, sometimes smooth, and we find relief from the constant contention for control that fills the human world. During the summer, when rangers riding screeching four-wheelers control the parks, we have to sneak in. Often, we avoid the beach altogether, and instead climb a high dune where we can at least see the lake. Autumn rejuvenates me, because then the summer folks return to their indoor lives, and we can again enjoy the forest trails and beach. Once more we can tune ourselves to the sand scrabbling beneath our feet, the scents curling upwards from the fallen leaves, the iridescent flashes of a turkey feather rolled between thumb and forefinger.

. . .

The frozen weather that drives others indoors had just begun when I took a Friday morning off from work to enjoy a leashless, lawless swing through the woods and a reunion with the shore. I'd walked only a few minutes when the silvery tang of adrenaline coated my tongue. At first, I did not understand why.

Then my brain registered it, ten paces ahead, another ten to the left: a new loafer, chocolate nubuck, hanging from a left foot about eighteen inches from the ground. A navy ragg sock disappeared into faded jeans. A tailored leather jacket bunched between his back and the tree. His head was turned away from me, so I couldn't see any insignia on his black ball cap. Short brown hair bristled into a well-trimmed beard.

I stopped walking.

This is a dead person. Deep breaths flooded my blood with oxygen, preparing.

Walk on. Remember, if you see something bad happening, pretend you don't notice, so the crooks don't come after you. I'd learned that one as a graduate student at the University of Chicago.

I stood near the viewing benches of a bird watchers' theater, which overlooked a bog shining like licorice, considering.

Probably just a dummy or a prank.

A dead person, my gut snapped. *Go.*

My legs carried me forward again, slowly. The dogs ran ahead, tails wagging, intent on the beach. I cast another glance at the body—no more than the whisper of a look.

Don't look!

I stared at the ground, a red-tan mix of sand and forest rot. Those shoes and the leather coat had seemed fairly nice. Not likely that anyone would dress a dummy like that, even for the most realistic of pranks.

My mind stalled, then insisted on one more look as I walked.

He hung from a bright white clothesline, tied to the juncture of a branch and the tree trunk only inches above the head. The right hand reached up, wrapped around a higher branch. The left arm crooked over another branch, wrist limp, hand hanging down. The right leg hung over a third branch, as if he tried to take the weight from his neck. The left leg dangled straight down, toes reaching for the ground.

He fought this. He lost. He died.

On the ground beneath him sat a jumbo-sized Burger King cup, still half-full of dark liquid, straw jutting from the spill-proof lid. A crumpled food bag lay nearby.

My steps slowed. Who has a picnic before they kill themselves?

White panic exploded along my spine, spilling shimmering heat into my brain and legs, and I stood motionless again.

Someone did this, tied him, watched, sipping soda until his reaching stopped, ate a hamburger in the cold, making sure.

Is the murderer still here? Is there more than one?

I wanted the dogs near me, but terror stripped speech from my throat. They seemed to have entirely missed the dead body hanging there.

If the murderers think you haven't noticed, they'll leave you alone.

I walked again. Someone might be watching, plotting to keep me from returning to my car. If I turned around on the path, I would only have to walk about two hundred yards to my car. Going forward, even taking the shortest trail, meant nearly two miles in this stinging isolation. If I turned around, I could get to the car in less than a minute.

I envisioned the park's layout in my mind's eye, a panorama shot from a helicopter. I saw the water, blue and white-edged, and the beach, flat, empty, and rising up the dunes into the woods. The dark green shadow of the pine forest, usually so peaceful, with gulls or a heron flying overhead, now throbbed with red and yellow hues, seething in its distance from a telephone or a lockable door. Shadowy figures lurked behind the trees.

If you turn around, they'll know you saw. They'll come after you, to silence you. Keep walking.

I watched my purple and white Sauconys barely ruffle the path as they walked deeper into the woods. I knew that this was the sort of thing soon-to-die teenagers did in bad movies, but I thought only of how I might reduce these murderers' motives for killing me. I had to pretend that I didn't know they were there.

◆ ◆ ◆

Most days I go to the beach bringing questions, and the mixed forms of the space created, not constructed, offer me answers. I pay attention; I smell winter in the wind and hear mermaids twanging country-western tunes beneath the ice. The seamless intimacy of lake and shore consumes my boundaries, invites my connection to the vast lake and sometimes vaster droplet, each containing worlds much bigger than my own. They ignite me.

◆ ◆ ◆

I climbed high along the back dune, circling south above the death. As soon as I could no longer see the body, I reasoned the murderers could no longer see me, and I began to run.

Before long, I could not distinguish separate heartbeats in my pounding ears. I swung my head to study every tree trunk large enough to conceal a person. I listened for nearby movement, but could only hear my heart and the racket from my asthmatic lungs.

I looked to the dogs, expecting reassurance. I had always believed they would attack someone if he assaulted me, but they hadn't investigated the death site at all. Would they see a murderer if one were tailing us now?

Up the next steep hill, my lungs crackled like tissue, and I knew I had to slow down or pass out. I remembered a favorite cartoon from childhood: the Bugs Bunny version of "The Tortoise and the Hare," in which that galumphing turtle drawls his philosophy of life to the smart-alecky Bugs. Bugs's legs blur in a circle, he runs so fast; but he still loses. Would someone watching me see my legs blurring too?

"Slow and steady wins the race," I chanted out loud, forcing myself to slow down, to breathe as deeply as I could without coughing, verbally rocking myself into a calmer pace.

I bent toward a rough and rooted hill, like a rider helping a horse clear a wall. I stretched my arms out in front of me, reaching for an invisible rope and pulling. My lungs clicked but did not seize, and I kept on. Soon I'd be home.

Home. When I got there, I'd have to call my boss, because I didn't think I should go to work. And my mother. She'd never believe this. No one would believe this. As I descended toward the trail head, I thought of the friends I would call, of their astonished reactions.

I arrived at the parking lot, and just inside the lip of the woods I stopped to survey the place. I saw only my station wagon and the red pickup that had been there when I arrived. It had frost on its windshield. I should have noticed that before.

I have heard about criminals hiding under parked cars until they reached out and grabbed their victim's ankles, the modern adult version of the monster under the bed. I looked. The coast seemed clear.

Somewhere to the west, waves slapped against the beach. They were not for me today.

I didn't want to do it, but of course I had to, so I grabbed the dogs' collars, called them to heel, and bolted toward my car. My hands drove the key into the lock with one smooth movement as my eyes scanned the perimeter of the grassy picnic area. I opened the passenger door and the dogs leapt inside; then I slid in, too, and locked the doors. My hand wavered near the ignition.

Please start. Cars never start in horror movies.

My eyes continued scanning the edge of the woods. I slid the car into reverse.

Call the police.

The engine's hum matched my panic. I didn't have a cell phone. I lived more than twenty minutes away. I had to find a phone.

♦　♦　♦

I read once that there are no naturally occurring horizontal lines in nature except for the backs of animals—and a water horizon. All of nature moves upward or in a circle, mimicking the cosmic plan. Most horizontal lines, and the rectangles they help construct, are human creations. That's why I break the rules nearly every day, sneaking to sanctuary like a criminalized pagan. Time on the beach with dogs takes the sharp angles from a tired face and smoothes the edges of a tried soul.

When the structures of our lives collapse, we seek something to hold onto: an edge, a boundary, a beach where we can see the beauty in overpowering chaos and experience the solidity of land at the same time. The edge of the littoral space gives us a way to shore up against the collapse. We can reinvent ourselves, allow the chaos of imagination to rumble over the sand, shifting its shape, creating something new for ourselves.

♦　♦　♦

It didn't take long for the police to determine that the man I found had killed himself, but that didn't help me. Death had overtaken my sanctuary. I tried to go back the next day, and the next, and found myself possessed by terror. The lone jogger I passed could easily have murdered me if he wished to, and for the first time I knew it. Fear spit from bone to bone, and I couldn't see, couldn't hear, couldn't feel any of the peace I'd always come for.

. . .

This hanging man's life had been extinguished, my sanctuary violated. What I loved about the woods was the rough weaving of energy in a pattern subtle beyond my understanding. But occasionally I got glimpses of the weave, and felt amazed and relieved by my own powerlessness to change it, by all of humanity's powerlessness to change it. I felt as if I'd shared a small bit of the cosmic tapestry.

The dead man had made it a cosmic joke. I raged. How dare he do this to me! Hadn't he thought about what it would be like for someone to find him?

. . .

Almost three years passed. I visited the woods, but only with others, never alone. No one blamed me, but I couldn't help loathing my own ridiculousness. After all, no one had actually threatened me; I had imagined the danger. Someone else had suffered, and in those woods.

Then one day it hit me: I refused to follow the park rules because they restricted the very freedom that gave the woods their spirit, just as my imagination gave me mine. I had chosen these woods as the best place for my own small rebellion, just as the dead man had chosen it for his ultimate one. I realized he had not changed the tapestry of my life, but simply revealed a new pattern within it, one which I didn't really want to see.

So, one cold morning, I went back alone.

I stood firmly on the trail and looked across the space between where I had stood and where he had hung. I envisioned him there once again, remembered the sharp adrenaline in my mouth, and the rasping loss of my voice. Then I walked off the path and back into my imagination.

I stood at the base of the tree and looked up its trunk, amazed at its height. I estimated it at nearly sixteen feet around, an old jack pine, with many stubbled branches. I speculated about how he'd climbed, where he'd sat when tying the rope. I took a deep breath and leaned back against the tree, right where he had been.

What had he thought of, sitting there between midnight and two A.M.? What had it been like in the thick dark, listening to bare branches click in the breeze, deciding to die?

I remembered my own darkness in these woods after I found him. Had he, too, envisioned danger everywhere? Did he feel terror or grief or helplessness he would do anything to escape? Was his act one of rebellion, like mine—an insistence on the recognition of the individual as empowered, as worthy, as uncontrollable?

My dogs and I walk freely in those woods again. I've stopped raging at the dead man and myself, and I feel only fleeting fear.

Occasionally I wonder: was the man whose body I found hanging from a jack pine perhaps more alive at the moment when he acted against the law of life then he had ever been?

Getting to Water

CLAUDIA SKUTAR

*lways there is a desire to wade into the calmness of Huron, even with the moon skulking just over the horizon, a witness so reflective that some nights a woman must pull back from her watch on the shore into the protective arms of the pines. Even so, the water holds a silky future, an answer to the question she asks daily of the horizon.

. . .

I wanted to see, so I chose a small tree limb for a staff, cut away the leaves and twigs with a jackknife to smooth out the bark for my hand. Even though I was twelve, I was determined to walk by county road to Sturgeon Point, six miles south on the map from my family's rented cottage between Black River and Harrisville on Huron's shoreline. The point appeared on the map to jut out somewhat from the Michigan coast, and I thought that this would afford a different perspective of the lake than the one I had from our place.

For some reason my father did not refuse to let me go. Instead, he allowed the walk, but only on the condition that he would follow me the six miles by car. As it was the only bargain he was willing to strike, I set out with him following a few hundred feet behind me at a crawl on the shoulder of the road. The walk itself was direct and easy on the blacktop; I adopted a steady pace. At times I would be well ahead of him; at times he would catch up and settle in close with the car, only to let me move ahead again.

◆ 66

Over the two to three hours and six miles of the trip, many cars passed us from both directions. More than a few drivers stopped to inquire of me whether I was okay, and it was a relief to finally turn onto the dirt road leading from the blacktop to the point. I passed a park with picnic tables, barbecue pits, swing sets, and at the water's edge was a beach of smooth sand. I walked to the water while my father waited, parked in a spot near the road. As it was a cool day in late summer with little sun, there were few people around, and I was thankful. The horizon line, a set of points on which I thought I could fix and get my bearings, was lost in the grey clouds that crowded in on it. With the exception of the clearing cut long ago by state or county workers to make the park, the landscape was thick with trees. I could see nothing of the surrounding shoreline, only the open water before me with its muted horizon. The point afforded no advantage in view.

I went back to the car, disappointed, rode the six miles back to the rented cottage with my father in silence. It was my father, not the landscape, whom I had seen differently, seen something unexpected that I didn't like.

Lake Talk

HEATHER SELLERS

LAKE AS WINDOW

It's May, and hot in Michigan. Marianne and I hike the Livingston Trail, branch off to the ridge, and scoot down the dune to the beach, where we walk along the lake in the hard, flat wind. We've warmed up with the chitchat through the woods. By the time we hit the beach, the wind is strong, loud, and difficult. We're at the secrets, the good stuff, the deep talk. My hand is a little visor. She's yelling.

"It was after I committed suicide," Marianne says. "I think that's when we went out. It was Nancy's boat. I don't know. I don't remember. It was cold. I would rather walk than sail."

You didn't commit suicide. We can't hear each other unless we yell. *You just tried.* I can't say this, even in a whisper. I can't say this, even at the lake. It's funny, how I want to correct her. Stop her from talking about the suicide as a success, something *she lived through.* Does she think she's a different woman now? Sometimes she acts like she's the walking dead now—real cheerful, post-person ghost. Or a new person, the one who didn't die. Someone died that night, and this is different-Marianne now.

"How have you been, really?" I holler into the wind.

Wind yanks her wild gray hair back and polishes her whole face. Her cheekbones, her brow bones, the frame of her. She's got gigantic brown moons for eyes, full lips. I see her skull architecture, how beautiful she was and is.

"I've got my grandson Jebediah this weekend," she yells. Then she turns her back to the sea. Points up into the dunes. Elegant Italian fingers, perfect nails, like tiny shells. "Oh gosh, when I met Tim, we made love right there—up there. Can't believe how bold I was!"

Marianne names two kinds of birds. I just want to sit down on the sand, lie back, forget about time. Now I am a grownup always thinking about time, the next errand, the dinner plan, the Must Be Done things.

We walk up into the dune. The grass is flattened, mowed by the wind. We have a favorite log, in a hollowed-out place, for sitting. We're low now, can't see the lake; it's just a big mood out there, humming unevenly.

"Are you taking your medicine?"

"No," she says.

I'm stunned, but I don't say anything, I let the breeze pour into my mouth. All this is being shouted. We don't need to shout anymore, we're bunkered in the dune, but we're in the habit. "Does Tim know?"

"I DOUBT IT!"

I push her off the driftwood.

"Are you going to report me?"

"Yes," I say. I don't know. I take my medicine.

"Let's go feel the water," she says.

We stand facing the water—everyone does—letting our toes get wet. Feet spread, hands across our chests. Today, the lake is the color of asphalt, oily. The lake doesn't do anything. It's blank. Just a big old hole.

"Well," says Marianne, at the top of her lungs, "I don't like what that medicine does to my sex life. I miss that."

I watch a man in dolphin shorts frolicking with his two giant poodles. I do not point out she and Tim would be having no sex *at all* if she were dead.

"You have to talk to the psychiatrist. You can't just do this."

She pushes me into a wave, and I lose my balance more than I want to.

"I need supervision," she says, bending over to pick me up.

I can't believe she tells me anything.

Marianne is Italian. Her husband is German. She's smooth, strong, a marathon runner, career Planned Parenthood administrator, mother of three sons in various states of twenty-something boy disarray. Our running group got the call from Linda, who operates the police scanner down at the township. *Marianne was taken away. They think permanent brain damage. Did you notice anything wrong?*

Later she told me—in exactly this spot, in the confessional that is the beach—every day we ran, she was thinking, *If I throw myself in front of that car, on Park, up at the corner, I'll be knocked to the side of the road, and not in the way.* Every car that passed, she had to think about that. If it would be a good choice or not.

I've had that too. It's very distracting.

Then the lake gets distracting. It starts to call out what can only be termed a siren song, and Marianne and I are susceptible to such enchantment. It's hot, it's May, we don't have enough to do, we have too much to do.

We're hiking back. Not talking. Quiet. The woods are quiet. "See that?" she yells. "That's an ant lion. Remember when you didn't know what those were?" We take turns with the little lion who cannot talk, letting him scratch up our palm, rush up our arm, his little buggy mane all Important and Worried.

I can see why humans go crazy. Learning the names of everything we give names to. Quizzing ourselves, pushing, walking, cooking, loving. The three boys with collapsing lives, looking for women who will help—the grandson, the husband, the dead father. It's like we're in a soup.

These walks to the lake are envelopes—the good, yelled part stuffed down in. The words kiting around down there across the sand, the waves, the cold water, everyone's secret words: maybe the worst of us.

"You can't just stop taking it," I say in the car. Marianne is gripping the seat, her teeth clenched tight. "You have to take it. I'm calling Tim and then I'm calling your doctor."

"You're kind of a bossy thing."

We pass five irritable-looking deer, motionless in the grass by the parking lot.

Marianne flips down the mirror on her visor and goes about straightening her hair. Sand falls into her lap, sparkly. "Don't you love the lake? Doesn't it just feed your soul? Oh, that was wonderful."

But it doesn't.

And it wasn't.

It was more like homework, like duty, and pretend.

LAKE AS MAD GIRL

Once I saw a fireball of lightning go down Milton Street.

The ball, the size of a human head, flashed, when I noticed it, from down by the Simses' corner. I was on the porch, watching the storm, and the thing, this basketball of white fire, zapped up the street, about waist high. I could feel it singeing and surging past my porch, down the middle of the street and out past the Jenkinses', straight on down past the stop sign, and I didn't see where next.

The heat was on my arms. I was thinking to call my boyfriend to come see. But my hair was streaking out of my pores, and I felt blind and thrilled and terrified.

♦ ♦ ♦

Anna is ten years younger than me, and she never stops pulsing at you. A lot of people can't really take it, she's just too much. I like a person who gives you something to work with. She's oceanic, a microclimate; she soaks you up and rains down on you.

Anna is a summer friend. We go to auctions around West Michigan, driving to Borculo, Burnips, West Olive, Drenthe, Dorr, North Dorr, and Zeeland. We avoid the unscrupulous auctioneers, and those who charge entry. We bid on Bakelite, ancient wool coats, men's bathing suits that people think are women's.

Anna knows *everything*: what people in New York will pay for old flowered tablecloths, what makes Eisenberg costume jewelry more significant than Napier, Monet, Coro. She knows about stoves and ladders and old buggy whips. She helps a farmer identify nineteenth-century spoon rings. She is tall and blonde and silky-willow, gorgeous, pale, sweating, huge, vintage-clad in a flowered skirt, a bustier, fat sandals, and blue-gem flower earrings.

We leave the last auction—I have a black coat she says is from 1895, maybe 1896, appliquéd with black felt. Seventeen dollars and fifty cents. She has a Bakelite bracelet from the 1940s, and a metal stand made to look like ivy her mother will like for the porch. Twenty dollars and one dollar. We also have two "fun boxes" you pay a dollar for, cardboard cartons filled with junk—or *junque*, as we like to say.

One day after an estate sale, lemonade, and a fifty-cent ladder and two more boxes of who knows what, we drive in my old car to the beach at Laketown Township, up 184 stair steps and down 156 stair steps, with our boxes. Anna is never out of breath. Her skirt flares in the wind.

We settle on the beach to sort. She's wearing 1940s underwear, a whole little frock unit, lined and crotched and totally modest, so she can offer her skirt, unzip it, and voilà, trendy beach blanket!

We dump our boxes and start to make piles. "Oh, this is good," she says. "You have great stuff. Do you know what this is?" She picks up parure, bracelets, a turquoise roadrunner with silver eyes. Plastic divided plates. "If you don't want these . . . do you know what this is? Look, I have a whatchamacallit! That's really what it's called!" A viewfinder, a cocktail shaker, some Pyrex custard cups . . . she totals the value at $500. More in New York.

The wind picks up. The beach is empty. It's high summer, and just us.

"Well, we made $498, minus your gas costs. This is a fantastic haul. Probably the last good haul. Stuff is picked over. The Chicago people have discovered all this. It's pretty much over. Whoa." She stops, cranes her neck to look up at the sky, hunkers into herself. "Look at that! Oh. Oh no! Oh boy."

"Whoa," I say. For once, Anna's enthusiasm, her ability to be impressed, is understated. On the lake, a tier of fulsome black clouds cloaks the entire coast. The lake is black. The sky is gray, backlit. The clouds are so rare-fierce and wild, my first thought is *in New York these would be valued at* . . .

"We should run for it."

"The stuff," I cry. I feel like a kid, in over my head. I feel I have underestimated everything.

Anna's already gracefully swooping everything into her skirt, folding the skirt into dollops and panels, and in her peach silk 1940s underwear, she's cranking across the dark, thick, cold sand. The thunder is immense and Bach-ish.

"Do you feel the ions?" she says. "I've never seen anything like this, except one time when I was fourteen!"

I can't keep up. A shot of lightning rattles across the beach, past the steps—it's a true streak—a line, like you'd draw trying to get a half-dead pen to work. Jagged, scratchy, there and not there, an indentation in the sky. A dozen more of these etchings of white light.

Anna is screaming, holding her skirt of base metal and plastic and unsorted jangle, running up the stairs.

"We should go under the stairs!" I scream.

I turn, very much thinking *Lot's Wife*, and there's the ball—a basketball of something more intense than fire. It's a sun, winging out of the black dragon clouds sitting on the water. My hair stiffens, my neck bristles, my arms are flimsy and tingling. I've got the two cardboard boxes, mostly empty in my hands, and I fling them on the dunes, and jump off the platform landing, and dive under the pine stairs.

The ball passes over us, just over our heads. By inches.

Anna, above me, dives under a bench. Screaming.

I feel like everything about Anna is attracting lightning, the jewelry and treasure we've pillaged from the De Noor estate, the Belkin farm, the Van Ommen sale—the world wants its stuff *back*.

"Metal nails?" I yell. I want to be smart, I want to know the details, like she does. It's hard being with someone so young who is so much smarter. Also, it would be good if she lived. But I feel it's her energy, her torrent of words and knowledge and huge press of personality that has conjured this storm.

It isn't, at this point, raining. The ball has gone over our heads. Anna, who doesn't swear, is saying, "Oh my gosh, did you see that?" I am cringing, from the ball of light which could come back and kill us dead, and also because I am afraid she is going to start explaining the electromagnetic issues, parsing the history of lightning, teaching me big bang theory.

We cringe in this moment, which seems to last a really, really long time.

If it would rain, then the lightning would obey, retreat, hit the lake, and shrivel.

The metallic taste in my mouth scares me. I think of my fillings. I think of my heart. I feel my blood. "Are you okay?" I yell.

Thunder, the kind you'd get if you were deaf and in hell, drowns out my words.

"Should we run for it?" she says.

Arrows of lightning, low in the sky. Pieces of sky shine like movie silver, torn screens. She dives back under her bench. I look up through the slats and see her underpants.

My tossed-away boxes flap into the steps and bound down to the beach, one towards the water, one towards the grass. Moving so fast, the few remaining items—some handkerchiefs, a doll, plastic bead necklaces—aren't falling out. The whole world feels held together by centrifugal force.

I think of the glacier; I think of the little towns: Holland, Graafschaap; and I press myself flat, like a dog, under the landing, into the sand.

If it would rain, I keep thinking. Less fire. Safety.

"What should we do?" I yell. I feel furry, incompetent, and indecisive.

Anna yells, her hands a funnel above me, "We have twelve seconds; we can make it to the other side of the dune. Let's go! This is the worst place to be! Follow me!"

And I do, casting my body forward after my annoying wise friend, through a cut marked, "DO NOT TRAMPLE DUNE GRASS RESTORATION IN PROGRESS." We hurl ourselves down the dune to the parking lot, and lie flat in a ditch between the sand and the macadam.

"Oh my gosh," I say. We're in my car. The soaking has begun, but I feel safer wet. "Once I saw one of those. In Florida. For awhile I remember thinking I was dead."

"These storms come off the lake," she says, "in a matter of seconds. What we just saw was . . ." and she explains exactly the phenomenon, she has specific nomenclature, she's on top of the physics.

Anna.

I don't want to know.

I want no more information. We sit in the car—the rain is in shower curtains on the windshield and Anna explains. No more balls of fire, just the regular old zigzag Zorro action in the sky above.

I'm a thirty-three-year-old kid with a driver's license, and all the stuff I ever wanted. The thunder and lightning continue, and the sky opens up and it rains even harder; the lake is dumping itself inside out on our heads.

"Let's go dance in it," she says. She's vibrating.

In the parking lot, we do a kind of witch-spree dance. The rain comes down thick and painful and beautifully lit from within, each drop a bauble. It's like all those 1950s earrings, all those blue and black and gray milky rhinestones, rain down on our heads, our backs, our necks, our arms, our cowering, beautiful, conjuring selves.

The lake itself, transformed into a trillion bits of treasure, pelting our sweet, smart skins.

Water Lessons

Jacqueline Kolosov

At Glencoe Beach, my mother, my sister, and I would follow a steep stone path several stories down, winding our way through exotic perennials, robins and blue jays and black birds chattering from the shrubbery. As soon as I touched sand, my skin began to tingle, my shoulder blades loosened, and my whole being yearned for the water. The sun overhead, the scream of the gulls, the hot white sand, and the glittering awe of Lake Michigan—everything about that wide open space—claimed me.

The beach was the one place where my sister and I had our mother all to ourselves. No one and nothing else could command her attention here. We'd line up our towels alongside hers, then take turns smoothing sunscreen on our faces, shoulders, arms, legs, any place the sun might mark us.

As we hunkered down on our towels, tunneling deeper into the sand by wiggling our bottoms and our feet, our mother would tell us stories about growing up in Slovenia on a farm not far from the Adriatic Sea, a body of water that I pictured as the sensuous inside of some exotic jewel, the water so warm you could melt into it.

Accompanied by their own mother, my mother and her two younger sisters often headed for the cerulean brilliance of the Adriatic. "We didn't go far out," my mother explained, "for none of us could swim well."

"But why?" my sister inevitably asked.

"Because we didn't have swimming lessons," my mother said, with a smile.

As I grew older, I began to more deeply appreciate and to admire the slow, steady breaststroke my mother had learned after coming to the States during her teenage years. My mother's resolve to swim well seemed a marker of her decision to thrive in a new country, where she had to learn a new language and a new way of life. In the big city of Chicago, her farmer parents went to work in factories, while my mother and her sisters went to an urban Catholic school. As a young woman, my mother took a secretarial job in a fifteen-story building with a view of the lake. She enrolled in design classes at the nearby Art Institute, slowly learning to sew the clothes she admired in *Vogue*. After she met my father, she'd wear her handmade dresses as they walked along the lake's rim, holding hands and talking about their future.

At Glencoe Beach, the swimming area was ringed with buoys. Squat in the middle floated a light blue raft the neat shape of a chocolate bar. Reaching it remained, for all children and many adults, the biggest challenge on Glencoe Beach. It wasn't the distance of the raft from land that made swimming out there a big deal; it was the water temperature—cold, cold, cold. Plenty of people plunged underwater, shrieked, then turned back, even in August.

Unlike the spinning dizziness of ballet or the confident, charged focus of soccer, swimming was something I was good at. I climbed in, glided and stroked along the boundaries of the swimming area, then returned to shore. Swimming made sense. As for the cold, I once heard someone call the water "refreshing," and it was. Swimming in that buoyant water inevitably helped me to measure how far I had come in the past year. How many breaths did I need to take? How long did I need to adjust to the chilly water?

At first, my mom or dad insisted on accompanying me to the raft, but when I turned ten and swam three miles in the community pool, I was at last allowed to swim out to it alone. Remarkably, I did not feel any fear. Instead, my body relaxed into the pulse of the waves. I'd raise my head up and out of the water, then plunge beneath the surface, synchronizing the forward movement of my arms with the thrust of my neck and shoulders. That first time, feeling very grown-up despite the awkward skinniness of my hips and chest, I hoisted myself out of the water and onto the raft, joining the bikini-clad teenagers who sunned themselves there for what seemed like hours, the blonde fineness of the hairs on their bellies and arms sharply delineated by the bronzed warmth of their skin. Lying in close proximity to their hushed voices, I listened in, trying to tap the source of their allure, and wondering if that allure would one day be mine.

During the years before I grew up and left home, my one regular swimming companion at Glencoe Beach remained a seventy-year-old woman who appeared—without fail—just before dusk, to tuck her silvery hair beneath a daisy-covered cap. She was one of the strongest swimmers I have ever seen, her breaststroke confident and steady, as if she could swim all the way to Chicago. I admired her without ever stopping to consider why. She and I never spoke, although we always nodded to each other companionably. The summer I turned twenty-one, she disappeared, and I felt as if I'd lost a kindred spirit.

The summer of 1992, when I was twenty-four years old and recently married, marked the end of my rootedness in Chicago. Come September, I would begin a doctoral program in English Literature at New York University. My husband, Joshua, and I planned an August move.

One afternoon at the beach, a small airplane brandishing a banner for chocolate or some other sweet passed overhead. Instead of making a joke or telling me he was hungry, Josh turned to me and said, "The airplane's following me." I tried to convince myself that he was kidding, but gradually and ominously, Joshua's behavior moved into a landscape of the surreal. He spoke of conversations with brilliant, dead philosophers. He quoted easily and extensively from his favorite writers—Saul Bellow, Milan Kundera, Martin Buber—committing whole pages to memory with an ease that astonished and terrified me. His talk became more brilliant as it became more manic. He spoke fast, and over the course of some two weeks, he gradually stopped sleeping.

Then, one morning at the start of June, he shook me awake. I opened my eyes to wild, pitying eyes. "What's wrong?" I asked. "What is it?"

"You look so young," he said.

Twenty-four *was* young. I laughed uncomfortably. What could he possibly mean?

"I can't believe you're forty," he said.

My insides seized up. I stared at Josh's frenzied face.

Moments later, he seized his head between his hands. "Help me," he sobbed.

Immediately, we walked the eight blocks to the university medical center.

Two hours later, after meeting briefly with one of the doctors who took a lot of notes yet said remarkably little, Joshua was admitted to the psychiatric ward. I watched a nurse take his arm, then lead him down a stark white corridor. Meanwhile, I went home alone to the apartment and climbed into a tub of very warm water. I lay there for hours, continually refilling the tub, going so far as to heat water from the kettle when the faucet turned cold.

Some three or four days later, a new doctor met me in one of the pristine rooms. I stared into the white lights, and he fed me the diagnosis: manic depression, clinically called bipolar disorder. I learned then that the cyclical, often hereditary illness was marked by a brief period of elation, and in Joshua's case, by incredible lucidity. Many intelligent, creative people suffer from bipolar disorder, an illness that typically manifests itself in one's late teens or early twenties. Stress and change can exacerbate the illness or bring on an "episode." Was I responsible for Josh's episode? After all, I was the reason for the move to New York . . .

Over the next week or so, Joshua floated within mania's bubble, and I felt as if I was talking to a stranger. If the mania was hard to bear, the illness's antipodes proved far worse. The depression that followed left Josh listless, exhausted, numb. For a time, he lost passion for reading, writing, food, conversation, laughter, sex. Josh, whom I'd met during my freshmen year at the University of Chicago, had anchored me as Lake Michigan did, and now he was sick. I felt myself treading water, just trying to keep my head up so that I could breathe.

My family and friends supported me, but I don't believe they knew how I felt—how could they? My practical mother, who came from a close-knit Catholic family, gave me advice that at first I didn't know how to apply. "Stand by Joshua's side. He's your husband. You need to be strong now, strong enough for both of you."

Initially, my mother's words seemed impenetrable, unusable—until I pictured the calm rhythms of the breaststroke she had worked so hard to master. In memory, I saw my mother's face rise up out of the water as she took a long breath. I considered all that she must have been dealing with during my childhood years: two growing daughters, an aging father who was going blind, and a husband whose work as a civil engineer in Chicago during the 1980s was not going well. Despite all the challenges in her life, after completing her own half circle around the swimming area, she walked up the beach, and she looked content—and strong.

Thinking about my mother in this way, her advice no longer seemed so opaque. "You need to be strong now." In her own way, I realized that she was telling me that I needed to find that unbreakable center within myself so that I could begin to rebuild my sense of myself as an individual and as a wife.

So I went back to the lake. I now lived on Chicago's South Side, a good hour's drive from Glencoe Beach and home. But physical distance wasn't the only reason why I needed to find a new landscape. Glencoe Beach belonged to the protected girl I had been. I had to discover a place that required me to wrestle with it.

Almost every morning, I drove the old LeBaron into the city and parked on one of the residential side streets. With my beach chair slung over one shoulder and a canvas bag full of novels on the other, I would make my way to the lakefront. This part of the lake belonged to the buzz of the city. Such a strange juxtaposition: the azure green of Lake Michigan set off by the rows of elegant old apartment buildings and modern high-rises that snaked their way along Lake Shore Drive. Occasionally I'd pause at the newly opened Starbucks to buy an enormous cup of hot tea. The regularity of the routine centered me.

I spent days on Oak Street Beach. I watched mothers arrive with their children, and fathers, too. Affluent North Siders came, but working-class people, college students, and tourists came also, a commingling of twenty-dollar aluminum lawn chairs and sporty, upscale models; picnics of Dr. Pepper and Doritos alongside Perrier and gourmet grilled-vegetable sandwiches. Old people with thick European accents found their way down from the air-conditioned high-rises to set up elaborate sunshades, opening portable coolers full of chilled grapes and beverages. They would sit for hours, gossiping and reminiscing along the water's edge. Lovers strolled hand in hand, the surf tickling their ankles. Once in a while, an executive in a business suit would arrive, only to roll up his pants legs, walk out into the water, and then stare out at the horizon—thinking of I don't know what.

But there were desperate, rootless-looking people at Oak Street Beach, too: homeless men and women who came to sit on the sand in their layers of heavy clothes, often wheeling shopping carts heaped with belongings right up to the water. Many talked to themselves. Once, I saw a twenty-something woman with scarred legs and a beautiful but scarred face lie down in the hot sand and begin to laugh and mutter to herself, as if there were a host of other people within her single body. Perhaps, I thought, there were, painfully reminded of the strange other person I now knew lived inside my Joshua.

Along with the children from the nearby brownstones and luxury high-rises came children from the housing projects. Abandoning their street clothes on the sand, clad only in loose underwear, they ran full speed ahead into the waves, laughing delightedly and sometimes fearfully—could they swim?—as the waves brushed up against their ankles or calves.

Most afternoons, I counted at least four languages being spoken: English, Spanish, Polish, Russian, and usually German or French. I thought of my own mother, young and newly immigrated, but I felt too fragile to participate in these lives. Still, I liked the company of so many different kinds of people, all of us sharing in the soothing pleasure of the lakefront, the hum of the traffic audible in the near distance. I couldn't help but wonder how many of these people came to the lake for strength, as I did, how many quiet faces camouflaged volatile spirits.

As in summers past, I spent a lot of time in the water. Now, however, no buoys defined the boundaries, and there was no raft to focus on as destination and refuge. Instead, there was just the wide open lake running into the horizon. Plunging beneath the cold surface, I swam the breaststroke as my mother had, very much aware that with every breath, I could look up and orient myself. This reassured me as I swam further out, occasionally hearing the lifeguard whistle or call through his horn: "You've gone too far . . ." Maybe.

Most of the time, no lifeguard signaled my return. No one was going to— *no one could*—define the boundaries for me now. When I looked back toward land, Chicago's indifferent skyscrapers seemed to stare back at me. But in the other direction, it was all wide open space: possibility or dissolution, depending on how I looked at it. As I forced myself to face the unknown, I took comfort in knowing that some thirty miles up the lakefront, children would be tunneling into the sand on Glencoe Beach, just as I had.

June turned into July, and slowly, like my mother learning to swim, I began to see the possibility of another kind of future. For the next several years, Joshua and I lived in and around New York City. From there, we moved back to the Midwest, though not to Chicago. Instead, we tried to settle into life in a small town in northwestern Ohio, and it was there that we finally decided to end our marriage.

That same year, I walked the Camino de Santiago, a pilgrimage that begins in the Pyrenees on the French border and runs across Spain to Santiago, a medieval city about fifty miles from the Atlantic Ocean. I came to Spain to walk out of myself, as thousands of pilgrims had been doing for centuries. I came to discover the person I could become.

During my four weeks of walking, I passed many rivers. They seemed to suggest that I keep moving, keep searching for a source. And I was searching then, yearning towards my next destination. I reached the fabled city of Santiago with calluses and a lithe body and spirit. After laying my sleeping bag down on the floor of a monastery, I headed outside to sit on the steps and gaze out at the city below. As the twilight sky changed from bronze to a dusky lilac, I listened to a young man sing in Spanish, and I let my mind float out over the city, the way it often did on those days and nights when I sat beside the lake and dreamed, opening myself up to the future and meditating upon the past, as if from the serene distance of another lifetime.

Although I resolved nothing that night, one thing became absolutely clear: I needed to trust uncertainty, and I could not help but think of Lake Michigan. *The waters are always in flux. Welcome change, upheaval, the unknown. Yet always remember that the waters are contained by land. Flux and containment.*

Early the next morning, I took the bus to Finisterre—literally earth's end. There, I walked slowly into the ocean. As I swam out into the cold Atlantic, I opened my mouth, and salt water quickly filled it. I recalled the words spoken during the marriage service: "You are the salt of the earth." In spite of all that I had lost, I believed I would be able to heal, grow, change. I needed to relax into the current. If I trusted the rhythms of the water, I would be safe.

I've settled, for now, in dry, dusty West Texas, where I have found productive work as a professor of creative writing and literature, good friends, and a man whose passion is fly-fishing and water birds (the stuff of another essay). Joshua and I keep in infrequent touch. After finally finding a psychiatrist able to help him successfully manage bipolar disorder, he has found happiness in a second marriage and a rewarding job.

I know that in time I will have to move back to a large body of water, and there are many days I dream of returning to Chicago. For now, I anticipate the periods when I can go home to Lake Michigan. I return during summer, when Glencoe Beach awaits me like a cherished friend who keeps me connected to the loved and protected child I still carry within myself. From Glencoe Beach I can look south along the shore towards the city and Oak Street Beach.

I also return to the lake during the winter. When the day is clouded over— an opaque white like a newly stretched canvas—the lake seems internally focused, pregnant or waiting. Sometimes there is a silence about the water, often crusted by a meandering layer of snow, and there is a silence within myself. Both silences seem to scintillate with possibility.

If I seek a text in which I might find my way into the future, that text resides in the waters of Lake Michigan. I gaze out at the endless vista of water, my eyes coming to rest on the almost indeterminate point where water meets sky. Reading. Listening. Waiting.

Perhaps, in my seventies, I will return to the hot August months of my childhood. Like the graceful old woman with the daisy-flowered swim cap, I will appear on the shore of Lake Michigan at dusk and swim out into the cold water, thinking about how far I have come and wondering, comfortably, where I am going.

Elemental Fine

Leigh Allison Wilson

Water

I first saw Lake Ontario on an April day in 1984, from the top of a hill on East Second Street in Oswego, New York. Down this street, crisscrossed with telephone wires upon which pigeons fornicated in large numbers, I could see a rectangle of dark, almost navy blue. I gasped when I saw it, as though the sight of the lake was itself an immersion.

There are reasons for this. In East Tennessee, where I grew up, there was of course water. Lots of water. When the Tennessee Valley Authority rolled up its sleeves in the thirties and forties, damming up dozens of rivers across the region, within half a decade the entire state suddenly puddled up as if an immense rainstorm had come and gone. But people lost farms, lost homes, lost graveyards. Lots of water gained at the cost of lots of loss, loss of places that begat memory, loss even of the proof of memory.

But my childhood, because of the dams, involved picnics beside pristine new lakes. Once I took a motorboat ride across the surface of a lake, and halfway across, my uncle told me that down below, dozens of feet below, was the bedroom in the house where my grandmother and grandfather probably conceived my mother. I had a penny in my pocket and I dropped it over. In my child mind, where time had no boundaries, I imagined the penny listing downward, like a rose petal, slipping into a glassless window between two bullheads, and falling on my grandmother's pillow—a good luck charm for her daughter to come, and the daughter to come after that—me. In retrospect, it didn't work.

But I have always believed in the necromancy of water, its alchemies and its transformative mysteries. I dream of drowning. My mother believes that she once drowned, four hundred years ago, during a life as a servant boy for a rich family; apparently she fell into a well. My dreams of drowning, though, are good dreams. I breathe water. I cannot cry. Sometimes I fuck like a fish. And in this way, water has become for me an element beyond time, beyond physics, beyond even luck. I believe in water, am faithful, full of faith, in water. I am very glad that my body is 79 percent water. I worry, sometimes, about the other 21 percent. When I first saw that navy blue piece of Lake Ontario, I gasped because I knew I had come to a place I could call home.

WIND

The wind blows so hard off Lake Ontario that at odd times my entire house shivers and groans like a big elderly dog stretching in a dream. The lake here is always "the Lake"—as though there are no others—the way people from Manhattan say, "the City" or Christians say, "the Book." In Tennessee people say, "the lakes," even though they might mean a particular lake, a specific place; the plural, for Tennesseans, often means a singular. There are "messes of spinach" and "bothers of work" and "troubles of adultery," a litany of plurals that can sound as if the world is being described in zoological terms. Tennesseans are a synecdochical people. Those who live near Lake Ontario are too, in reverse—if you live near a lake that big, the singular always blows away the multiple, the episodic, the aggregate. On the shores of Lake Ontario I have fallen in love, lost that love, fallen in love again. And although I am originally a Tennessean, I have become accustomed to the worldview of a Lake Ontarian. I tend to say, "the Love" in the loving moment, though there have been more loves than one. I say, "the Love" in just the way everyone around here says, "the Lake"—Lake, Love, and in between the wind blows, hard.

The season I'm thinking about, the fall of 2001, the winds blew particularly hard off Lake Ontario. That fall I discovered that the one I loved had fallen in love with someone else, a friend. This was a hard thing. As a matter of fact it blew me away. Still, I had for months already begun to wonder about myself and that love; *the* Love had already turned to *a* love—perhaps had already turned into something more like desperation and not love at all. I'm not sure there's a figure of speech for this, but if there were it would be named by a frightening made-up word, like "metastany." Impossible to know, sometimes, which way the emotional winds are blowing, but that they are—and hard—is mostly beyond doubt. The peculiar power of wind is that it can eat away, over time, even a block of marble, and the human heart is a vulnerable thing. That particular fall, the winds off Lake Ontario and my own internal winds were in terrible harmony, a terrible expense of spirit. At night I could hear the naked limbs of trees scrabble against my roof. The air itself seemed grayer, full of a kind of exhausted energy, like an old woman bent on clearing a dinner table before everyone was through. Sometimes, listening to the winds blow, I thought I might be dying soon.

One night I lay in bed, and in a despairing reverie, I imagined my ex-lover with the new lover. For some reason their hair was entwined on a pillow; a greenish tint pervaded the scene. Water, I thought, they're underwater, they're living in the lake. And I immediately felt betrayed—not by the two of them, the two lovers, but by the lake herself: betrayed by Lake Ontario who had enfolded them, dream-like, in my mind's eye. While I pondered this newest betrayal, I became aware that the water dripping continuously onto my forehead was not part of the reverie. It was really water. Water dripping onto my forehead from a leak in my ceiling. Why the leak sprang into being right over my head as it lay on a pillow, my mind full of various unpleasant couplings, I cannot say. But as anyone who lives near the lake can tell you, all water—the water you drink, the water you shovel endlessly in the form of snow, the water that condenses on your skin when you walk through an early-morning forest banked by fog—all the water around here originates from the lake. Lake Ontario had not abandoned me.

EARTH

That very night I resolved to fix my house, to fix myself. I resolved to fix things. Here it seems important to say that my reactions to the first sight of Lake Ontario—and subsequent sightings and meditations—always hinge on the beauties of a *piece* of the lake. Often, my heart soars from a glimpse of it at the end of tunnel of trees, or framed through a window, or clipped weirdly between the smokestacks of a power plant. My admiration for Lake Ontario is a kind of piecework, the parts of it intimating a whole my imagination can't quite stretch to embrace. I feel my arms are too short, my blood too anemic, my IQ too low. I love the colossal body of this water in sections. And so I began to fix my house in sections, hoping that I too would get fixed, a piece-work of the soul, or at the very least I would quit these midnight paranoid imaginings.

I contacted my neighbor, a contractor named Mark, the man who had orig-inally built the house. He came over and looked around, actually stepping on my bed to get a look at the leak in the ceiling. There was a pan on my pillow to catch the water; his stockinged feet tilted the pan sideways, almost but not quite spilling it. "You have a problem," he said. What I heard was, "You have *A Prob-lem*," for I was convinced I had many. He pointed out that he hadn't built the bedroom addition, some other guy had, some cheaper guy who went broke dur-ing the building of the addition, and so he, Mark, wasn't responsible for the shoddiness of the work. He had warned the previous owner about the cheap guy, but she had ignored the warning. "Fine," I said, "but let's fix it."

A bunch of men swarmed my roof in late November. It was the week of Thanksgiving, a week of lake-effect snow that came down in flakes the size of baby's fists. When frigid Canadian air rides across the open and warmer waters of Lake Ontario, the result is lake-effect snow, and it is often relentlessly ex-pansive, an uncle who won't quit telling bad jokes though the whole family has gotten pissed off. The workmen came during a lake-effect snowstorm and pulled off all the old shingles and tarpaper on the roof over the bedroom. For a while, all the banging and stomping seemed in weird consonance with the falling of the snow. Then a great silence fell. One of the men tiptoed into the house, hat in hand, wondering if I'd go on the roof with him. I climbed a lad-der and joined a group of men, all of whom were staring down at my roof. Snowflakes hit my hot cheeks, disappeared instantly, then ran down off my chin. We were staring at two-by-fours that had been laid down to form the sup-port of my roof. They had been laid down every which way, laid as randomly as if the earlier workmen had thrown them there from the lawn below, then tarpapered over them. The jumble put me in mind of the films they showed us in high school, the ones to keep us from doing drugs: spider webs created by spiders on acid, although frankly those films were exactly why I had always wanted to try acid. Still, I wasn't crazy about the possibility of that first roofer being on the hallucinogen himself.

They rebuilt that whole section of the roof over the course of the next few days. Unfortunately, as they rebuilt, they uncovered more sections that also needed rebuilding (sections, I might add, that couldn't have been built by that earlier broke, mind-tripping builder), and so I ended up with a roof of plastic wrap as winter set in. At night I could sense the house breathe, hear the winds off the lake pucker up the plastic and lay it flat again. My roof's renovation was "in progress," the way lake-effect storms around here are said to be "in progress"; that is, it seems possible they will never end in your lifetime. My house felt dwindled; my own skin felt dwindled. I began to have some more paranoid midnight reveries, this time involving plastic and peeled skin and brittle ice on top of large bodies of water.

Near Christmas, the men moved inside. Unbeknownst to me, large sections of dry wall in my bedroom and the office off the bedroom had been ruined by repeated dousings of water during repeated winters. I say "sections" because that's what the workmen called it: sections that expanded until really it was everything, but we all kept calling it sections. It seemed cheaper that way. It wasn't. Every time they pulled down a new section of dry wall they found more moisture rot and pulled down another section of dry wall. Cloying, almost damp white dust permeated the air of my home. It occurred to me that my house, like my body, was 79 percent water, 21 percent something else, and that 21 percent was no good. One night in December I woke up from a terrible dream, turned on my bedside lamp, went to the bathroom, came back, and on my pillow was the imprint of my head surrounded by white dust. I visited a friend in her office where one big window framed a gray piece of snow-ridden Lake Ontario, and when I got up from my chair to leave, there was a dusty white afterimage of my ass on the seat. The separation of parts and wholes began to be difficult for me. I imagined my ex-lover and her new lover as a completely filled-in crossword puzzle. I was an unfinished one, with maybe twenty-two across penciled in, tentatively.

By the eve of New Year's Eve, it stopped snowing. Against all the odds, and breaking a fair number of weather records, it didn't snow again all winter. They finished all the dry-walling New Year's Eve. They finished the roof, working overtime, New Year's Day. On Lake Ontario, large ships from Canada were able to make passage into Oswego Harbor well into January and beyond, because the lake never froze that year. I began, in my heart of hearts, to let go of my ex-lover.

FIRE

When I was growing up in Tennessee, well past the age I should have known better, I set fires. At first they were just little piles of sticks I'd light up in the driveway, staring with fascination as the sticks turned to not-sticks, disappeared into white air. After a while, though, I grew older and bolder. There was a small but disturbing incident in my bedroom closet. There was another, more satisfying conflagration involving an old shack in the woods. I stopped just short of burning down an entire subdivision-in-progress because I happened to meet a kid who was going to live in one of the houses. My last (and no one but I would say, best) blaze took place in the newly renovated lobby of my grade school—I lit the papier-mâché bonfire in the middle of some Native American mannequins. They had seemed cold to me. Things got out of hand; the mannequins caught fire and a baby-doll papoose burned up. I got kicked out of school for a week and sent to a psychiatrist. He told my mother we needed to take more vacations. We didn't take them, but I no longer set fires.

There is a moral to this, I learned, though you can't find it in a Hallmark card, and that moral is: Sometimes things have to burn.

That terrible fall and early winter of 2001, I burned. I drowned, too; winds swept over and through me, the earth itself shifted and became a plasticine sea, but mostly I burned. In the end I came out of my house, out of myself, my Self, burned down to the trace elements. And in that burning I grew whole again. I could feel all of my watery parts spread and connect across all possible surfaces. The following spring I made new friends, rediscovered and revalued old ones. That summer I met a new lover. She is the Love, of course, but now I see her and myself and these new and old friends—and even the workmen who renovated my house, the children they talked about with pride, the children those children will have—I see all of us as creatures of an immense, interconnected body of water, our watery limbs and torsos connected in a fantastic water world across this planet. Sometimes I want to drop a penny upon us, to wish us good luck. Memory and the proof of memory, it seems, are all in our heads.

In April of 2002, exactly eighteen years to the month after I first saw Lake Ontario, I sat beside a bonfire on the lake. Someone talked about how the Iroquois, in naming the lake "Ontario," had meant to call it "fine lake." It looked mighty fine from where we sat beside it—immense, dark blue, never ending, full of possibility. A friend turned to me and asked, as if she had just remembered a bit of something, "How are you doing?"

And I said, "Fine." I said, "I'm doing fine."

Gifts

sually at the lake, we don't argue, instead we look across the water and see no end, and so cannot speak, ending the spell of not ending, our voices, our words unable to seem infinite, not that we required infinity of anything. We required only that the lake be big enough to stretch beyond our limits. Deirdre and I were capable of riffs, anger, contention, and any of that could be healed, was healed, leaving evidence, the smallest mental and physical scars of reunification, but the lake healed without seams, as if nothing had happened. Even frozen water butchered into cubes melted into one full glass, one unity of water. As ragged as the water became during storms, the repair of the ravages of fury was simply for the fury to stop.

—*Thylias Moss*

Fog. Like delicate tatting, it weaves silver filigree between white birches and gnarled cedar roots, coating with the tiniest of drops the spider webs and orange-and-pink woods orchids along its soft path. It makes no sound but all things are aware it has arrived.

—*Michele Bergstrom*

I nearly missed the mist on the bay this morning. There's just a remnant on the far shore, and fast receding. I wanted vertical feet of it, silent, cropping up before my eyes from the express gray-green of the surface. I start with the mist because it never reads *People* or *Entertainment Weekly* or *Us.* I'm sure it understands there's nothing personal in not having any staying power, evaporating with a suck into general circulation. It doesn't hold a grudge. Next day, watching from its new incarnation, cloud, ambient moisture, it doesn't offer cynical advice as the rind of the lake again peels off into air.

—*Belinda Kremer*

The weather on Lake Michigan can change very quickly. When the wind's out of the north, the waves can build over the entire fetch of the lake. I've seen waves over fifteen feet, and very close together. The harnesses are on, and everybody who doesn't need to be on deck is below. How you react depends on whether it's big winds and big waves or if it's just waves. A storm is kind of exciting once you get everything settled. When you've got the right sails on and everybody's strapped in, it's kind of fun looking around at the weather. You say to yourself, can you believe this? Can you believe these waves?

—*Nancy Garrity with Bonnie Jo Campbell*

The Importance of Dunes

A N N I C K   S M I T H

umor. The Old English word tastes sweet, like peaches. One dictionary definition says, "Any period regarded as a time of fruition, fulfillment, happiness or beauty." This pure and easy concept of summer is beguiling, but fraudulent as nostalgia. I remind myself that summer's peach must have at its heart a pit, a seed, the hint of bitterness.

All the summers of my childhood, I lived on the beaches of Lake Michigan. My second-story bedroom faced west, toward the lake. I slept with the sounds of waves lapping or waves crashing, waves roaring in the gusts and thunder of an electrical storm. There were gulls diving, and thin-legged sandpipers on the beach where I stood. When sky drops into lake and waves pull at your toes, any summer child knows she is on the edge—a small person in a great blue world.

The creatures who lived in the sand were also small and sometimes stinging: sand fleas, burrowing wasps, red ants, beetles, a swarm of ladybugs on my baby sister's bottom. I tried to catch minnows in the shallows where a warm urine-colored stream ran into the lake; my little sisters and I hopped after frogs and trapped tadpoles in jars so we could watch their astounding tails turn into feet. Alewives washed up on the beach some years, so many and so rank we

---

Editor's note: Annick Smith and I collaborated here to combine two earlier essays by the author, the original "The Importance of Dunes" (1994) with "Thanksgiving" (2001).

would rake them into a pile a foot high, dig a deep hole, and bury them to keep our beach from smelling of fishy death. We tried to catch the gold, black-veined monarch butterflies in nets, but I hated the powdery feel of their wings and the clumsiness of my fingers.

Once I witnessed the killing of a snake. My father's cousin Paul, on furlough from World War II, had come to visit. He was slim, dark, romantic—the only soldier I knew. I was riding his back, playing horsey on the beach, when a curious movement where nothing should have moved froze him. A gray, diamond-marked twist of driftwood had come alive at our feet.

"Rattlesnake," Paul screamed and dumped me in the sand. He grabbed a large stick and clubbed the snake to death. I was more scared of Paul's violence than I was of the snake.

After the war, Paul would give me his Purple Heart, but he had been wounded beyond any healing. He would change his name to Paul Armstrong (Hungarian Jew turned All-American Boy), ditch his European-educated ways, and become a busboy in greasy spoons from Kansas City to Baton Rouge. He would descend into catatonia until scientists invented antipsychotic drugs. Then he grew fat, lived in cheap hotels in Chicago, and peeped into windows at naked women. One evening he choked to death on a five-inch slab of steak. I never really knew Paul—except for our encounter with snakes. I like snakes.

◆　◆　◆

The beaches where I discovered venom are some eighty miles from Chicago, along the Indiana Tollway and Interstate 94, past the stinking refineries of Calumet City and the steel mills of Gary, on Michigan's cupped southwestern shore. My family spent summers in the resort town of Lakeside until I was seven, then bought an unfinished house in a beach community called Tower Hills Shorelands near Warren Dunes State Park. My parents put in plumbing, paneled the walls with knotty pine, built a flagstone terrace. Sixty years later, when I visit my aged mother, I sleep in my old bedroom on the second floor, and waves still sing through the open French windows.

In Lakeside I learned to be ashamed of my body. My Hungarian parents had come to America from Paris, where I was born. French children played nude on the beaches; so did I. My parents were photographers. They liked to take pictures of me at the edge of the waves—my plump legs, my little bucket.

One hot July afternoon when I was two, a policeman accosted my father. "You better get that kid off our beach."

My father was perplexed.

"You're lucky I'm not pulling you in."

"But this is America!"

"You bet it's America. This is a Christian community."

The nuns in the convent adjoining the public beach had complained. I was rushed into panties, never again to feel unconscious in my body while in the company of others until I was grown and a mother and bathing in hot pools on the Middle Fork of the Salmon River, deep in the Idaho wilderness. Here is one value of wild places: You are not important there. You are a leaf, a common weed.

Life begins on a beach. Unlikely plants poke out of pure sand: marram grass, a razor-edged green pioneer waving to its followers—sea rocket, bugseed, winged pigweed, cocklebur. The beach is a desert, and that must be why, when I finally lived some months in the Sonoran Desert, I felt drawn to it, happy in the spare, thorny blossoming of life. Each cactus, yellow poppy, palo verde, finger-leafed mesquite emerges as if newly created from rocks turned to sand. The Yaquis have a name for their desert: the enchanted world of flowers.

Ancient creatures who emerged from waters to colonize beaches have left us legacies. My sisters and I often walked on the lakeshore among green- and rust-colored pebbles, our backs stooped and aching, looking for fossils we called "Indian stones." These tiny, round petrified worm-animals with star-shaped holes were our jewels. My mother, who knew little of geology but liked to make stories, told me the fossils were a million years old. I could barely comprehend one year. The Indian stones strung around my neck signified time.

On clear August nights, we girls would lie on our backs on blankets, counting shooting stars. In Chicago, where my family lived in an apartment through the long winter, you could not see the stars in the sky. It was luminous, smoky, filled with the orange reflected light of the city. The beach became our planetarium. We learned the names of constellations. This was space.

◆ ◆ ◆

Foredune. The word is a seduction. Prevailing winds blow sand inland until the particles hit an obstruction—a tuft of little bluestem grass, a driftwood log.

The grains pile up against the windward side of an object and, having lost their momentum, roll gently down the sheltered side, forming a mini-dune. In this sheltered space, sand cress, wild rye, bearberry, horsemint, hairy puccoon, Pitcher's thistle, even prickly-pear cactus take hold. More sand accumulates, enriched by decaying vegetation and held secure by a network of tangled surface roots. Insects find sustenance, rodents burrow, songbirds fly from the oak forest to feast on seeds and berries. They are building a foredune.

The cliff behind our beach is formed by waves of winter storms slicing into foredunes. Severe winters cut the dunes back, leaving a wide, flat beach. Other years the water level rises, and the beach is a narrow walkway. The miniature mountains and cliffs rising from the beach to the more permanent tree-anchored dunes are my memory's password for play. When my sisters and I were waterlogged, blue-lipped, and bored with swimming, we would leap from our cliff's tiered ledges. I was Wonder Woman with a beach-blanket cape.

Above the cliff, our no man's land of foredunes swelled to a wooded ridge. On top, where the sand turns smoky gray in the process of becoming dirt, our white frame house sits among oaks, pines, and sassafras trees, its wide screened-in porch looking west over the lake to the setting sun. On windy days, when it was too cold to swim, we sisters would descend the steep, splintery stairs from the house, cross a wooden ramp over the gully that separates foredunes from the more permanent backdunes, and thread through thick, white-powdered poison ivy to the clearing where our cottonwood stood.

We nested in the tree and played house under its airy roof, collecting sand cherries and acorns for food, seed pods for money. A wind-borne cottonseed drifts to ground. Watered by rain, it may take hold. These trees grow fast, come to maturity, and begin to die within the span of a human life. I did not know that cottonwoods are the only trees that survive on foredunes. Ours was old in cottonwood time.

Some days we carried a lunch of peanut-butter-and-jelly sandwiches, plums, chocolate-chip cookies, Kool-Aid in a thermos. Some days we brought dolls, a deck of Old Maid, our doctor's kit. We spread our blanket. We climbed the silver-limbed tree. The sun dove toward the purple horizon.

Clang, clang, our Grandma Beck beat on the horseshoe dinner bell. "Annick, Kaati, Carole—where are you?" She would call herself hoarse, with her Hungarian accent, but we would not answer. We were too busy playing doctor. Who can forget the probings of child-doctor hands? The unbearable tickle and tingle of a metal stethoscope on a bare nipple. Most little girls play doctor with boys and eventually we did, too, but awakening to sexuality in such female-child intimacy will for me always be linked to foredunes, treetops, soft green light, the rumble of white-capped waves. It is the domain of sisters.

. . .

Blowouts are sand craters, scooped out of the dunes by swirling winds. Ours was maybe fifty feet deep, flat and round at the bottom, fringed at the edges with jack pine and white pine, dotted with clumps of blue-leafed willow, starry false Solomon's seal, the ever-present marram grass.

You might come to a blowout with a serious novel, as I did with *Moby Dick*, and be lost in an ocean humming with whales. You might bring a sketch pad, or try to write a poem. I would lie on my back and see faces in drifting clouds. The blowout was my place for dreaming, the inverse of mountains.

Occasionally my father would bring a model to the dunes to pose nude for arty photographs. We girls were not allowed to observe, but Kathy and I would sneak after them, the model in shorts, my father's neck strung with his Rolleiflex and lenses. They went in morning, when the sun slanted and shadows were possible.

Creeping like the Potawatomis, who once walked a trail along the shore, we tracked the grownups to the blowout. The model would shed her bra and underpants. We held our breath. We had smelled the woman's perfume. My father would direct the model toward the configuration of sand he wanted as background. Voices drifted up to us, sometimes laughter. They never touched. Maybe my father knew we were spying. He was sexy—dark and handsome. We knew he loved women. We were in love with him too. The blowout was a wild place where anything could happen.

It must have been tough for my mother—three daughters, gorgeous models, all this adoration of her husband. No wonder she sometimes nagged and slammed doors, broke down in hysterical weeping, escaped to the beach for solace. I see her in my mind's eye striding away from us—a petite, pretty, buxom woman with good legs and a floppy hat.

I always thought of myself as my father's surrogate eldest son, and he was my main childhood hero. I would not learn to sew like my mother. I did not cook or bake my mother's fine Hungarian pastries. I cut my thick dark hair short, wore jeans, knew the box scores of the Chicago Cubs, and preferred the company of men. And then, at eleven and a half, I was besieged by hormones. I became paralyzed with self-consciousness. Awkward, slumped at the shoulders, withdrawn, I flinched from my father's embraces, not daring to shout the danger I felt: "Don't touch me!"

On the beach in front of my parents and their friends, I took to shameless wrestling with a boy who lived down the road. I would drift far out into the lake with him, legs and arms entwined around a black inner tube, exchanging wet kisses. I wonder what I was trying to prove. That I was free of my father? A girl sexy as any model? Normal? Wild?

Freedom from self-awareness came only when I was alone in the sand and grass, or reading, preferably both. That is why I loved the blowout, even the idea of the blowout, where I could think, feel, daydream, and meditate with no one watching but the beetles and crows. I was lucky to have found this haven so early and so close to hand. The peace I experienced in my blowout has shaped my life to a degree I could not have imagined in my youth. I would grow up to be a solitary walker, like my mother, seeking solace in nature as others seek it in religion, booze, or drugs.

◆ ◆ ◆

Some anthropologists define and classify cultures by studying landscape patterns of habitation. One theory is called Prospect and Refuge, and I believe it applies to individuals as well as cultures. The roots of such patterns can be traced to Stone Age hunters and gatherers, and to the animals that were their models and their meat. Those who lived in the high, open grasslands and savannas sought a dwelling place of prospect for predation and defense, like wolves, where they could spot herds of ungulates or invading tribes. Jungle peoples lived at the fecund bottom of life, looking up to the monkeys in the trees, snakes curling like vines, the bright plumage of toucans.

But the places of greatest possibility and complexity—the places where higher cultures evolved—are at the edges of mountains and woods, looking down to a wider space. That is where our beach house sits, at the edge of an oak forest overlooking the lake. From childhood through adulthood, I have known artists and aspired to be one, and in my experience, artists will choose prospect over refuge any day, unless they can have both.

Carl Sandburg once lived down our sandy road in Tower Hill. Just before we bought our place, he moved a few miles away to a farm in Harbert, where his wife raised goats. My father took us to visit, but Sandburg was not home. What I remember are the goats. Gregarious, bearded creatures, they ambled on the sod-roofed house; one jumped on the hood of our Buick.

The dunes have been a retreat for Chicago artists and intellectuals since the early 1900s, and literary warriors were our neighbors and visitors. Young Norman Maclean would ride with Sherwood Anderson on what he called the "Yellow Peril"—the electric train that ran from Chicago to South Bend, Indiana —to visit his mentor, the historian Ferdinand Schevill. Nelson Algren came to drink whiskey on our porch, and we listened to his stories as the sun slid into the lake. The Greek American writer Harry Petrakis, another friend, still lives near New Buffalo. Ben Burns, who edited the *Chicago Defender* in the 1940s and was managing editor of *Ebony*, remodeled Sandburg's old studio into a spacious house. When he moved to North Carolina at age sixty-seven, Sandburg said, "It's only my ghost that's leaving the Middle West."

The dunes are full of ghosts. The oldest are prehistoric mammoths, mastodons, giant beaver. Retreating glaciers carved the Great Lakes, and our geologically young dunes blow up against moraines, drifts, and outwash plains. Under the sand are the limestone beds of a Paleozoic sea, piled up over millions of years before the coming of vertebrate life. Sand upon sand is the way I like to think about history.

In ancient times, 100 B.C. to A.D. 700, Hopewell Indians established villages and summer gardens near New Buffalo. A few miles inland from our beach, near the town of Three Oaks, they dug pits to store corn, wild rice, beans, and root crops. My family went to Three Oaks for fresh food—sweet corn and ripe tomatoes at roadside stands. We filled coffee cans with blueberries off the bush and picked bushels of Golden Delicious apples from the orchards.

A forest band of Potawatomis lived near St. Joseph, Michigan, where my Old Country grandmothers would go to "take the waters," easing their rheumatic limbs into the mineral baths of a Victorian spa. In 1838 the Potawatomis, casualties of white man's measles and smallpox and white man's wars, were packed off to a reservation in Oklahoma. One recalcitrant band moved to Cass County, Michigan, where a small group still survives. I identify with survivors; many of my relatives died in Auschwitz.

Most of the thronging wildlife that lived here did not survive. Bison were hunted out by Indians and whites by 1750. Even before white settlement began, during the trapper era in the early 1800s, elk and most of the beaver had been killed off. Timber wolves were exterminated a few years before most of the deer were shot in 1873, which is when the last wild turkey graced a pioneer's table. Before long, there were no more black bears, panthers, lynx, otters, or wolverines. And in 1880 the last flocks of passenger pigeons darkened the skies over our dunes.

Huge sturgeon once swam up local streams in the spring spawning run. Farmers netted suckers by the wagonload to feed to the hogs. At New Buffalo, fishermen caught 5,000 whitefish in one day. Most of this rich life is gone, but the deer and wild turkeys have come back. As a child, I searched for deer among the white oaks, red oaks, black oaks, dogwood, sassafras, and basswood in our patch of forest. I tracked old game trails, but never saw even hoofprints. Then about a decade ago, I was amazed to see a fat white-tailed doe racing across our beach at dawn. Deer, like rats and coyotes, are also survivors. Now they have returned in such numbers that people may hunt them in the park's northern sections.

The legendary forests that spread to the east—Galien beeches, maples, and the famous "oak openings" that James Fenimore Cooper described—live only in the imaginations of readers like me. Lucky for my soul, it is still possible to glimpse a sight of the aboriginal woods in the nature sanctuary of Warren Woods, near Lakeside. I remember taking Sunday visitors to walk among the giant beeches, the woods hushed and filled with sunlight at their tops, cool in midsummer along the green-shaded paths. Those walks were as close as I had come in childhood to what church is supposed to be.

The forest behind our house at Tower Hill is a spiritual retreat, with covenants that restrict development. I could not know firsthand the primeval deep woods of Michigan, but ours is filled with pussytoes, asters, and bastard toadflax. With my mother and sisters, I gathered wild geraniums in June, blue and yellow violets in May. Best of all was April, when the trees had not yet come into leaf, but the delicate white orchid-centered trilliums lit the earth in the aftermath of a spring snow.

I love to return to Tower Hill in early spring when our woods are ethereal, filled with a dank perfume from layers of rotting leaves, hushed except for the raucous blue jays that hunt eggs in the nests of red-crested cardinals. These are my family's sacred groves. We pray in our ways to the god of the deep woods.

◆   ◆   ◆

My sisters and I have come to maturity transformed and transforming like dunes that won't stay put. We who still think of ourselves as children have children old enough to be mothers and fathers. Very little remains the same except for Old Baldy, the highest dune, which we climbed as if it were Mount Everest.

It would be an expedition, with rucksacks full of snacks and towels. Kathy, Carole, and I, and several neighbor kids would parade past the church camp to the public beach, where bathers of all shapes, ages, and colors camped under red-striped umbrellas. Old Baldy loomed above the stove-hot cement of the parking lot, its steep flank hollowed like the trough of a wave. We'd race to the top, drop our loads, and somersault down. We landed laughing, our mouths filled with sand.

Anchoring the sloping backside of our mountain were thick stands of pine, poplars, and poison ivy. We swung on wild grape vines—"Me Tarzan, you Jane"—and the littlest kids had to be chimps. Behind Old Baldy, the dunes spread like the Sahara. In the moonlight, when I was seventeen and in love with a fair-haired Minnesota boy named David Smith, the great dune was our necking tryst. Once, rolling and panting at the edge of the woods, I forgot about poison ivy. The next week in high school, the gym teacher would not let me into the swimming pool with my crusty, oozing sores. I learned that love is full of perils. A year later, lying on the sand, Dave said: "I love your mind, your soul, your body." What more could a girl ask?

I married Dave Smith when I was nineteen. After he graduated from law school at the University of Chicago, we made our escape from the Midwest with six-month-old Eric. My trajectory from that time to now has been westward and upward, toward the last wild places, toward those who would share with me the ecstatic pull of landscape and sky. On the homestead Dave and I built in western Montana, I am surrounded by meadows. Bear and elk roam my woods, and coyotes howl from the deep grass. Desire for wildness is what I took from the beach, the foredunes, the blowout.

. . .

Think of a funnel. The Michigan dunes have been a gathering place for four generations blown in from Hungary and France and Montana, from New York, Chicago, Boston, California, and Texas. Dave and I bore four children who would learn to walk with us on sand. My sisters also married and had babies.

For thirty-five years, the eight cousins have spent summer days on our beach, bringing sweethearts now, spouses, and my mother's great-grandchildren.

Our family album is filled with elongating limbs and silvering hair—playing like these memories against the blues and browns of lake and sand. Some faces are gone: Dave, dead in 1974; Kathy's husband Chris, dead in 1976; Nelson Algren, dead in 1981; my father, dead in 1997. My mother is coming one hundred. I shudder to think of losing her, too.

The dunes are changing with us: more summer mansions, retaining walls to keep dunes from eroding, our blowout filled in by a Caterpillar bulldozer for a resort development. Accustomed to Montana mountains, I see Old Baldy small as an anthill. Perhaps it has joined the ranks of the aging and shrinking. Hang gliders fly around the big dune's pine-fringed pate; windsurfers slalom offshore. Four miles down the beach at Bridgman, where terrorist Wobblies once hid from the law, we stare at the ominous cone of a nuclear power plant. Lake waters cool its reactors.

My mother and I recently visited the dunes in November. As we drove into the state park, we spotted two young white-tailed bucks, their antlers like outspread fingers waved in greeting. It was a metal-bright day—surf roaring, the breeze scented with dried leaves and smoke. Gulls flocked on the sand, but mallards and geese had migrated south, or inland, where they stay as long as there's open water.

In the parking lot by the boarded-up, pagoda-shaped concession stand, a pigtailed girl who reminded me of me stamped her foot. "I will not leave until I climb Old Baldy!" she cried. Me neither, I thought.

I took Mother home and went back to the great dune. Eight middle-schoolers from Kyoto climbed ahead of me. Chattery as crows, they swung from cottonwood snags on top of the 240-foot dune. Looking east, I saw a red-brown roof of trees that masked orchards, vineyards, and towns, creating the illusion of primeval America. To the west was the white-capped lake. South lay our summer home on Tower Hill, but northward, toward the domed nuclear plant, the great Warren Dunes Natural Area opened wild and unpeopled.

I had stepped down into the nearly vertical slope of a U-shaped blowout and was sliding in deep sand when I heard a loud rustle from below. I scanned a patch of cottonwoods skirted by pale, waving marram grass, but saw nothing. Then I heard the sound again and a black shape emerged into sunlight.

It was a huge, heavy bird. The bird unfolded his wide black wings. He spread his unmistakable half-moon tail. I saw a long neck and red wattles. I held my breath. The rooster sailed stately over the opposite dune and into the oaks. He was the first wild turkey I had ever seen in the dunes. Tears came to my eyes. "Turkey!" I shouted. I was shouting thanksgiving to no one, and to all creation.

I knew winter was coming, the wildest season, when waves freeze in mid-motion, snow makes lace of the woods, and spindrift melds with sand. Winter on the lake is heavy and elusive as mercury—like memory, family, death, and, of course, like love—which is why I keep returning to the edge where water and sand create unlikely life. Here, after snow melts, there will be snakes in the marram grass, monarch butterflies so rare we don't dare catch them, and Indian stones from the Paleozoic seas. The French had it right when they said, *The more things change, the more they stay the same.*

In every season, the dunes are moving. That is the nature of dunes. They change with every wind. Their dance is monotonous, evanescent, and shifting . . . one-step, one-step, one-step. It is my heart.

Aboard

Mary Blocksma

*I*t's a lonely drive from Cape Vincent to Tibbetts Point, where Lake Ontario meets the St. Lawrence River. No one is here; the American Youth Hostel, housed in the keeper's quarters, does not begin its season till June. Like all Fourth Coast lighthouses, the Tibbetts Point Lighthouse has been automated, and the light, once fueled with whale oil, is now electric, this one visible on clearer days fourteen miles over the lake. A radio beacon has replaced the foghorn. Nearby, a little road hugs a shore that soon narrows into a water-flanked ridge. I park there and emerge. On my right, Lake Ontario tosses large and restless. On my left, countless terns swoop like small, sleek gulls through a swirling mist above a flat, dark backwater, hover, plunge, and flutter off, emitting high-pitched screams. Two tern species—inky black terns, white underwings and forked tails looking painted, unreal; and white, black-capped common terns, whose tangerine bill provide accents of color—mingle like a moving Escher. Slowly the swarm thins as the birds become aware of my figure in the mist, and the silences between their cries expand, merge, until all I can hear is the lake breathing.

After four wet days and nights, I crave a long hot shower, a warm dry room. I follow the scalloped shore and then lose it in dairy country, driving past black and white cows and bright white gulls, feeding together on shining green pastures. The gray, snaky road is sleek with rain. I'm trying to stay by the water as much as I can—the one rule I travel by, which sometimes requires the exploration of small roads not on maps—and right now I have no idea where I am. I'm not lost, really—there's no such thing as "lost" on a trip like this. I'm just turning right when it seems appropriate, a method of lakeside navigation that sometimes works and sometimes doesn't. I stop often to get my bearings.

. . .

Two old barges, with peeling white paint and dark red trim, angle up on a deserted beach as if recently crashed. Inside, white upholstered parlor chairs are pushed up to white tablecloths in a large room. Waves break against the far windows. I warm up with hot coffee while the only patron tells me over his plate of meat and potatoes that several years ago, a tug was towing livestock across Lake Ontario in these barges when a storm hit, the lines broke, and the transport washed up here. Seemed too much trouble to move them, so voilà, a restaurant. What? A motel? Not around here.

Henderson Harbor, a tiny village perched on a bay, stylish buildings interspersed with bait shops and boathouses, feels like a ghost town in the gloomy damp. It's getting late. I walk into an elegant old frame inn, shout about; no one is there. No one is on the streets either. A newer, expensive-looking restaurant up the street is closed. Still, I hear music, so I walk around to the back. A man appears, wielding a broom. Sure, we're closed. No problem, come on in. Have some coffee. What am I looking for? A modest motel on the water? Got the perfect place. He makes a call, can't rouse anyone, and says he'll try again later.

Tony Cocuzzoli's wife, Ann Marie, appears, and while we wait, Tony describes a nearby island where a petroleum company entertains its executives. "Miss Texas came by helicopter. They bring in trailer loads of ice coolers, fly in live turkeys and pheasants. You can land stark naked and they'll outfit you from head to toe for hunting and fishing. This is executive camping. You just go over there and shoot things." Area natives, the Cocuzzolis confide, find this hilarious.

As for the quiet town, I have just missed the annual Rod and Reel Derby, the biggest event of the year—all-out fishing, partying, street dances, thousands of people—so now everyone's recuperating. There's also a good wind, so the bartenders, surfers every one, are probably out "shredding."

Tony calls again. At last—a room.

May 22

A loon is fishing just past the clunking docks outside my window at the Sunset Motel, where I sit typing at a small table. This place is perfect. I am not just on the water; I can hear it lapping underneath the floor, in a boat "garage." No phone, no TV, but there's a hot shower and a warm room fragrant with lilacs that Jack and Phyllis, the owners, just dropped off. Outside, gulls sail past, swallows swoop, terns dive, and a northern shoveler, a mallard-like duck with a huge bill, just paddled in.

I have plugged in my automatic coffeepot to heat water for tea and instant soup. *The Victoria Day Show*, a funky Canadian radio program, is cracking me up. "Victoria Day" describes her taste in music as the sort of thing you might hear trailing from an old Chevrolet. She reads a poem about radishes from a book called *The Garden That Got Away* and sings along, off-key, with a group called the Rumaniacs.

My tape recorder has stopped working, so I'm waiting for an express-mail replacement from my father, who has taken an active, envious interest in this adventure. He has loved the Lakes since childhood, introduced by YMCA-sponsored camps and canoe trips. I seem to have inherited his fondness, if not for boats, at least for offbeat Great Lakes places. This is one of them.

. . .

I've backtracked, returning briefly to Cape Vincent to hitch a ride on a small Seaway pilot boat, which is ferrying Captain Richard J. Menkes, who happens to be the president of the St. Lawrence Seaway Pilots Association, out past the breakwater to the 579.5-foot *Olympic Dignity*. These foreign "salties" often take on special pilots to navigate the Lakes or the Seaway—Captain Menkes will pilot the Greek freighter downriver to Massena, where the ship may then take on another Seaway pilot to Montreal. The captain resembles an airline pilot—graying at the temples, courteous, with an air of authority. I arrived on time—but, he notes, just. He asks for my business card, which I do not have. I start feeling like a stowaway.

The trip is short—in minutes, Captain Menkes is climbing the ladder up the side of the ship. Heads of sailors pop up along the top, high, high above us, like birds on a wall. A woman! Foreign exclamations! More heads. Arms appear and wave at me. A rope snakes down suddenly through the air, and a bucket labeled U.S. Mail drops into the boat, is filled and pulled back up. A dashing, graying man hurries down the ladder and declares, as his boots hit the deck: "I'm the best-looking pilot of 'em all! And the crew, they made me an honorary Greek citizen."

He is Captain Richard Tetzlaff, and he has just brought the ship across Lake Ontario. Scheduled shortly to board another, he's anxious to get going. The pilots change every fifty to a hundred miles on the Seaway, he tells me. This particular ship is carrying steel, a cargo so heavy that most of the hold is empty. She is owned by the Onassis company in Monte Carlo, registered out of Monrovia. We pull away from the looming black hull, waving at the sailors, who shout down at us in Greek.

May 24

After a clean, clear dawn, over water like a satin quilt—fifty-one degrees, air somewhat colder—I head out of Henderson Bay on a powerful boat that would comfortably hold six, but this morning carries only me and Captain Jerry Read, a good-natured college student also known as "Mouse." Bill Saife, the fishing guide who offered me this free trip, is guiding a group of four men who, it turns out, did not want a woman on board. They think it's bad luck, Mouse tells me apologetically. Not to worry, I assure him. I am happy.

Jerry and I leave first, lowering the aerials to pass under a low bridge out to the lake. Bill's boat, in radio contact, is a few minutes behind us. "We're only going out about five miles," shouts Jerry over the roar of the huge motor. "We'll be fishing for lake and brown trout today. Later in summer we go so far out, you can't see anything but water—maybe fifteen, twenty miles. Salmon fishing starts in June, gets really good in August." He tells me he's lived in Henderson Harbor all his life.

Jerry slows the boat to a crawl. I steer while he rigs four sturdy fishing rods in the two substantial-looking black holders braced on the back of the boat. (There are more of these on the sides to accommodate a larger crowd.) Soon our lines trail off the back. "The real secret to this kind of fishing is knowing the water," Jerry tells me. "See that line between the light- and darker-colored water? That's where the warm water butts up against the cool water, and that's where we usually find some fish." We head in that direction.

It isn't necessary to pay close attention—each line is attached to the big orange weight and the release mechanism of a downrigger, a device that causes the fishing pole, usually bent, to snap up when a fish hits. It isn't ten minutes before I hear one go. Jerry rushes to the back to help, and after a short struggle I have caught a silvery, white-spotted lake trout. It isn't terribly large, but too big for a one-person meal, so I ask Jerry to throw it back. "We encourage catch-and-release," says Jerry as he does so, but he warns against handling the fish too much—the slime on their bodies helps them breathe and resist parasites.

Snap, there goes another pole. It is beautiful out here, this glassy emerald water, sapphire sky, silvery fish whipping out of the foam. This one is a Seneca Lake trout, Jerry says. It comes from the oldest strain of fish stock in the lake. He can tell this from the clipped upper fin. Maybe twenty inches long, the fish is all muscle. It has that taut energy, the grace of a dancer. "Let it go," I say.

About now, Bill radios in. Are we getting any bites? Jerry reports our catch. "Oh. Don't seem to be getting much here," says Bill. I smile. I can hear those guys now: "Beginner's luck," I hope they are saying. "Damn woman." Oh yes, I chortle in my secret heart. The witch is on the water, boys—watch out!

Back goes the line. I excuse myself to use the "head." To flush it I turn a switch, pump some water in, and switch the pipe closed again. Back in the cabin, Jerry tells me that there are three "lady" charter captains in the harbor. We are looking at blips on the electronic fish finder when another pole goes. Hey, I'm getting good at this. I pull in a little brown trout, round black ink spots on the top half, a few red ones along the golden middle. We head back—it's about ten o'clock and this one's just right for breakfast.

Back at the Quonset-hut headquarters, I pay $27 for the gas we used (my God, we were only gone a couple of hours!), which, added to my $15 New York nonresident fishing license, totals my breakfast at $42. Actually, this is an incredible bargain: the usual expense includes a guide fee—$400 a day—which I have not been charged, and all that elaborate fishing equipment, which I did not buy, and of course the beer that often flows, which I did not bring. I ask Jerry if this very expensive fish is safe to eat, and he says, "It's all in how you clean it. The contaminants are mainly in the skin and fat, so if you get rid of those, you get rid of most of the bad stuff." Jerry takes my fish to a big cleaning room and hands it to a young man, who casually whacks up my supple catch with an electric knife. He dumps most of the fish—head, tail, skin, fins, guts, and bones—through a hole in the floor—splash! "The snappers swim in at night and clean up," he says, handing me two thin fillets.

Outside the motel, I balance my mushroom-shaped propane stove at the end of the dock and fry my fish in the upside-down lid of my water bucket. While it's sizzling, Phyllis comes by and tells me about a *60 Minutes* team that came here about seven years ago. "They tested the fish, they tested the water, and they couldn't find a story, so they left and they never came back." She also tells me about a ninety-four-year-old woman who skinny-dips daily in chilly Lake Ontario, adding, "I think she'd be pleased if you'd mention her in your book."

I slip the hot brown trout fillets on a green plastic plate, sprinkle them with salt, butter a hamburger bun, and (water lapping at the pilings, sun shimmering on blue water) dig in.

Walking the Lake's Edge in Winter

JUDITH ARCANA

*E*veryone who knows Chicago knows winter there is cold, really cold, and pretty often filled with snow. The snow lands thick, in great dunes that blanket the city's dirt. Or it lies hard and gritty in the street, like the salt crystals scattered to break it down to slush. Or maybe the snow never lands; it just cuts, sharp and hard, slashed by the knife of the wind.

Not everyone knows what Chicago winters do with the big lake; few walk the ice edge in early February. Lake Michigan is so big it rarely freezes over, and the wind in winter moves the water much as it does in the hot months, lifting it into waves as clear in their hearts of grey light as summer's waves of green. The lake's body rises and falls all winter long.

By February of a freezing winter, the shore is no longer flat, and the lake no longer throws its fans across the sand. By February there are ice caves, built up and hollowed out by the waves, some four and five feet high above the beach. Most days the sky is low, colored milk, and sand suspended in the wave-carved ice is coarse enough to smooth freshcut wood. But when the low sky opens and the brittle winter light pours through, its pale gold illuminates the waiting shadow of the ice caves. Suspended sand glitters like gemstones; hollows become diamond mirrors.

Between Fullerton Parkway and North Avenue, a stretch with a breakwater of long narrow concrete piers, the ice caves gleam green and silver. Even the white of that frozen architecture glistens. New waves make no splash, but crack where they land. They shatter as they freeze.

I walked that shore in February. *I want to go to the beach*, I said inside my head, and pulled on high boots lined with fleece. My mind was changing like the landscape; I needed to be there. I needed the comfort that comes when inside and outside are one thing, no separation.

I understood this, why I was going to the lake, when I crossed under Lake Shore Drive and the cars roared over my head, trembling the walls of the concrete tunnel, rumbling its dark cracked ceiling. On the other side, the hotdog/popcorn/ice-cream wagon was boarded up, and the drinking fountains covered. There were no gulls, and after the roar of the Drive, the beach seemed silent.

Then, in that sudden quiet after the tunnel, I heard the creaking ice, moved to sound by the insistent lake, heard my bootsteps crunching the dense snow. I saw that the long piers were gone—no, they were invisible, a skeleton for the carved ice and frozen sandsnow.

No fish smell, but the smell of my own body rose on the heat coming out of my collar, warming my throat, wrapped in its layers of flannel and wool. I stumped over to what had been the summer edge of the beach, and stopped. There I saw that light was trapped in the ice, shining. The sand itself shone, silica and mica glistening like tiny stars in ice-locked space. The ice looked green as I approached it, silver-grey when I finally stood there, watching water from Gary and Milwaukee come to freeze at the tips of my boots.

Here was the science lesson made palpable: all about freezing, all about how one thing, water, could be many things, and yet be itself. Solid—the ice, and liquid—the lake, even gas—my wet breath like hot steam; and in all of these, itself. Was this true of me? My mind expanded like the lake at freezing, and took new shapes, like the ice caves.

Here was the philosophy lesson, biology of the spirit, teaching the physical nature of mind in Chicago, as fresh water mingles with salt when the St. Lawrence finds the sea, that briny offshore current freshening then, there, just there and then in a moment—and all of it changing: going, coming, moving, changing, coming on through the Great Lakes to me, here on this winter beach. Like the water that makes me, the water inside me, moving from lips to heart, cells to systems and back again in tides of myself, so this water, rising from the heart of the continent, surges from Mackinaw City to Toronto, from Portneuf to Riviere-au-Renard. Here was the lesson that teaches how everything changes, how transition is never complete, how whatever we are is whatever we've been, whatever we ever will be.

Getting to the Point

Leslie Stainton

I’ve never been good at math. Algebra intrigued but ultimately baffled me; I never risked calculus or trigonometry. Simple arithmetic was OK, but even today, when my twelve-year-old stepson asks me whether denominators need to agree in order to multiply fractions, I can only shrug. I hated my tenth-grade math teacher so much that I rejoiced when he kicked me out of class for an entire week after I'd insulted him.

Geometry was different. Not that I got it, but at some antediluvian level I appreciated the possibilities. The shapes were beautiful, the words evocative. Polygon, hexagon, parallelogram, trapezoid. These summoned images of other worlds, South Sea islands, barbarous rites. Even the familiar square, rectangle, triangle exerted a fascination. We learned to dance by heeding their outlines, bounced balls in and out of their chalked confines, banged at their resonant edges in the band room.

Geometry bespeaks a world where rules govern but variation is infinite. How big can a trapezoid be? How sharply can you angle a parallelogram? What is the circumference of the earth? Geometry surrounds us: It's in every corner of the gabled room where I write these sentences. It's in our buildings, streets, squares, cul-de-sacs, pencil points, ice cubes, lapels, computer screens, alphabet, land.

Geometry is unavoidable. Which may be the conclusion two French missionaries reached when they landed one March night in 1670 on the eastern side of a scalene triangle that protrudes into the waters of Lake Erie, on the southern shores of Ontario. *Pères* Francis Dollier de Casson and René de Bréhard de Galinée were not, of course, seeking geometry, but a safe place to hole up for the night, and ultimately a spot to build a mission. They hoped to convert the people they called "savage," the first residents of the Great Lakes region. Galinée, a mathematician by training, also planned to map their route.

They called the site "the long point."

"We had made that day nearly twenty leagues, so we were all very much tired," writes Galinée in his subsequent account of their journey. "That was the reason why we did not carry all our packs up on the high ground, but left them on the sand."

A great wind picked up as they slept, and washed the waters of the lake over their belongings. They managed to salvage the baggage and a keg of powder from one canoe, but lost everything else, including a cache of venison that had only recently saved them from starvation. Worse, "the entire altar service was lost," Galinée writes with palpable anguish. "This accident put it beyond our power to have the aid of the sacraments or to administer them to the rest."

Rather than pursue their mission without spiritual props, the missionaries turned back to Montreal—albeit by traveling another hundred miles west, then north through the Sault of Sainte-Marie. If he was at all moved by the discovery of a near-perfect triangle of land in Lake Erie, the mapmaker and mathematician Galinée made no mention of it in his narrative, the first written record of the point the French later named *pelée*, or "peeled," for its bare terrain.

Instead, Galinée focused on what happened next. Outside Detroit, he and Dollier found an immense stone idol, worshipped by the natives for its power to protect them as they sailed on Lake Erie. Still smarting from their loss, the Frenchmen took their revenge. "I consecrated one of my axes to break this god of stone, and then having yoked our canoes together we carried the largest pieces to the middle of the river, and threw all the rest also into the water, in order that it might never be heard of again," Galinée reports. "God rewarded us immediately for this good action, for we killed a roe-buck and a bear that very day."

Legend has it the stone fragments left behind by the missionaries retained the power of the original deity and continued to safeguard the Indians—a possibility the devout Galinée never considered. We seldom perceive things without blinders of our own making. Some fifty years after Galinée's rampage, another Frenchman, the philosopher and lawyer Charles de Secondat, baron of Montesquieu, hypothesized, "If triangles were to create a god, they would describe him with three sides."

. . .

A modern explorer approaches Point Pelee not by sea but by land, driving south from Leamington, Ontario, a small town distinguished, for an outsider like me, mostly by its proliferation of fruit and vegetable stands. The point itself is part of the Canadian national park system. At the entrance, one pays a fee and proceeds south through a forest on the western side of the peninsula. Signs warn that infant turtles, no bigger than a tablespoon, can cross your path at any moment. The place feels not so much peninsular as landlocked, a huge wilderness classroom with pedagogical displays of wildlife in action.

And yet there is a sense of progression. Like the infinitesimal turtles, or the intrepid Galinée, we move where instinct leads us. In part it's mathematical: how, and at what angle, will the long sides of this tricorn converge? In part it's the lure of water. But it may also be physiology. Because Pelee is the southernmost tip of Canada, the same latitude as Rome and Barcelona, and because we are a furless species that craves warmth, we plunge intuitively south, as birds do, toward the point, or what the French more aptly call *l'extrémité*.

Much of the six-mile route runs past an enormous marsh, also triangular, one of the last in a region once dense with marshland. The European settlers who followed Galinée and Dollier drained and diked much of southern Ontario in the name of agriculture—hence Leamington's bounty—but they left Pelee untouched, a rare vestige of pre-European-explorers topography. Fully 70 percent of the peninsula is marsh.

Galinée didn't mention the thousands of birds that are Pelee's primary draw today. Not even gulls, known to congregate on the tip of the point, appear in his narrative. For the birds, the Ontario peninsula is a last, reviving stop before crossing Lake Erie in the fall. In the spring, it's a restorative after the difficult flight back. Galinée had other things on his mind, of course, and he arrived too early for the spring migration.

Anyway, it wasn't until 1882 that anyone, at least anyone who recorded things, paid much attention at all to the birds. That year, W. E. Saunders, a naturalist from London, Ontario, came to Pelee to hunt ducks and found passenger pigeons instead, those indefatigable travelers, as well as hundreds of other bird species. Of his discovery, Saunders wrote, "I do not know that anyone had previously seen such a migration."

The birders followed. In 1908, Saunders and five colleagues from the Great Lakes Ornithological Club built a migration lab called "the shack" near the end of the point. A year later, a man named Norman Wood spent four weeks bird watching on Pelee at the height of the fall migration. Wood recorded dozens of species: thrashers, gulls, warblers, hawks, sparrows, sandpipers, herons, ducks, killdeer, snipe, crows, kingfishers, owls, eagles. Like other birders of his time, including Saunders, Wood identified many of his finds after shooting them.

Standing in the middle of the great Pelee marsh, where Canadian rangers have thoughtfully laid out a meandering boardwalk for pilgrims bearing binoculars and Peterson guides, I can't conceive of anyone shooting what soars above my head. Ninety years after Wood and his cronies fired their guns, the birds still come. Some, of course, have vanished. I have little hope of seeing a bald eagle, let alone two, as Wood did; the passenger pigeons Saunders marveled at are now extinct. But what I suspect is a palm warbler darts coyly in and out of the cattails, foiling my efforts to identify her. Confusing fall warblers, indeed.

Birds, who intercede between sky and earth, have long been auguries of both fortune and doom. By their flight, seers once predicted the destiny of kings and the mindset of gods. Even in my lifetime, the canary in the mineshaft has foretold life or death.

The gods of Galinée's age having scattered, we come to a place like Pelee in part to forge a connection with such mysteries. Children clatter along the boardwalk while their more earnest parents point to the sky. We are all looking. I catch the eye of a father guiding his young son up the stairs of a lookout platform, and we smile. Conspirators. As at church, our prayers are mostly private, but our communion is not.

By night, many migrating birds miss Pelee. It's only in the hour before dawn, as light begins to break, that they will descend to a lower altitude and spot the ground below them. By day, birds cleave to the contours of the shoreline, moving ever down, down, down as the land abruptly drops from the coast and races south to its dagger point. Fleeing arctic air, the pale yellow warbler who now flirts with me in the marsh will look down and see land and recognize it as a harbor. Pelee's cattails allow her to delay her treacherous journey over water. Absent icons or gods to protect her, she loads up on insects, and braces for Erie. I catch her briefly in my binoculars, then she's gone. Both stronger and weaker than I am, she is destined to stray further and, if my luck holds, to die sooner.

. ◆ .

Galileo taught that one cannot comprehend the universe without understanding the language in which it is written. "It is written in the language of mathematics," he went on, "and its characters are triangles, circles, and other geometrical figures, without which it is humanly impossible to understand a single word of it; without these, one is wandering about in a dark labyrinth."

Here at the tip of the peninsula, the land lengthens and narrows, shedding trees, rocks, driftwood, soil, and pebbles until there is only sand, and then it too dives underwater and disappears. The language of the place is clear. The labyrinth of trees and marsh are behind us. Sand alone remains, and birds—a clutch of gulls who brave the gusts at the extremity of the tapered land.

To the west of this triangle, along the beach that ruined Galinée and Dollier, dun-colored waves swell and roil and slam against the shore. The wind is battering. But if I turn my back and face east, the lake is as calm as bathwater. Where the two sides collide, inches beyond the last remnant of land, a huge liquid ring uncoils. It must be twenty yards in diameter. Long before one reaches the tip, signs in French and English warn of the dangers. No one, not even "the strongest swimmer," can be sure of surviving the deadly pull of this circular current, we're told. Don't even think of wading. Oblivious to their peril, the gulls on the point lounge and primp like teenage boys.

Writing at the turn of the twentieth century, Bertrand Russell observed, "Mathematics takes us still further from what is human, into the region of absolute necessity, to which not only the actual world, but every possible world, must conform."

Geometry has brought me to this extreme. Although this is not the end of the earth—barges and the low, long silhouette of an island are visible on the lake horizon, and I stand, after all, near the center of a continent—it feels like it just the same. The medieval Finisterre, sought and feared by pilgrims, where earth ended and the endless sea began. The dark waters, mansion of the dead, beyond which nothing is certain. Here it is the wide and dangerous lake that is capable of swallowing birds, swimmers, ships, missionaries, or Indians in their fragile canoes.

To his crude map of the long point we now call Pelee, Father René de Bréhard de Galinée appended a note. "Lake Erie—I only mark what I have seen of it, whilst waiting to see the rest." The lens of faith through which Galinée viewed the world let him approach the unknown with a certainty most of us crave. Although this inconsequential spit of land had robbed him of the sacrament and deprived the natives of salvation, Galinée nevertheless labored over its shape, ultimately sketching something that more closely resembles a pustule than the lean mathematical figure it is. Still, he got it. At some level, Galinée understood that even he must conform to the exigencies of this place, however savage it might seem.

No one stays out here long. It's a relief to turn back from the point with its hammering winds and head north into the shelter of trees. Just inside the woods, not far from the tip, I spot a trio of monarch butterflies, the first I've seen today. What could be more absurd? A few hundred feet from the end of the world, three paper-weight beings with bright orange wings flit with the indolence of children from tree to tree, then pause to levitate. It's a temporary condition, I know. Like the yellow warbler, they're destined to fly south, over the great lake and then hundreds of miles beyond. By the thousands, they come here each fall to stock up on the single plant that can sustain them on their improbable trip—milkweed, of the genus *Asclepias*, derived from Asclepius, Apollo's son, god of medicine. On the brink of the unprotected world, in these gently rustling leaves, the butterflies tremble with what I can only guess is pleasure. Our separate journeys beckon.

Leap

ANNA MILLS

"This water is clearer than Jamaica." Eve stands knee-deep on the shore of Madeline Island. A wave swells against her legs and subsides, a greeting from the gray-blue horizon. I think how odd the world is, to have deposited her on an island in Lake Superior where people look a second longer at her dark skin and her red-black dreadlocks. She grew up with a warm ocean, a kaleidoscope of fish. We arrived this morning in Bayfield, a flowery town on the south shore. I bought gumballs at an old-fashioned candy shop while Eve got coffee. We drove onto the ferry and climbed to the deck to watch flat water shining. The wake foamed and boiled, and Madeline Island moved closer—a forest lying on the water. Soon we drove off the boat and passed a grocery store advertising cheap smoked fish, and then a circus tent called "Tom's Burned Down Café." The buildings disappeared, and the leaves made clouds over the road. We camped at Big Bay State Park among pines and tall grass and then set off over a bridge through the swamp to emerge on the beach. Now we are lounging. The flies buzz, but the sun is constant and the long stretch of sand almost empty.

"I'm going in." Eve throws her towel to me and bends to test the water. I know how it feels, cold but not freezing. Looking north past the red rock arm of the bay, I see only water, as wide as the ocean. The world rests, simple and remote like the smile on a Buddha's face.

Soon we head back to our picnic table to eat bean stew wrapped in tortillas. I spoon yogurt into mine. We haven't brought a stove, so we eat it cold, a strange salad with cumin and curry. When it gets dark we find ourselves without firewood, our minds jumping to faster music than the rustle of the campground. We climb into Eve's old sports car and drive. There is Tom's Burned Down Café, a tent on the edge of town surrounded by wild orange lilies. Rusted iron sculptures lead to the entrance—I think I see a teepee, a spinning wheel, and a bouquet of flowers, machine parts jutting out at odd angles. We climb the steps past hand-painted signs: "Life begins when you get one," and "Don't worry about what most people think—most don't." A woman stacks glasses behind the bar, and a man with a bushy beard tunes a fiddle. A dog of no recognizable breed sniffs the fireplace. Eve asks for Jamaican coffee, as always, and then teaches the bartender: "You have coffee? Just add Kahlua and rum." We learn that the café actually did burn down. Tom pitched this tent in the ashes on a foundation of wrecked cars—the bartender points to one through a crack in the floorboards.

The next morning, Eve and I set out along the shore. In the still forest a short way from the lake, mosquitoes swarm. She slips her arms inside my shirt to protect them and hugs me as we walk. We meet no one. The lake disappears and reappears through the trees. Hundreds of birds call, but we don't know their names. When I look into the forest, it is hard to imagine that red rock and waves lie close. Heavy green air, earth, and a dark ceiling of leaves seem to swallow the world. I watch the white skin peeking through my sandals and hope the bugs will miss it.

The coves tempt me, and I pause when the path swings by a cliff. Should we get in? I haven't brought a bathing suit. "Nudist," Eve teases. I admit I want to feel the water sweep along all of me. I always want to. We make our way down the bank, grasping at roots, and then walk out on a low, rocky promontory. Soon we slip in, breasts and bellies exposed: a brown fish and a white fish. I go under and blow out my breath and sink toward the round boulders, like great eggs. Silence, skin alive with touch, clean like ice. I surface. Lake Superior offers itself, ringed with stones. It's not so cold that I won't plunge again and again.

We wade out, but don't bother to dry ourselves in the humid air. Instead, we brush off thick drops and pull on our clothes. My shirt clings. I want to kiss Eve with wet lips, but she is absorbed in finding the right stone to skip. I wonder if she used to squat that way as a tomboy. For half an hour we search for the flattest rocks and send them towards the horizon. Then we scramble up the bank to the trail. After a long immersion under the trees, we emerge at the northern end of the island. A few ledges jut out from the shore, their red forms the last solid matter before a long, liquid gray. I wonder if the water is deep enough to jump. I see a way down, and my veins pound toward the moment. Eve refuses. As a girl, she played in the ocean but never learned to swim; deep water scares her.

I hand over my camera, dump my backpack, and because I am a crazy girl, I shed my clothes again. The rock feels gritty as if it would rub off on my hands. I lower myself towards a table that runs to a point a few feet above the water. I scrape a knee and feel almost glad—a badge. The table narrows like an arrowhead. I walk slowly toward the point, feeling the ridges with the soles of my feet. This is the culmination of silent pines, flies, yellow sand, skipping stones, and a tent built on ashes. I look into the lake and see no shoals, only the blue-brown water, milky, opaque. Then I look north toward reaches where there are no footholds, no leaves rustling. We have outrun ourselves. The water spreads as wide as my arms, rocking, not breaking like the ocean. Surface and sky lie against each other like bodies. If death comes like this—vast, intimate, sensuous—why ever fear?

I turn and pace back. I pinch my nose, count to five, and speed forward. Leap. White thunder, the pain of the slap, and then the cold world enclosing me. I paw like a monkey and surface sputtering. I paddle to the rock with a grin of desperate, unveiled joy. Eve catches me with the camera, eyes wider than human eyes, crawling out with the lake at my toes.

Bodies of Water

Lisa Lenzo

_M_y love for Lake Michigan began with another large body of water. I was eight years old and had flown with my family from Detroit to Sanibel Island, and one afternoon during our vacation, I decided that I would walk around the entire island by myself. I started down the beach, chanting while I walked—_I'm walking out of civilization, I'm walking out of civilization_—until my mother and the other beachcombers turned into dots and disappeared. Trudging through water and sand, climbing over whole sideways forests of driftwood trees, I gazed at the sky and the gulf, listened to the crashing of the waves, and drifted into a reverie unlike any I had ever known. The boundaries between me and the water and the sky had disappeared—it was as if I had reached out and joined with them, even as I continued to walk in my own body and on my own feet, and as if the sky and water had reached in from the horizon to join with me. I felt in my bones that I belonged to the water and the sky, to the driftwood and the sand and even to the dead jellyfish I'd seen, and that they were a part of me.

When I was seventeen, I returned to Florida with my family for another vacation. Worried about my future and suffering from a mild depression, I walked by the ocean for most of each day by myself. I walked for so many hours, from before sunrise till suppertime and again after supper, that I developed a case of sun poisoning, but that didn't deter me; rather than retreating indoors, I put on a long-sleeved shirt and long pants and kept walking, dipping my clothed body in the ocean to stay cool. I felt strong and healthy and free. I felt so good that I considered not going back to Detroit and to school, but just staying in Florida. I was pretty sure I'd be fine if I could walk by the water each day.

But in the end I concluded that I couldn't manage to live in Florida on my own, so I returned to Detroit, where my depression worsened. When I'd reached my breaking point, I fled north of the city to live in a tent on rolling land that was dotted with tiny lakes and threaded with creeks. A month later, feeling stronger, I moved across the state, for what I thought would be just the summer, to live and work at a camp on an inland sea, an ocean without salt, Lake Michigan.

I lived in a cabin perched above its vast, shifting body, and was lulled to sleep by its lapping and awakened by its storms. I walked beside the lake and swam in it, diving in and out of its waves, and my new boyfriend taught me to sail on its surface. I began to call Lake Michigan "the Lake" in the same spirit that native peoples call themselves "the People."

At the end of the summer, I stayed on as the camp's winter cook, while Mark, my new boyfriend, became the year-round caretaker. Three and half years later we married, and soon after, I gave birth to our first child. Steffie was born with severe hydrocephalus, water on the brain. She lived only one hour and forty-four minutes. My waterhead child, my lovely, flawed girl, I held her briefly when she was already dead, then gave her over to be burned to ash.

Sorrow had already struck us in the months prior to Steffie's birth, with the deaths of two of our grandfathers and the suicide of Mark's aunt. Then, three weeks after Steffie died, my brother's legs were crushed in the cardboard compactor at his summer job and had to be amputated. Mark and I would tense each time the phone rang, and stunned and grieving from all that had happened, I would wake in the night and not know why I was crying. For my baby? For my brother? I went back to work two weeks after Steffie's death, but I cried more nights than not for the next couple of months, while Mark, lying quietly beside me or holding me stiffly, retreated deep into himself and didn't cry at all.

Fourteen months after Steffie's death and again hugely pregnant, I sailed with Mark out into the lake with Steffie's ashes wrapped tightly in a kerchief. As we sped away from the shore, I opened the kerchief out over the boat's edge. The ashes and bits of bone were quickly gone. There was only the choppy water, the flapping kerchief, my empty hands.

Our second child, Cloey, was born healthy and strong. When she was a baby, I took her swimming almost every summer evening. Dixie Elder, the camp's nature director, would watch us from the porch as we set out toward the lake. Dixie had taught lifesaving to the camp staff until she was well into her seventies, and she had swum in the lake daily during her frequent summer visits. But that summer she'd turned eighty, and she wasn't strong enough anymore to walk back up the bluff. Instead, she'd rest her gaze on the lake from above it, and every evening when I returned, carrying Cloey up the hill, she would ask me about the water, and I would tell her how it was. Rough or calm, warm or cold, it was always good.

I was happy then at times, yet Steffie's death had created a deep divide between Mark and me, and on most of those evenings, Cloey and I swam without him. It's a common fallacy that the death of a child brings parents closer—in fact, the vast majority of married couples who lose a child end up divorcing, and eventually, despite counseling, that's what Mark and I did. I'll never know, had Steffie lived, whether we would have divorced for other reasons, but it's clear that our years together were divided into two distinct parts: the easy years, before Steffie's death, and the difficult years that came after.

In our last years together, when I was thinking of leaving, Mark wouldn't use words to try to convince me to stay. Instead, he'd ask me if I wanted to go for a walk, and then he would lead me along the camp's wooded trails, walking beside me without touching me. We'd pass under the beeches whose pale, tiny leaves I'd watched unfold after our baby's death, amazed that spring could go on as if nothing had happened; we'd drift by the tall maples that Mark and I had tapped for their sap when our love was still clear and untainted. We'd end up at the lake, staring out over the water, and still Mark wouldn't speak; he wouldn't try to use words or his own merits to plead his case. Sensing me pulling away, he would show me the land and the lake to try to convince me to stay, knowing that their hold on me was stronger than his own.

I finally left Mark and my home on the lake when I was twenty-nine and Cloey was six. In my new life inland, my days were filled to overflowing with working, going to school, and taking care of Cloey, but at least twice a week I drove to a lakeside park and hiked through rolling duneland, under maples, beeches, and pines, and down the highest bluff to the water. Those walks were my therapy, my recreation, and my communion. Twenty years later, they still are all these things to me.

I walk through the woods to the lake and look out over the water and name what I am thankful for and ask the questions I'm mulling over, and the answers are clearer when I'm looking out over the lake.

Or I'll swim out into the lake, not stopping where the other swimmers stop, but stroking out past the second sandbar, then rolling over and floating on my back with the sun shining down on me, then stroking out farther. Floating, swimming, floating, lollygagging my way out, I'll turn around now and then to look at the shore, at the shrinking people on the beach, until they're so far away that they hardly look human. As a child I'd chanted, *I'm walking out of civilization, I'm walking out of civilization.* Now I am swimming out of it. The water laps at me, overlaps me, soaking my hair and my skin. It enters my ears and my mouth and, if I'm not careful, my nose. As I stroke, it streams over me, caressing each inch of my flesh; I frog-kick, and it swirls at the mouth of the channel between my legs.

A gull lands on the water near me and floats there like a boat, reminding me, by how effortlessly she sits, that she's more at home out here than I. Still, the lake is a sort of home for me. My first daughter's ashes are long dispersed and dissolved—it's been twenty-six years since the lake took them in—but part of her remains here, and so part of me remains here, mixed into the water. My body of water is mixed with this body of water, held up by it, held close.

The Salmon

LORAINE ANDERSON

*T*here is a stretch of beach along Lake Michigan where I like to walk in times of great moment. That is how I came to be there one December day, wearing two layers of everything.

It was the day winter finally hit northern Michigan. American and British missiles were slamming Iraq. The U.S. House of Representatives was crashing against President Clinton, and the Ship of State was sinking fast.

Mostly, though, it was the morning of my fiftieth birthday, and I needed to catch my breath. It had been one of those years.

The walk down the beach was not to be, however, and neither was catching my breath, at least that's how it seemed at first. The cold, harsh wind pummeled my back, whirled around in front of me, and sucked the air from my mouth. The creek I usually leapt over was wide, wild, and calf-deep as it emptied into the Big Lake.

So instead, I turned inland and followed the creek back into the dunes and woods until the trail ended in a thicket guarded by a huge pine. I leaned against the tree and watched clouds march across the sky. They scattered occasionally, and the sun sent shafts of light that dappled the creek and draped a golden sheen over a giant evergreen several hundred yards across the creek.

I could hear the wind and waves roaring and crashing into the beach. In my little eddy along the creek, though, it was quiet and still, and far away from city living and working in a cubicle without even sight of a window.

That's where I was when I first saw her—an aging, dark fish swimming around some submerged logs. I moved forward. She darted back and then stopped at a safe distance, facing me.

I remembered ancient tales told by Pacific Northwest Coast Indians. The salmon is a powerful symbol in their mythology. More than a plentiful food source, salmon give life so that life can go on.

I kneeled down for a closer look. She didn't back away. Her body was rotting the way salmon do after spawning. Part of her lip was gone, maybe torn by a fishing lure. White lined the nostrils on her snout. It seemed strange that I would meet up with a dying fish on a day I was celebrating something I saw as transforming.

The winter air crept into my bones, but I didn't want to leave her alone to die. Somehow, my understanding of life after fifty years seemed entwined with her death—and not in any pessimistic sense.

I stood there for a long time. Two other fish flicked by. The salmon didn't move. Her lower fins had come to rest on the creek bottom. Her tail was still. She seemed suspended, lifeless. I think she died right there in front of me.

For some reason, I felt immeasurable gratitude, both for her life and mine. When I left that spot, I understood something about the cycle of life, death, and renewal that I hadn't before. I accepted it, too. Maybe the fish was a coincidence, maybe not. I do know she was a gift.

Surfin' USA

Diane Wakoski

On a recent summer day, my husband Robert and I were sitting on the beach at Lake Michigan with Judith Minty and her husband Ed. I was the only person on the beach wearing long trousers. Despite a massive layer of heavy sunblock on my skin, I wished that I had worn long sleeves too. So I was wrapping a towel around my arms, as well as covering my bare feet with sand.

At sixty-three, and pale as a moonlight mushroom, I am paying the price for those years of trying to be a "California girl," golden, tanned, and ripe looking. My very pale, dry skin that is thin and ages badly in every way seemed beautiful to me when I was young. One of the only beautiful things about me. When other teenagers had acne, I had skin like opals.

Then, when I moved to New York in 1960, I saw how different I would appear with a tan. Sleek. As if I were fashionable. And sexy. So my smooth pale skin, when I could manage it, I turned into a golden skin, wore miniskirts with bare legs and sandals. My arms were always slender, even when I gained a little weight. I called them "my Wanda Landowska arms," imagining them poised over a harpsichord, and I wore sleeveless blouses and dresses whenever the weather permitted. Often when it didn't. I started wearing bangle bracelets, which often made me close my eyes and shake my right arm like a nymph. I would gaze at my braceleted arm as if I could be a magician, do sleight-of-hand tricks. As if I could be a ballet dancer, with the tanned arms arched up over my head like the center panel of a triptych.

My legs were also okay, and especially looked good when they were tanned. They are too short for my body, as my former sister-in-law, Rhoda Sherbell, a sculptor showed me once in an informal anatomy lesson. At one time she decided to make a life-sized (huge!) bronze sculpture, which she first modeled in clay, featuring several contemporary American figures—I think it was me, Aaron Copeland, and Casey Stengal, or something like that. At any rate, I posed nude for her—with a good tan, of course, for one of the things a tan did for me was to make me love my naked body. My tan would become better than Victoria's Secret underwear.

In the sculpture, she made my legs proportionally long, to go with my long-waisted torso. Wow, did that sculptured figure look beautiful! The architecture of the body is something we forget unless we look at paintings all the time, I think. Odd. Just writing this makes me want to get in touch with Rhoda and ask her if she ever finished that sculpture, or if after my divorce from her brother, my first husband, she eliminated the Diane Wakoski figure before she finished the work and had it bronzed. She models in clay, is so skilled: a genuinely old-fashioned sculptor who has never been fazed by contemporary fashions. I loved sitting in her studio with the smell of the wet clay, and feeling a part of the world of ancient Greek and Roman beauty.

Sitting on the beach on Lake Michigan conjured up so many images from my attempt to create the myth of the California beach girl in my poems. The California beach girl that, in fact, I never was. Robert and Judith and Ed had waded out into Lake Michigan, which was very shallow near the beach. The water, for the first time in the many years we have visited Judith and Ed during the summers, was not icy. It was cool and animal-warm at the same time. Perfect swimming weather. The sun was crashing down on us like an elevator, and I did feel deprived, though it was my own choice, sitting there on the hot beach, fearing what the sun was doing to my body. And I knew the water was utterly refreshing, because when we took our walk along the beach earlier, I walked in it with my trousers rolled up, though not enough so that they didn't get soaked up to the knee. I watched Ed and Judith, who are my age, playing. I watched Robert swimming and playing in the water. Very few other places do adults play.

I don't swim. All my life I have had so many fears, and water is one of them. Yet I long for it, and when the sun is pressing hard and I am on a beach or near a pool, the desire sometimes to immerse myself and find myself swimming is strong. I am not sure why, during all those years of sunbathing, I didn't at least buy a raft or water toy and just paddle around in lakes or pools, letting the float hold me. My hideous experiences at Fullerton Union High School, trying to learn to swim in order to fulfill a graduation requirement, flunking it every year, keep me distanced from any idea that swimming could be fun. In retrospect, I don't know why they have to teach you to put your face in the water, to swim in some traditional way. I could have worn my glasses, kept my face out of the water, and learned to dog paddle around perfectly well. As it was, the only thing I ever learned to do was "the dead man's float." Seems prophetic somehow.

One summer I did have fun in the water. It was the summer I spent in Greece with my second husband, MW. We lived on the island of Hydra, and we could take a boat to a beautiful little public bathing beach with a kind of cove, a bar, and an all-ages swimming area. I floated around on a raft, my arms pillowed on it and my torso and feet in the water, paddling slowly in utter bliss. That is, until I looked down into the clear-as-Etruscan-glass water. I saw what probably was the shadow of my body on the float, and I panicked. The first time, I thought the shadow was a giant squid. So help me, panic is full of clichés. I was sure some terrible sea creature was down there and after me! I'd kick like mad, paddle myself back to shore, and flop down on the float as a substitute beach blanket and work on my tan.

I grew up with ideas of Hollywood glamour from the '40s, so two-piece bathing suits were always the ones I chose. Betty Grable with her amazing pinup legs, Petty girls: these were paper-doll images that I grew up thinking should be what women in bathing suits looked like. Again, those unfortunate short legs I had. But I found that this almost didn't matter when I started wearing bikinis. Not the skimpiest, but low cut on the belly. And my small breasts made it easy to wear a skinny string top.

Judith remarked on a young woman wearing an interesting bathing suit that was really one-piece but was cut away across the waist in the back, with the top and bottom only connected by a little strip in the front. Electric blue against the girl's white skin. Dark hair. I flashed back on the woman, right out of an Antonioni film, who wore a malachite-green topless one-piece bathing suit and was always at our beach near Hydra. Her tan was the perfect bronze of today's trendy SUVs. The green glowed against this stranger's skin and reminded me of the two colors of copper, its bright polish and then the verdigris. She was a kind of bionic woman, a perfect swimmer. Belonged on a yacht. I wanted to have her body. What a summer of longing I spent in Hydra, 1973.

When Robert came back from swimming, wet and so handsome, I felt like I was in a movie, talking to the star. Of course I am fat now, my thick ankles pale as slugs, my legs like short pillars, and my arms like baseball bats. My skin is like the moon's surface, covered with moles and blotches, age spots, and without a single unblemished patch. This is the result of all those years of tanning, and constantly reminds me that even with sunblock I shouldn't let my skin be exposed to much bright sunshine. I had Robert's white tee shirt wrapped around the bare parts of my arms, as I sat there, and my feet and ankles buried in the sand. I wore a wide-brimmed straw hat that completely shaded my face and protected my scalp, and the rest of me was covered with jeans and tee shirt. An old woman at the beach in a French movie.

Here's what I was thinking. One of the reasons I have been drawn to beach culture since my teenage years, and why it is so representative of American adolescence, is that the beach is the only place in America where it's all right to dress expressly to expose your body. It's where you wear sexy bathing suits that invite other people to look at you and see you as sexually attractive. It's permitted as a peep show. No touching, of course, though we all know that it easily leads to the *Beach Blanket Bingo* of our teenage lives. Americans embraced the two-piece bathing suit early on, and then the bikini. Nude beaches still are rare, except in New Age areas like Northern California. And they are usually patronized by people who want to view the naked body without the sexual gaze.

You aren't welcome at a nudist beach or camp if you are going to get a hard-on or ogle the other men and women. The first thing I noticed when I once went to a nude beach was how fat and ugly most everyone seemed to be. I think of the Diane Arbus photo of a nudist couple. Not sexy.

Americans go to the beach *to feel sexual,* and to be given permission to feel that way. Not to act on it, for the most part, but to look at everyone with sexual eyes. Americans don't have a healthy attitude toward nakedness. We might be Puritans who take Genesis as our main testament. We view nakedness as purely sexual, as if we had just finished eating the whole fruit from that Tree of Temptation and can only look at our sexual parts as wicked seduction. So we don't want naked bodies at beaches. That would make us admit that we are casting the taboo lascivious gaze. However, most of us like skimpy bathing suits. We like any bathing suit, actually, because it allows us secretly to cast the sexual gaze and not feel guilty about it.

I saw a prepubescent daughter at the beach that summer throwing sand flirtatiously at her dad, then flinging water, and finally running with him into the water to wrestle a little. I don't think there is anything wrong with this; however, doing this anywhere but at the beach might make it seem prurient. There, it was part of a normal human eroticism that does not necessarily result in sexual contact. The family romance was safely guarded in this beach sport, probably imprinting the girl with an image of a future husband who would be fun and handsome and protective, as her father was in that beach play.

I suppose this is why the Beach Boys were a more important band than the Beatles. They were American, and Brian Wilson was writing about the way we allow ourselves to coexist with our taboos. The girl joy-riding in her father's car, "Little Deuce Coupe"—"I'll have fun fun fun 'til my daddy takes the T-bird away." "The Little Old Lady From Pasadena," who refuses to give up her freedom even though she drives slowly. The hypersensitive teenager, living his rich fantasy life "in my room." So many lyrics that express the great American dilemma—how can we be pure and human, both at once? How can we hang on to our pleasures while still obeying the rules? Poor Brian Wilson never found a way to do it, but his songs are priceless visions of our culture's evasion of its Puritan heritage.

Being "human," oddly enough, is always defined as wallowing in our animal instincts and the primitive urges we all possess. Yet supposedly, we also define "human" as specifically above animals, knowing how to suppress or control our "animal instincts." So, it is both human to be naked, and human to wear bathing suits. The latter is more American.

I only seem go to the beach once a year now. That is what Robert and I should do when we retire: move to the beach. However, that will probably not happen. Undoubtedly I remain, as I have said elsewhere, "A Failed Beach Girl Out Of The West."

Hunting the Moon

GAIL LOUISE SIEGEL

The moon finds hiding places in the city behind gas-station marquees, fat cottonwood branches, and courtyard apartment buildings. It even tucks away behind billboards.

Moonrise is at 10:01 P.M. tonight and I am determined to find it, having missed it yesterday from sheer lack of gumption, and the nights before due to murky skies. So I drive to a close, convenient spot—the big park two blocks from my house, with its soccer pitch and baseball fields, sledding hill, and schoolyard. It's a promising, wide-open space. I pull into the lot. A boy is sliding into second base under the lights. I park facing east and ignore the giant fluorescent globes dangling over the game. There are scattered stars, streaks of cloud, but no moon.

I'm the only lunatic here. Everyone else is looking west, toward home plate. It's too early for the moon to clear the trees.

So I try my luck at the mall parking lot. But the glare there is even worse. Grocery-store floodlights create a virtual daylight. Moonless and defeated, I head home.

Then, two blocks short of my street, I am inspired. I turn east to Lake Michigan, where I'll have a clear shot at any moon that might come up tonight. I race. My eyes keep straying up between trees; I train them back on the road.

At the lake I hit pay dirt. Turning off Sheridan Road, I see her, rising slowly out of the black water like a holy melon—the full moon. And I'm not the only one who's come to look; cars line the street. I poke along for a parking spot.

I notice a white truck with "Commercial and Residential Carpet Cleaning" written on the side. The driver guns the engine and then cuts it off. He leaps from the truck and breaches an opening in the hurricane fence along the beach. He stretches out on the cold sand and props his head on a rock. He is seriously hunting the moon.

Around him, the sand is littered with bodies, basking in the moonlight. They are sprawled on blankets, huddled inside of coats, heads resting against backpacks. It's a private club of lake watchers and moon worshipers, more sedate than the runners and dog walkers rimming the shore at sunrise. More reverent than the vacationers dotting Ludington's dunes while the sun sets toward Wisconsin. More sober than the cocktail set mingling on the patios of Negril as the sun sinks into the Caribbean.

Watching the sun come and go suddenly seems mundane.

The moon, floating above the water, catches her own reflection in Lake Michigan's eye, and the lake, in its inimitable, rhythmic voice, whispers back. It's an intimate tune, suited to the night.

A breeze ripples the glassy black sheen of the water, and the lovers on the sand draw close. In the windy hush, we are all lovers now: the man in his truck, the couples on the beach, this woman in her car. And not least of us, the earth's preening satellite and this vast, dark lake, crooning softly its constant, seductive song.

Ghosts

To live on this lake is to never go straight home. My mother taught me, even if it's only for eggs. You're out, go, look. And I do, for moonrise, frigates, mornings' red lake sun ladders, white waves. My parents, old when I was born, gave me this lake, and the lake me. Even in storms they'd wrap me in cotton and wool, set me on shore: the excitement of a hunter's moon, a beaver moon, on a midnight loud lake. The lake swallows lights and turns back stones and feathers and bones. When I was seven, an eight-point buck smashed out of a wave and ran a hand's distance from all my surprise. Up the beach, partially covered in sand, a dead doe. The lake swallows lights and gives back deer. My parents are gone. Still, I go every day to the lake, send prayers by crows, and warblers, and lake. My mother taught me this: Never go straight home.

—*Susan Firer*

I've talked with divers who, drawn by the litter of the past—several centuries of mastheads, rudderposts, gunwales, cargo hulls resting on the bottom—explore these waters. One man told me he found a wedding band embedded in a sunken ship's boiler. He's a scientist and sometimes gives lectures at local schools about cycles of life and decay in the lake. Once, on a quiz a teacher gave, when he had finished, a student wrote, *Organisms fall to the bottom and are covered in sentiment.*

—*Jackie Bartley*

The two square miles of Healy Lake Ranch were sold off piece by piece several years ago, and I miss my time there. I miss the smell of frost in the morning, the gold of sunlight splicing the treetops. I miss wandering the dirt roads in the morning, identifying animal tracks. My sisters and I all had a lesson in field dressing a deer. We can bait hooks, reel in fish, recognize tree species. We know the sound of coyotes at night, and loons in the morning. In each of us is a connection with nature, with deer that invited us to watch their simple routines and remarkable bodies create paths through the woods.

—*Amber Briggs*

Manitou Passage

GAIL GRIFFIN

We boarded the idling bus in the dark, dragging the duffle bags we'd packed the night before. We had brushed our teeth and thrown cold water on our faces, but we were still buried in sleep, silent. Frank, the camp's ancient, irascible bus driver, cranked the bus doors shut and wrenched the gearshift into first. As we rolled down the lane toward the camp entrance, most of us sank back into sleep, heads against our duffle bags. It seemed to take hours to get to Leland, but even as we pulled up to the dock, the air was just beginning to fade to the gray before dawn. By now we were mostly awake, stumbling off the bus, blinking and sniffing the fishy, watery air. We filed onto the boat, found seats, and began buckling on the bulky orange life jackets as our counselors instructed. Another long wait, and the boat's engines ground to life. As we chugged out of the mouth of the Carp River, the wind off the big lake quickly swallowed the harbor smells, swallowed our voices and our breath. The water was beginning to shine in pale yellow-pink sunlight. Above us, bleating gulls floated and banked.

. . .

Within the ornately structured universe of Camp, our other lives in Cleveland Heights or Bloomfield Hills fell away like dreams. Camp rituals and nomenclature assumed an absolute reality. The week's calm order of classes, meals, songs, evening entertainments, and cabin life was broken by the occasional day or overnight expedition elsewhere around northwest Lower Michigan. We never knew and never wondered how these trips were scheduled; a list simply appeared in the Lodge. But we did understand the hierarchy. Little kids went to the Cherry Farms overnight, sleeping among someone's fruit trees on the Old Mission Peninsula, which bisects Grand Traverse Bay. Slightly older girls went on "the Boardman"—a day trip by barge down the river of the same name, which curls through Grand Traverse County. The oldest and most accomplished canoers got tapped to go on "the Manistee"—a three-day canoe expedition down that more serious river. Between the Boardman and the Manistee was what we called "the Manitou," an overnight on South Manitou Island.

So I must have been about twelve or thirteen at this first encounter with Lake Michigan. I had flown over it once, on my first airplane, to Chicago with my father the year before he died. I had seen the bay at Traverse City. But I confronted the great water called lac Dauphin by the French, Michigamme by the Ojibwa, that morning as we left Leland, the wind in my face, the sun rising behind me, the boat lurching against the roiling water.

Was it on that trip that I first heard the legend of the Manitou Islands? I seem always to have known it; but then, you can hardly escape it in northwestern Michigan, inscribed as it is on placemats, burned into shellacked slices of pine, painted onto the walls of museums of local history, illustrated in children's books. Supposedly of Ojibwa origin, it begins with a great fire in what is now Wisconsin driving a mother bear and her two cubs into the water to swim for the opposite shore. The mother bear crawled out on the other side and, looking behind her, saw her exhausted cubs sink below the waves. Gitche Manitou heard her howl of a prayer and turned the cubs into islands, one small and round, the other long and thin. Their mother, collapsed on the shore, was frozen in place, where she could always see them. Her great, long, sandy flanks, rising four hundred feet above the water, are now called Sleeping Bear. As of 1970, she is a national park, she and her lost babes.

From the first, I hated the story. It wasn't quaint or magical, lyrical or inspirational; it was brutal and horrifying. To this day I avoid it. Tales of mothers separated from children, of children left behind clawed at my stomach, churning up primal fear and grief. In my only recurring dream, I came home from school to find strangers in my house, my mother and brother having moved away. I had learned that elemental lesson—that people die, that they leave forever—at the age of nine. When my mother sat down next to me in the kitchen and told me my father was dead, I instantly knew an even worse truth: that she could die too. I could be left behind, with my bigger brother, flailing in the waves as she disappeared.

I think she may have sent me to camp the first time, the summer after Dad died, to teach me that she could leave my sight for an entire month and yet return for me. Camp quickly provided a brilliant alternative to the complications and confusion of real life. It was isolated, and at once secure and full of challenge, a deep green island in the north woods that had imprinted themselves deeply, on the mythic level, in my earliest summers at my father's hunting cabin near Grayling. There were horses and water, my two greatest passions. It was a world of girls. I moved under the pines, through the sunlight dappling the soft, powdery earth, and felt a belonging I had never known. I entered into the Camp rituals easily, with deep satisfaction. I also rose through the strata of achievement in swimming, in archery and riflery, in riding and canoeing. Early in my Camp career, I slept among the cherry trees and woke with cold dew covering my sleeping bag. In a subsequent summer, I floated down the Boardman in the deep afternoon chiaroscuro, watching the trees slide by above my head, iridescent dragonflies darting along the banks. And now, I was girl enough for the Manitou.

◆   ◆   ◆

It means *spirit* in Ojibwa. From the west shore of the Leelanau Peninsula, the islands float on the horizon, long and blue. Often they vanish into mist for days. On a bright July day, when they are "out," they seem to be moving against the surging water. They lie only ten miles out from Leland; I remember thinking that morning how close they looked. But as the boat plowed through the waves, the islands seemed not to come any closer, but to recede.

Elusive, even deceptive. They are in fact the southernmost points of an archipelago stretching up to the straits called *Michilimackinac*, consisting of the exposed tips of a great limestone ridge buried by the melting glaciers that created the Lakes. When two coeval developments—the opening of the Erie Canal in 1825 and the advent of steamships on the Lakes—collaborated to create a rapid water route from Chicago all the way to New York, the little Manitous rapidly became central players in the Great Lakes navigation saga. For, as I saw that morning as it finally pulled into focus, South Manitou Island is graced on its southeastern end with a crescent-shaped natural harbor—the only one between Chicago and Mackinaw, some three hundred miles of water. It curves into the lake like a hand—which, by 1840, extended rest and shelter, food and water, and access to the cordwood that fueled the ships' engines for the next leg of the journey. From Chicago to Buffalo, a steamship would eat three hundred cords of wood.

For vessels not intending to stop, the islands took on another kind of significance. When a ship's captain coming up from Chicago achieved Pointe Aux Becs Scies—"Sawbeak Point," collapsed over the years into "Point Betsie"—he had a decision to make, as he studied the blue shapes in the northern distance: west around them and out into the open lake, or east, hugging the shore, through what became known as the Manitou Passage. The latter saved him some sixty miles and the violent weather of the open lake. But the shorter route sent him into a perilous obstacle course of shoals and rocks and tricky winds of its own. At one point between South Manitou Harbor and the town of Leland, the lake bottom rises to twenty feet below the surface. Called the Manitou Shoal, it was the undoing of innumerable ships attempting the Passage. Over 150 wrecks lie on the lake floor of the Passage, some of them still visible—some, like the *Three Brothers*, broken up off South Manitou in 1911, disclosed suddenly, decades later, by the shifting of the island shore.

Not all of those sacrificed were seamen. Some of the wrecks were smaller, starker. In 1878, a boatman took Aaron and Julia Sheridan and their infant child out from South Manitou for some pleasure sailing. As their two older children watched from the beach, the weather shifted and the winds came up. The sail swung the boom around, knocking Aaron, Julia, and the baby into the water. He disappeared instantly. Julia clutched her baby with one arm and the gunwale of the boat with the other, but soon was washed away. The next day, the boatman staggered up onto North Manitou. For days after, the locals watched the two Sheridan children walking the beach, wailing, waiting for the bodies to wash up: the Manitou legend reenacted, roles reversed.

• • •

It's hard to feel the danger and hauntedness of these waters on a bright summer morning. As the transit boat chugged over the Manitou Shoal, I was ecstatic, lost in the vast blue, the dazzle of sun on water. Maybe, off to the west, the long brown line of a freighter pulled toward Mackinac. I wasn't yet aware that my family's history is tied up with the Great Lakes. Even symbolically: the first white sailors on the Lakes appeared in a vessel called *The Griffin*. My paternal great-grandfather, William Griffin, a bushy-bearded Canadian of Welsh descent out of Montreal, was a captain on the Lakes. The details of his life seem to place him further east, along the St. Lawrence River, perhaps into Lake Ontario or Erie. But I like to wonder if he came this far, if he knew this lake too, if he spied the Manitous coming into view and chose the Passage, reading and memorizing its dangerous, complicated story. He seems to have come from a large family that emigrated down from St. John's, Newfoundland, in the early nineteenth century, always settling in seaports. Were we a family of sailors? Are my own people among the spirits haunting these islands?

. . .

By 1839, when the Griffins were moving southwest, the Passage was already notorious enough that plans were underway for the construction of a light on the "perched dunes" of South Manitou, which rise from their limestone base over three hundred feet above the waves. The first light was replaced in 1872 by the one that still stands, 104 feet tall, a red and white tower worthy of Virginia Woolf. The morning that I stepped off the boat onto the South Manitou dock, the light had only recently been abandoned by its last Coast Guard crew. At that point, in the early sixties, North Manitou, the larger island, was off limits, privately owned and sparsely inhabited, a dark mystery three miles away. Back to the east, the mainland was a dim blue-green line broken by the white of Sleeping Bear. We hiked to our camping spot, set up camp according to counselors' instructions, and took off to explore the island—which is small, a mere ten miles of shore.

It was the first of a certain kind of experience I would have across northern Michigan in the course of my life—the sense of being in a place that *had once been*, a place abandoned to the quiet of a long dream, the silence behind and beyond the noise of life. A ghost place. The Upper Peninsula is full of them. We circled the lighthouse, tall and still and dark. Off the southwestern tip of the island we saw, rising eerily from the water, the top mast of the *Francisco Morazon*, run aground only a few years earlier. We visited the cemeteries where the early settlers lie buried. The story persists that in one cholera epidemic, so frantic were the healthy to get the bodies underground before the plague could devour the island that they buried some prematurely. It is said that the sound of their moans and their fingernails clawing their coffins can be heard in the wind at night.

There are calmer spirits, too. Near the southwestern shore of the island is the Valley of the Giants, a stand of tremendous old-growth cedars. The rings inside some of these ancients tell a story that circles back to the time before Columbus. They sway and whisper in the wind; in the fullness of their time they fall, disintegrating into the sand within the sound of the water they have always known.

As the sun sank behind the island, I gathered firewood. I toasted Bisquick on a green stick, peeled away the black skin, and ate the lukewarm dough. I speared the hot dog that had fallen into the fire and finished blackening it to taste. I washed it all down with the sweet grape or cherry potion called Bug Juice. I ran up into the brush, yanked down my shorts, and peed in the woods. When the sun, after hanging low in the sky for hours, finally dropped into the water and the air went suddenly chill, I felt my sunburned skin. Around the fire I probably listened to the story of The Hook—or told it—shivering and giggling maniacally to ward off the cold and my own fear. With such stories, we both accommodate and hold at bay the spirits around us, the things that never were, or that once were and are no more. I fell asleep listening to the primal rhythm of waves surging in, drawing back, a sound at once formidable and comforting. In the morning I ate sandy blueberry pancakes with more Bug Juice, rolled up my sleeping bag, and helped carry everything down to the dock to wait for the boat. Frank would be waiting beside the bus in Leland. We would drag our sunburned, sandy selves back into Camp, celebrities of the hour, surrounded briefly by the aura of Elsewhere.

I took one souvenir back with me—a skull, probably of a deer, that I had found bleaching on the beach on the far side of the island. Shreds of pale, desiccated, woolly matter hung from its bones—brains, I was sure. It smelled acrid and dry. Some of the other girls and the counselors were grossed out, amazed that I wanted to take it. I carried it not only back to camp but back home, where my mother tolerated its presence provided that it lived in the garage. During the winter when I sniffed it, slid my fingers across its smooth bones and into its empty eye sockets, dislodging tenacious sand crystals, the sound of the water and the haunted silence of the island filled me.

My personal *memento mori*, an odd souvenir of summer camp. I wasn't a particularly morbid girl, though I have always felt a weird intimacy with death and a peacefulness in cemeteries. I think what I found on South Manitou, though, was not deathliness, but a place where life and death rocked into each other like crosscurrents, losing their boundaries. A "point of intersection of the timeless / With time," T. S. Eliot called it. The haunted past of the island, the eternal present of summer, both collapsed into the whispered promise of the waves—*always, always*. Perhaps it was on the spirit island that I, standing on that charged cusp between girl and woman, first felt some inkling of the great secret, that eternity lies at the quiet heart of constant change, the shifting of sand, cycles of decay and generation, the beat of great waters.

To this day, in the midst of Real Life, I have only to close my eyes and think myself there, by the waters off Sleeping Bear's shoulder, looking out on the Spirit Islands, and I am instantly at the heart of the mystery, the stasis in the motion, the changelessness within the constant change. In some way I too am lost in the Manitou Passage, caught in the shifty winds, the songs of the dead, where time is water.

. . .

The sandy skull in the garage still hangs in my imagination. In my fifties, I struggle to learn to look steadily at that source of childhood terror, the loss of my mother, who approaches ninety. I asked her recently if she feared death, knowing the answer.

"Oh, no," she replied quickly, firmly. "I might have some fear of the physical suffering, but death itself? No."

"What do you think comes after? Anything?"

She thought momentarily. "I don't know. I think . . . you merge into something . . . very *big*."

"That's funny," I said. "That's how I think of it too." I paused. "If you can, after you're gone, will you tell me there's nothing to be afraid of?"

Her voice went soft. "I'm telling you *now*."

Shortly afterward, I spent some days at a house on Lake Michigan, just where the shore curves from Point Betsie toward the mouth of the Platte River. The first night, I woke in darkness very suddenly, in that momentary confusion and panic when you don't know where you are. Then, from the open window, I heard it—the sound of the waves, thrashing onto the beach and dragging back. Instantly I knew a deep comfort, an engrossing safety and contentment that felt as old as childhood. I fell immediately back into a dense, peaceful sleep as profound as dark water. When I woke, the sun would be shattering to diamonds on the lake. In the far distance, the high dunes at South Manitou's tip would be breasting the waves, as if the island were moving.

In the Apostle Islands

Judith Strasser

The Sand Island Lighthouse Volunteer

Two years ago, her second husband died. Lung cancer. "Love is so blind," she says. "Until we were married, I never saw that he smoked." She was a nurse in Chicagoland. She cared for him, changed his dressings, gave him back rubs until he died. "I loved that man dearly," she tells me. "But Harold, forgive me, I'm glad you're gone." She lives in a lighthouse. No plumbing, no electric. Propane on the blink. Tourists arriving all hours. "He'd never put up with this." She wouldn't have it otherwise. The virgin pines. The solitude. The sunrise and sunset views.

The Hummingbird

It takes a week to get up the courage to swim in the June lake. The best times are mornings: the sun's on the sand, and often the breeze is offshore. I choose the moment carefully, put on my suit, load up with books and sunscreen, mosey down to the beach. Perfect: I wade in up to my waist, splash chest and arms . . . I'm in and out in less time than it takes a hummingbird, later, to buzz the porch fuchsia and find it's just my old Speedo, hung from a nail to dry.

County Road

The settlers are gone, cabins rotted or burned. What remains: the schoolhouse foundation, moss-garden-capped concrete; a Model T, sunk to its fenders, kneeling under the trees. A trail—choked with balsam and alder, roadbed rutted, muddy, sodden—a permanent bog of memory bordered by sentinel trees. *Penny candy from the co-op; Noreng's berries, big as hens' eggs, too juicy to ship anywhere; dances—pump organ, squeezebox, fiddle, everyone at the school; crossing the ice bridge for mail; Mrs. Hill's famous ham; the nor'easter that took Harold Dahl.* Crawl over tree trunks, muck through jewelweed, tread bear scat in blackberry brambles, swim sedges over your head. Lose the trace in the marsh. Turn back. This is no wilderness. Still, you've come to the end of the road.

Ripples of Azure and Grey, An Excerpt

RACHEL AZIMA

The first time my mom and I visited Alpena, on the shore of Lake Huron, we came on a geology trip. Following a stop at a gypsum mine, we had come to Alpena to hunt for fossils. After this first taste, my mom and I grew obsessed with finding fossils, returning again and again to look for more. During our drives up north, we'd talk about the searches to come. "I hope we find some trilobites!" I'd say, and my mom would agree. The Holy Grail of fossils, trilobites were rare in the Devonian rock we searched in. We knew it was unlikely that we would find one of these peculiar, ocean-dwelling creatures, the cousins of horseshoe crabs and sow bugs, but this made the idea of finding one all the more alluring.

It was odd to think that this land, even this lake, was once covered by stranger seas. Here in Alpena, the fossil-bearing limestone was laid bare, the evidence of Michigan's even more watery history crumbling out into the open. Glaciers that began scraping over this region a million years ago made both our lakeshore dallying and our fossil hunting possible. The soft seabed of the Paleozoic era, the layer where our fossils rested, offered a malleable landscape. It yielded willingly to the creeping ice, soft sandstone and shale giving in, preparing the way for new inland seas. The Great Lakes emerged once the glaciers receded, this ice that cut away the layers and gave us glimpses of a deep history, life hardened and preserved in stone. And these fossils were what we wanted: tangible links to a distant past.

Our first morning in Alpena brought the start of our quest. We'd set out, armed with paper and plastic bags and my mom's startlingly wide fossil-hunting hat. A moment always arrived when our whole mission nearly fell apart: we'd pull up to the gate of our search site, Three Mile Dam—a small dam on the Thunder Bay River, about three miles from Lake Huron—and we'd see the "No Trespassing" sign. My mom would tense up visibly. "I don't know about this," she'd say, looking around, probably picturing men in pickup trucks with shotguns just around the bend. One time, the gate, which was usually open, happened to be closed, which my mom saw as even stronger evidence that this was a bad idea. "Are you sure you want to go?" she said, stopping the van in front of the gate.

I bounced in my seat impatiently. "Come on, Mom! We drove all the way up here—we have to go! If anyone sees us, we'll just tell them why we're here. It's not like we're doing anything bad. Why would they care?"

After a brief hesitation that seemed interminable to me, she groaned and got out of the van to open the gate. "A great way to start my law career," she grumbled, getting back inside. She put the van into drive and we headed in.

As we climbed the rocks beside the dammed river, there was no escaping the August heat. We squinted up at the sky, willing the big clouds that just barely skirted the brightness to make a move and plunge us into shadow. The artificial waterfall of the dam held an even roar, mocking us with all its powerful, just-out-of-reach coolness. The forbiddenness of this place gave it an extra charm in my eyes, making us more like Indiana Jones as we plundered the dam for treasure.

At first, it was hard to see the fossils as anything but more greyish rock. But gradually, as the sound of the water seemed to ebb to a hum, our eyes adjusted to gradations of texture and form. Soon, anything with a ripple jumped out at me: most were shells, some a familiar shape, like ordinary bivalves that needed a good washing. Others were elongated, their ridged surfaces pulled to narrow tips on either side, stranger than anything I knew. And the tiny disks of crinoids were scattered everywhere. "Look at this one!" I'd shout, grabbing a piece of rock with a well-defined shell embedded inside. I kept everything that caught my eye, unable to let go of a slab that had one perfect brachiopod, a slightly longer-than-normal crinoid stem. If a fossil appealed to me in some way—if it were a hair different from the one I'd just seen—I wouldn't be able to part with it. I tossed them in bags haphazardly, figuring that if they had survived hundreds of millions of years already, they wouldn't break. Mom was more selective, picking and choosing, keeping in mind our basement already cluttered with relics.

Even more exciting was the discovery of a fossil with a different shape: something that wasn't a shell, a form that seemed more insectile. And it never failed: if there were a knobby piece that could be a trilobite, my mom would find it. "Rachel, come and take a look at this!" she'd call out, and I'd run over so we could breathlessly examine a mysterious fragment she'd found. And this time, it finally happened: she held out a bug-like piece, a semicircle followed by slender bands, narrowing to a rounded end. It was oddly curled, almost into a ball. "What do you think?" she asked eagerly.

I peered at it, felt its ridges. "It has to be one," I said. A trilobite. Despite my devotion to my mom, I was jealous of her skill. I returned to my own searches, doubly determined to find perfect specimens. And I wondered: how could these creatures persist for such unimaginable lengths of time and remain recognizable? The earth held its memory more accurately than its human inhabitants, but surrendered it only in these fragments, pieces that held inscrutable stories in states of surprising perfection. At home, I'd look up the names of the fossils I had found, though the names did them no justice. A "blastoid" looked like a stony bud, not something out of science fiction. And I found the artist's renderings of the Paleozoic sea laughable. The images were too familiar, like any other ocean—not nearly adequate to the mystery of these odd forms, their fascination.

That night, when I would try to fall asleep, the fossils would still be there, a mosaic of a thousand ridged pieces pulsating behind my eyelids.

◆ ◆ ◆

Once we were thoroughly baked, eyes exhausted from the search, it was time to leave the dam with our loot and return to the edge of the living lake. Sometimes we'd wade in the water, sometimes just sit and think. I didn't swim—I had never learned how. Just a whiff of moist air laden with the insidious odor of chlorine made my heart pound. But on these shores, as I walked and stretched my stiff muscles, I always felt at ease.

One night we lingered late, stretching out on the rock to look up into the dimming sky. The lake was in a pleasant mood, sucking and slapping the rocks below us. The expanse above us slid almost imperceptibly through all the colors of the spectrum, blue and violet slowly giving way to a luminous grey. The sky receded further and further into shadow, until it was just dark enough to let stars emerge. One by one, they revealed themselves from the darkness. "Look, Mom! There's Vega of the Lyre!" I exclaimed softly, pointing out a bright star with a bluish tint, nearly directly overhead. Proud of my knowledge of the constellations, I pointed out the Summer Triangle, Cassiopeia, the double star in the handle of the Big Dipper, all the tracings of mythology I knew. At home, where our view was hemmed in by houses and trees, my dad and I were the star watchers; my mom never wanted to go outside and wait for meteor showers. But here, in the warm summer air, I had a chance to share with her. And in the vastness that stretched over the water, the whole process was made plain.

"What's that?" my mom exclaimed, startled. She pointed to the horizon. A full moon was just peeking over, uncannily large and bright. Quietly, we watched it rise over the water. Then once it reached a certain height, we noticed some disturbances in the lake. We sat up and stared. Fish flickered everywhere, triggered in some mysterious way by the moon's pull: tiny shadows leaped out of the water and splashed back down in shards of moonlight. Scattered over the surface of the lake, they made the water seem alive.

    * * *

We never wanted to leave. Looking back, it would be easy to see Alpena as simply pastoral, a site of escape, the wild away from home. But Alpena wasn't just something to split off and squirrel away like the *mucrospirifers*, the fossils with tapered ends that my mom stored away lovingly in the gold of Godiva boxes, carefully labeled in her clear block letters. My internal geography is more complex than that: Lake Huron haunts me, has become the standard against which I compare every scene.

I hold now to this great lake and to the fossils we hunted, those reminders of older water. Tokens of memory in small, ancient shapes, hues gone but forms intact. All these colors and textures stay with me, ripples of azure and grey, dreams that open out into histories. I count on this persistence, this knowledge that even delicacy can survive.

The Souls of Trees

Susan Laidlaw

*I*t is a soft night. Calm, secret, and still. My feet dangle over a ravine which a fallen oak has spanned and made into a perfect suspended chair. I am ten feet up in darkness. The tall, gray shapes of pines and oaks surround me. Ahead, where the ravine spills into a swamp thick with tamaracks and ferns, the darkness blackens into a shade impenetrable by my cone-laden eyes. There is no moon, and very little sky light makes it through the heavy canopy above. I am a human unhoused in the night without so much as a flashlight.

My other senses automatically intensify. The thick scent of compost rises up from the forest floor, where broken oak leaves and pine needles decay into a nutrient-rich mulch. My ears (always quick to tune in when darkness obscures my sight) home in on a variety of sounds. The clattering noise of claw on wood as some animal—probably a raccoon—climbs a tree somewhere to my right. I can tell it's going down by the *clatter, clatter, screeeeeee* sounds it makes as its claws dig into the tree and then relax, sliding down the bark. Behind me, the unmistakably delicate footfall of a white-tail as it moves along the deer trail that leads to the cornfield. An almost ghostly sound, these soft footfalls, betrayed infrequently by the snap of a twig or the crunch of brittle leaves. The steady song of the whippoorwill fills the hollow night.

Tonight the wind is gentle. Often the wind in northern Michigan can really blow. Not the gales of the plains, but huge, undulating breaths of wind.

It rushes through the white pines, making the sea of trees sound like the roar from nearby Lake Huron. It will rattle oak leaves together, spinning them in opposite directions so they meet with a scuff and spin again. *Scuff. Spin. Scuff.* But tonight, there is hardly a breeze, but a stir; not quite a blowing, but a tugging, wrapping, twirling. Enough to bustle the leaves, but no more. This stir breathes soft, cool air onto the back of my neck and through the minuscule hairs on my face. It is so slow, I can detect its patterns as it capers across the exposed parts of my skin. The night is so expansive, the dark so deep, I am suspended in it. At this moment, in this place on the oak, with the patters of the forest moving around me in the dark, I feel numinous. I close my eyes and sway.

◆ ◆ ◆

The Ojibwa believed that the woods around the Great Lakes were occupied by certain spirits, mysteries, invisible realities, or in the Algonquian language, *manitous*. The belief in these deities dignified the land and the animals for the Ojibwa. Children were taught early on that these manitous could not be separated from life or the trees, soil, water, wind; indeed, they should be regarded with respect and deference. Kitchi-Manitou was the creator, also called Great Mystery. He was responsible for the earth, seasons, time, souls, and the cycles of life. In addition to the Kitchi-Manitou, an abundance of other spirits inhabited the forests and beyond. The Pau-eehnissiwuk lived on the water's edge. The Zauwabeekummook, the copper manitou, dwelt in mountains and escarpments. The Waimetik was the heart of the oak. Matchi-auwishuk, the Evil Ones, were used by parents to frighten children into obedience. But perhaps the most loved were the Maemaegawaehnssiwuk, the little people, who had a special care and regard for children. These manitous would console grieving children and protect children lost in the woods. Sometimes, the Maemaegawaehnssiwuk would become playmates with children who had no one else to play with.

When I was eight, I had Maemaegawaehnssiwuk friends. Of course, I didn't know that's what they were called, but I did know when I went into the forest, many shy, invisible creatures would come out to keep me company. I had to earn their trust by showing my respect for their home and my reverence for them. We would wade up the creek, hide behind decaying logs, and pretend all humans were bad. The animals were not afraid of us and could even talk to us by silent telepathy. They depended on us to warn them when dangers approached. When I detected danger, I would climb a tree, cup my hands over my mouth and give the warning call of a screech owl so all the spirits and animals could scatter and hide. I wanted to be more like them, a part of the wild, so I would roll in dry leaves and rub skunk cabbage over my arms and legs.

There was one hemlock tree that curved over a creek near a cornfield where I would always go to wait for the manitous to come and find me. I would sit in the curve of the hemlock and drop my feet, toe by toe, into the freezing water until each foot was red from numbness. As I waited for my feet to get used to the cold, I made little leaf boats and set them to sail down my little tributary. From my tree, I would watch them swirl and bump along the narrow creek, and wish one would successfully make the trip all the way to the swells of big Lake Huron. By the time my feet were numb, my friends would have found me on my hemlock, and we would splash into the woods by way of the creek. When I was older, I would come to this tree and read, or rest, or contemplate, or write bad poetry. Eventually the bark on the curved part of the tree became smooth and glossy from use. I brought my first boyfriend to this tree, thinking it fun to share with him this hidden mystery, this part of me. He thought he would surprise me by carving our initials into its bark. I stared at the wound: SUZ + CHAS, drops of resin pooled up around the letters. Curled pieces of bark lay scattered on the bank of the creek. I felt bile roll into my mouth.

◆ ◆ ◆

Michigan dew already begins to settle on the thick bark as I slide my way across the oak and onto the bank of the ravine. My feet crush the leaves beneath them with a *chrsst* and I hear a large, startled snort behind me. I have been sitting so quietly for so long, I have become part of the nocturnal landscape. In those moments on the log, I felt I could have fed any animal from my hand. Now my movement has revealed my otherness and there is momentary confusion from a nearby white-tail. *Crack*, whoops, I didn't feel that twig. The deer bounds a few noisy steps to the right, stops again, and snorts a warning call. A quick, strong, wet-sounding noise. I press my lips together, gather a pocket of air in my cheeks and—"*psffht*"—snort back at the deer. I hear the leap, the rush of fern and shower of ground debris as the deer flees another yard and stops again. The deer stomps in agitation, two muted thumps from one of its front hooves. Feeling slightly amused, I speak out loud. *"Heelllooo* out there!" Whirl, leap, gone. It is silent except for my heavy words which still hang about me in the disturbed air. I am immediately sorry I spoke.

I start my way home by way of one of the main deer trails. This trail skirts the edge of a ravine, crosses through a small clearing, weaves behind the cemetery, and links up to the two-track that will lead me all the way back to the barnyard. As I walk, I carefully feel my way with my feet so I don't make any more offensive noises. My father taught me this trick, to let my feet develop a consciousness of the forest floor so I could learn to walk silently without having to stare down at the ground. As I get older, I find myself forgetting the feel part of my walking. My feet bungle along and I lose my way, too caught up in the turmoil of traffic, deadlines, and agendas to notice the smaller, slower landscape of the natural world.

I try to stay connected to the landscape around this farm. Whenever I come to this place, I walk about with my field guides and notebooks, looking up different species of fern and trying my hand at a sketch or two. I know when the indigo bunting will return in the spring and which autumns the frost comes early. I am sure I could walk blindfolded from the cemetery, along the lane, all the way back to the farmhouse without losing my way. And yet, I remember a time when I believed if I looked hard enough, I could actually see the souls of the trees; I knew that the peaty earth I walked over was alive and could feel each step of my not-yet-size-nine feet. Such a connection! Where is that affinity I once had? The veneration? The distinct feeling that every piece of the forest is alive and I am somehow a part of its living dynamic? Through the years, the wonder has crept away.

•   •   •

Lymon Yellowhair is a spiritual leader of the Lakota nation. We became friends the summer I helped him build a sweat lodge on a section of the Poudre River that ran through the plains of Colorado. The first time I participated in a sweat, I thought I was going to suffocate. They closed the flap of the lodge for the last prayer session, and in the pitch black I could hear the snapping of the fiery rocks we sat around: twenty-one river stones that had been roasting in a fire for five hours prior to the ceremony. The heat was inescapable. My hair was soaking wet, and every time I took a breath, fire rolled into my throat and seared my lungs. Singing and praying filled the small, round lodge, but I was too distracted to listen. Lymon told me if the heat got too bad, I could call out "Mitake Oyasin," meaning All My Relations, and the flap would open; but I felt too embarrassed, too much of a *waschitu*, and determined to stick it out. I dug a hole in the earth floor and breathed into it, pulling the cool dampness of the dirt down into my lungs.

When the flap finally opened, and we were sitting in the breeze by the river, Lymon explained to me the importance of concentration in the lodge. He said the Lakota come into the lodge and pray together to be whole together; that it is important to bring the outside world into the sweat lodge, so that we are praying with the earth, the animals, and the sky. It is a chance to establish a connection with everything around us, to *feel* what is around us as much as see. He said I will know when I have this connection because I will be able to look around me and see the earth breathe. I was always struck by those words: see the earth breathe. Every week for a year I participated in these sweats. I began to tie clumps of tobacco in small cloth "prayer bundles" of yellow, red, and green. I would sometimes tend the fire, watching the rocks toast away for the hours leading up to the sweat. I burnt bunches of sage. I learned the words to the Lakota songs. The heat no longer bothered me in the lodge; instead, I felt it purify me, sloughing off the mental grime of school, work, and stress. I sang and prayed and felt a connection to the people around me; I even felt a return to my connection with the natural world. But I never saw the earth breathe.

◆ ◆ ◆

Stepping out of the woods on my journey back to the farmhouse, I look up to find the Milky Way and am met instead with a carpet of color. The night is awash with myriad hues pulsing and shimmering across a silky black canopy of sky. The aurora borealis—and it is spectacular! I run the last half-mile across the open field, through the barnyard, and onto the soft, cool lawn in front of the farmhouse.

Lying on my back on the grass, I can feel little bits of moisture soak into my T-shirt from the dew already collecting on the ground. Overhead, the sky is rippling like drapery in the wind: greens, purples, reds, yellows, blues, and oranges mix together on a vast celestial palette. I have never seen the borealis this active or this kaleidoscopic. The colors dance upwards from the horizons to the apex of the sky and stop right before they all connect together, leaving a small hole at the center of the heavens that I imagine crawling through and looking to the other side. Then, the colors retract, shrinking back down to the horizons to shimmer and sway before exploding back up to the apex again.

The lights appear so close, it seems as if I could climb the tallest white pine, reach out my hand, and pull it back stained with streaks of green and red. I could grab hold of one of the colors and be included in the dance, swept up weightlessly into this proximal space. The brilliance is astounding: my head starts to roll; for a moment, I close my eyes. I can feel the entire planet moving under my back, slowly spinning its cosmic course around this solar system. For a fleeting second, the corporeal and ethereal come crashing together. I think of the words of Buddhist master Thich Nhat Hanh:

> *Breathing in, I know I am breathing in.*
> *Breathing out I know I am breathing out.*
>
> *Breathing in, I see myself as mountain.*
> *Breathing out, I feel solid.*
>
> *Breathing in, I see myself as space.*
> *Breathing out, I feel free.*

I open my eyes. The colors are still there, streaking through the atmosphere in luminous sheets. I roll onto my stomach and observe the earth. I see blades of grass moving, I hear katydids rasping, I smell green and brown and can feel the pulsation of life. The earth is breathing. I know my place.

Storm Light on
Bois Blanc Island

KATHLEEN STOCKING

his is an island that could wash away in a storm is my one thought about
Boblo, as a fierce wind tries to blow us from our narrow path and into
the raging waters of Lake Huron a few feet away.

Boblo, or Bois Blanc, is a small sandspit of an island off Cheboygan, and
"us" is me and two people I'd met briefly on the ferry a few hours earlier. And
I have just run into them again, walking along the shore with their little dog,
Spike.

Spike is making progress. The other three of us are barely holding our
own. The wind is incredibly loud. The sound is like that of a train. Invisible.
In the air.

Bob McCoy is a stocky, curly haired, well-spoken, young-looking, and el-
egantly dressed man who says he has taken an early retirement from the family business and now spends his time traveling between his Chicago and Boblo
homes. Taffy McCoy, his sister, is plainly dressed, a professor of sociology; her
area of expertise is the sociology of mental illness, the process of who decides
who is insane in this society. Spike, who looks like a poodle mutt, is in fact,
Taffy tells me, a rare breed of French canine, a bichon frisé.

We are on an ancient concrete sidewalk that runs between the beach and a
row of abandoned-looking, turn-of-the-century summer cottages up the bank.
The sidewalk goes for a ways and then, where it has become crumbled by age
or covered by sand, disappears and then picks up again a few feet further on.

I had noticed Bob and Taffy McCoy on the boat because I had been humming—so happy had I been to be on a ferry and facing into the open water and unaware that anyone saw or heard me—and had glanced up to find someone looking at me, and they had smiled at me, spontaneously, in a rather bemused and kindly way. There had only been a few passengers on the ferry and a bearded captain named Virgil.

On the ferry crossing that morning the air had been gray and humid and the waters of Lake Huron pale and placid with an oily, greenish cast. Now the lake beside us—technically the Straits of Mackinac here—is wildly dark and troubled, roaring with waves, and above us and around us there is an exciting but disquieting mixture of brilliant sunlight and black clouds, both.

Up the bank the row of cottages facing the lake looks disconcertingly unchanged since the early 1900s, almost more like photographs of cottages than actual cottages, and as we walk the time seems to become other, as if I've slipped, or the place has, into another plane of reality or time. Even Bob McCoy, who describes himself as a bon vivant and a raconteur, seems to belong to an earlier, more leisurely period in American resort culture.

The wind is so strong it is almost capable of holding us in place. Later I will learn it got up to fifty-five miles per hour that afternoon, but at the time it just seems fantastic, a tropism, an entity unto itself, like nothing I've ever encountered before and a part of the place.

This is the kind of weather in which ships go down in the Great Lakes, and we are all giddy as one of us reminds the others of the girl whose car blew off the Mackinac Bridge a couple of years earlier—like a scrap of paper, one of the newspapers had reported—and into three hundred feet of dark water below.

Bob and Taffy tell me their father began bringing their family here thirty years ago. "We came here when there was no electricity," Bob says, "no phones." Their brother drowned while sailing off Boblo some years earlier, they tell me, and their memory of that brother and their attachment to the island keeps them coming back.

Bob spends his time reading, walking, cooking, and entertaining the rare houseguest. Taffy comes up when she can, often bringing gourmet food items from downstate and her research materials. "We do a lot of cooking," Bob says. "Supper can take all day."

I ask them how many people like themselves are on Bois Blanc, telling them I have just come from the island's one-room schoolhouse, where Lani White is the teacher for four students, all boys, one of whom calls her "Mom." When a man came to the door with the mail, two boys said, "It's Uncle Al."

Each student had work that was individualized to their particular needs. In the back corner a student at a computer keyboard clicked away behind a partition. Lani White agreed that she has what most would regard as the best of both worlds: modern teaching tools and small class size in a beautiful island setting. She said they could finish the standard curriculum in less time than it would take her in an ordinary classroom, and it gave them a time for the exploration of subjects in greater variety and greater depth. She said she had taught downstate for years and missed having other teachers to talk to but treasured the time with the students and the natural resources of the island.

I whiled away the afternoon seated at a tiny desk next to an enormous wasp nest that Lani told me "Uncle Al" had found on the island. At recess the students played with garter snakes, giving the snakes rides down the slide.

Bob gives me a thumbnail sketch of the sociology of the island saying that there are two primary groups, the summer residents who have second homes on the island, and the people who live there all year. The population in the summer he estimates to be about two hundred people, and he thinks there are about forty permanent winter residents. He says islanders often marry each other and even when they get divorced, if they remarry, it's often someone from the island. Everyone seems to be related in some way. There are many tourists in the summer who come over on the ferry for the day or for a few days, but in the off-season the island is blessedly peaceful and quiet.

We don't talk then for a while, the wind is so loud. I follow Bob's glance toward a small sandy road and next to it a big field of grass, blowing. The wind riffles the grass and smoothes it, like animal fur, making ripples in it. Meanwhile, the clouds above are creating marbleized and shifting shadows on the grass below. It is mesmerizing.

We bore into the wind, using our heads to make a path for our bodies. A sudden shift in the sky, and the sun shatters the cloud cover, throwing light a thousand ways. Distant thunder roars like jets at a county fair. The lake looks like it could eat us alive, if it could only crawl up onto the shore where we are.

There is a wide, soft-looking, cornmeal-colored beach that extends as far as one can see in either direction. Bob and Taffy say there is good swimming "in the summer." August is barely over as we speak, and so I divine that summer is the key word here.

What is it like here in the winter?

"Winter is a challenge," Bob says. "What they do is take a line of trees [and place them in holes in the ice between Bois Blanc and Cheboygan]. If the trees stand up, you can go across. If the trees are lying down, you can't go across. Last year two people drowned. They were crossing at night [in a snow-mobile] and they got off the tree line and they splashed into the Straits." Their bodies came up last spring.

This has been my year for islands and the people who live on them. I can't get enough of them. I think I am looking for the islands in my own psyche, the lost and undiscovered parts of myself.

I have fantasized about islands—not so much as places to live or places to escape to, but the coming and goings, the ferry rides, attract me. I see in my mind the way the boat leaves the harbor, then I see the open water, then finally we lose sight of the land behind us and there is nothing but sky and water before us, then slowly the island reveals itself on the horizon and we come bumping along at last into the dock; then I want to go and take that ride on that boat to that island, and then I do.

Islands are places where you can be changed—like Circe's island where Odysseus's men were changed into animals—and then changed back again. Where you can transform yourself into someone else, or imagine you can.

Islands are not the mainland, so by definition they are not bound to the same rules as the mainland. One of Shakespeare's last plays, *The Tempest*, where all manner of magical things happen, is set on an island. Thomas More's *Utopia*, about a perfect community, is set on an island and became such a classic it added the word and the concept to our language. Thomas Mann's metaphysical *Death in Venice* begins on an island and continues, through several boat rides and gondola journeys, in a watery Venice of the soul. Aldous Huxley's fictional Will Farnaby, dying of the disease called Civilization, goes to rejuvenate himself on an island in the book called *Island*, and the real-life painter Paul Gauguin spent much of the last third of his life living and painting on South Sea islands. There must be something to it, this craving for islands.

I think it's in part that our civilization is moving so quickly into new realms, where picture phones, human clones, virtual-reality games, and travel by trains running on magnetic tape tracks in the air are just around the corner, and where we daily contend with things unimaginable twenty years ago or even twenty weeks ago—ceaseless voice mail, e-mail, car phones, modems, computerized shopping, handitellers—that our so-called modern conveniences, our sorcerer's apprentices, have sometimes seemed to all conspire to create a pace like centrifugal force that spins us until we see ourselves flying out or up or back into the quietness of an island where the world of before seems to still exist and we can reestablish that ancient connection between ourselves and the universe.

"There's a log home Yves St. Laurent would *kill* for," Bob says in diva tones, indicating an elaborately built log cottage—the kind the Rockefellers built in the Rockies a century ago—"but I could put my walking stick through any *part* of it: it's so porous [from insects]."

Bob says a small colony of artists, including a few musicians from the Chicago Symphony, were here at one time but, with the exception of one or two, they died or moved away years ago and have not been replaced by other summer residents. Waste disposal on the island is a problem; the island dump has been closed. The cost of getting things to the island and off the island is high. "There are no new people moving in. Houses don't go on the market. The property stays in the family. I bought my house from my father." He estimates that 80 percent of the island is in the hands of the state (54 percent of the island is state-owned; the other 46 percent is privately owned, but about half of this acreage is heavily restricted by state and federal environmental laws, I learned later) and that the other 20 percent "is in the hands of a very few people who are not motivated to sell."

Bois Blanc Island is only twelve miles long and seven miles wide and today it *feels* small. I can feel the edges of it, sense its size in the intensity of wind and the sound of the water, can imagine myself walking its circumference, can imagine knowing all the people here by name within a week.

We move from the walk along the waterfront to a path through tall pines. There is a thick carpet of pine needles beneath my feet. It is dark under the evergreens and quieter here farther from the shore. It begins to rain lightly. Taffy says she fantasizes about this island as their secret hideaway, a place to come if the bomb drops.

We pass an Episcopal church where the gray cobblestones of a homemade archway fatten in the rain. Then we continue on down past several boarded-up cottages closed for the season and then onto a mossy, gravelly trail to the McCoys's.

Bob McCoy has redone "the children's cottage," and the narrow walk to it is bordered with tiny, brightly colored flowers. As we go up the steps to the screened porch, a young male houseguest skips sideways satyr-like down the front steps, followed by clouds of steam scented with bay leaf, off to the store before it closes to get some cooking ingredient.

Inside it is all deep blue-greens, light pine floors, reading nooks with soft cushions in designer fabrics in muted shades of blue-green. "It never looked like this when we were growing up here," Bob says when I compliment him on his decorating. "This was where we put all the cousins when they came."

I passed the one small store on Boblo open at this time of year, and it sells everything from bait to diapers; no fresh fruit or vegetables were in evidence. I'd been told the post office is the center of social life, and the bar. Other than some commercial fishing and some harvesting of maple syrup, there's no commerce to speak of; there's no industry, no hospitals, no judges, no lawyers, no courts, no libraries, no art galleries, no Laundromat. It is a sweetly undeveloped and softly beautiful place.

"It's easy to lose track of time here," Bob jokes. "Line up ten people and ask everyone what day it is—if two people agree, then that's what day it is."

He offers me a cup of coffee. "Boblo" is how islanders pronounce Bois Blanc, he says. On the mainland, before I arrived, I heard it pronounced "Bwha Blanch" and "Boys Blank" and everything in between. It is a French phrase and I was told on Bois Blanc that it meant "white wood" for the birch trees everywhere. I later heard that Bois Blanc was a French Canadian term for the American basswood and that that might be the now-forgotten origin of the name.

Bob hands me an old sepia-toned brochure that shows two handsome men in knickers in a wooded setting. He says it is a remnant from the island's former Wilderness Club, a rustic but high-toned turn-of-the-century club for the very wealthy. People came up the big lakes by steamer to stay there for a week or for the entire summer.

He gives me a Wilderness Club menu for Sunday dinner, which, along with prime rib and roast lamb, includes such delicacies as boiled ox tongue and green apple pie. The one puzzling item on the menu is "reception flakes," which we speculate might be some early version of Wheaties.

The Wilderness Club brochure is written in a breezy manner, with dozens and dozens of connecting clauses, reminiscent of what Gertrude Stein called her "money" style, in which she wrote for magazines when she toured America in the 1930s.

"The Wilderness Club is composed of men who invite kindred spirits who want to live more fully; men, who through the exactions of the hours of business subconsciously perhaps, anticipate the day . . . when they may throw their cares away and live close to Nature—out in 'the open,' men who have not as yet become so deeply entrenched in today's forced and unnatural manner of living and striving to accomplish, that they have entirely lost interest in the broad uncultivated fields . . . men who want to be boys again, to 'let down,' to give vent to the sprit of play . . . to romp, to swim, to fish, to stroll about in Nature's playground unhampered and unsought."

Aside from the question as to what "reception flakes" might be, what happened to the people who ate them? Where did the men in knickers, men who want to be boys, go?

Bob tells me the Wilderness Club burned down. He asks if I recall seeing a large grassy area near the road and when I nod, he says, "That's where it was."

When Michigan was first opened for settlement in the 1830s, many homesteaders lived on islands. Islands were more accessible and inhabitable than anywhere else and provided an instant livelihood in fishing and a steady income in cutting cordwood for the steamers that plied the lakes. After that the ships went to coal and oil fuel instead of wood, and simultaneously, the interior of Michigan developed more roads and became more settled. By the 1890s the population on the majority of the various Michigan islands was dwindling and by the 1950s many of the islands had been all but abandoned. There has been a resurgence of interest in islands, largely because by the 1980s lake frontage on the mainland had become both prohibitively expensive and extremely hard to acquire.

After a short time, I thank the McCoys for the coffee and for showing me the Wilderness Club brochure and go back out into the strange rain-and-sunshine afternoon. Travel makes me feel stimulated and enervated at the same time, exhausted by learning new things and excited by it. Now I am feeling a strong need to find my motel room and be alone for a while. I make my way back down the small sandy road that leads to the one-room schoolhouse so that I can retrieve my satchel of books and my duffel bag.

The sandy road to the school has a ribbon of lavender-tinged light above it. Only five months before I had been home on the Leelanau walking behind my house on an old logging trail where there had been hundreds of small milky-purple butterflies floating in the path like a low, living cloud. With a jolt

I realize I've thought of this because the patch of sky above me is the exact pale blue-violet shade of those Lepidoptera.

Behind me, at the shore end of the road, the lake roars. The sound surges down the road in waves that wash and eddy around me like water.

The school's shed entranceway smells of the rubber of the indoor-outdoor carpet and the mildew of old wooden walls, bringing back memories of the smell of wet galoshes in the cloakroom of my own days at the small old red-brick schoolhouse in Glen Arbor. "Kid Zone," reads a poster with a smiling turtle, his amphibious hand raised in greeting. Under it are the words, "Enter with Care and Love."

I stand in the warm, stale air of the shed, out of the wind, while the dusk deepens in the pine woods around the school. I stare momentarily at a child's worn, red jacket hanging on a hook. There is a poem above it, written in flowing script. "If once you have slept on an island," this poem by Rachel Field begins, "You'll never quite be the same. / Oh, you won't know why, and you can't say how / Such change upon you came, / But once you have slept on an island, / You'll never be quite the same."

For a moment I feel the child's jacket could be mine, or my child's, the time of the poem—from the early 1900s—the time I live in. Lately, I've begun to suffer from a terrifying sense that I am a ghost in my own life, a doppelgänger of myself or past-life versions of myself or some other person, and I can't tell if this is because I'm in transition, or is an aspect of travel itself, or because past lives have become a metaphor for the pace of modern life.

A *New Yorker* cartoon recently showed two earnest daters, and one says to the other, "I wasn't anybody in a previous lifetime either." We can only imagine that this was offered, and received, as a reassurance.

Outside, the schoolyard is quiet in the gathering shadows of late afternoon. The bare, sandy loam smells sour, the way schoolyard sand smells when it's been played in forever. Here, only a few hours earlier, garter snakes took rides down the slide. I glance back at the school. Lani White said the snakes live in the foundation. There is still a strong wind. I can hear it like loud bees in the trees above my head, and there is that terrifying dull roar of the waters of Lake Huron washing up the tree-tunnel road, like the sound in a culvert.

As I drive, the pines along the narrow two-track from the school slowly sway like grass or ferns—like the giant prehistoric gymnosperms that they in fact are—first far in one direction, and then far in the other.

This is a seriously potholed road and I make my way along it cautiously, not daring to drive more than ten miles an hour. Where, I wonder, do they fix cars on this island? The air, washed by the storm, is pale and bright. There are stands of birches here, mournful and white as ghosts, their wispy branches sweeping the ground like old women's hair.

Perhaps a mile beyond the ferryboat dock, a large tree falls across the road. It is just inches in front of my car. It shakes the ground. It shakes me. After a minute or two, I get out and look at it, feeling even as I do absurdly helpless: there's no way I can move this tree. My father always traveled with an ax in his car—and knew how to use it. I should have learned when he wanted to teach me. I manage to get around the tree by going through the woods, nearly tearing the oil pan off the bottom of my car as I do.

My motel, adjoined by a restaurant and party store, is on the water in a dark stand of trees. The store is closed. The restaurant is open, but empty. The glassed-in kitchen is dark. I see only my shadow, darkly reflected. There is a black pay phone on the wall, and on a chalkboard there's a sign that announces that dinner tonight will be spaghetti. I stand waiting, wondering what to do.

The soul, I think, staring past and through my own reflection and into the darkened kitchen, must be mica-like, must look like a mirror, if it looks like anything, and fill with light and become drained of light, as the person does.

I move toward the tables and chairs in the center of the room. Then I get my briefcase of books from the car. These are books I've brought with me, and some new ones I've just bought at Cheboygan's Logmark Bookstore. The Logmark Bookstore was astonishingly sophisticated, more like the Gotham bookstore in Manhattan, even to the distracted and bespectacled booksellers, than anything one would expect to find in a faded lakeshore town three hundred miles north of Detroit.

I get myself a cup of tepid coffee from the pot that's sitting at the side of the room. I feel terrifyingly tiny, so small a bird could swallow me. I feel myself waver and place my hand, palm down, on the cool Formica top of the sideboard for a moment before making my way to a table.

I sit in one of the plastic chairs at the table and look out onto the water, where the storm is raging. I read Blake. I read Homer. What does it matter that I nearly died from a tree landing on me? Across thousands of years I transcend the illusory closed horizons of place and time by associating with other minds.

Since this is also where I am to get my key to my room for the night, I just keep waiting, and reading, thinking surely someone will come. Finally, after a half-hour or so, I decide to call the number in the phone book that I had called to get the reservation in the first place, a week earlier.

I am relieved when someone answers and says they'll be right down. While I am talking on the phone to them I am reading a sign on the board next to the phone that says: "WANTED—woman to Cook and Clean fish, dig Worms and make lures. Must have GOOD BOAT and motor. Please enclose picture of boat and motor." I had seen this first several weeks earlier in the Northland Restaurant on Drummond and more recently at the Engadiner in Engadine on Route 2 in the Upper Peninsula; it had been mildly amusing then, but by now time and repetition have flattened its humor to a point of diminishing returns.

I wait quite a while. I had told them on the phone, when they asked, that I would probably want supper—thinking that maybe ten people would show up, or at least the members of their family—but no one comes.

I am shaking and feel very cold. It occurs to me that I might be in shock. The tree missed me by moments. No one is coming and it's getting dark.

Finally the woman arrives and gives me the key to my room. I pay for the room and the coffee, and tell her I am going on down the shore to the only other public place on the island, the Bois Blanc Tavern, which I've heard is a few miles further on.

"Can't miss it!" she says. She seems relieved not to have to make me supper. "Right on the road!"

The road is alternately dark with puddles and in other places gleaming white with puddle-sized lozenges of newly washed gravel, all from the hard rain. *The road looks like a Dalmatian*, I think. Here, the shore of the island is much rockier. In places, the gravel road is very close to the gravel shore, and almost indistinguishable from it.

The Bois Blanc Tavern is a long, low, weather-stained slab-wood structure. Across the road is a gravelly and marshy escarpment into Lake Huron, startlingly pristine and wild, in contrast to the bar. Now, again, the sun is out, but the storm-wracked waters of the lake do not create a mellow mood. The bar parking lot has room for thirty vehicles, but today there are only three, all of them trucks.

A strong wind blows a very large, empty hospital-refuse-blue plastic barrel all the way across the wide sweep of gravel parking lot during the entire time I am walking from my car to the wooden ramp up to the front door. The barrel on the gravel makes a light musical sound, reminiscent of the Caribbean, the Rastafarians—an oddly tropical touch here on the shores of northern Lake Huron during a storm.

Inside, a very nice lady who looks a lot like Dolly Parton welcomes me to sit next to her at the bar. She is as willing to talk as I am needing to talk, and she fills me in on the island lore as I sip a Diet Coke. There are about ten people here, mostly men who mostly look like country and western singers. They have no coffee here, and people on both sides of the bar seem surprised that I don't order an alcoholic drink.

I know little or nothing about bar etiquette and wonder if I *should* order a drink. I couldn't feel much more out of my element if I had stepped into the intergalactic bar in *Star Wars*. I am considering ordering a drink to relax me, when my mind flashes back to that time a few months earlier when I was a guest speaker at a ladies' book club in a southern Michigan city, and two glasses of white wine and club soda worked like truth serum.

All the book-club ladies wanted to share—as ladies love to do, so a midwife friend of mine tells me—and since I was the guest, they just kept asking me question after question. Each of my answers triggered another raging round of questions—they'd never heard of anything like that in their lives or met anybody like me, ever. When they were done, I was a damp spot on the carpet and the book tour was over.

"Thanks," I say. "I think I'll hold off on the drink."

Then the barmaid, Susie White, the sister of Lani White's husband, offers me an "initiation drink." She says it will be on the house, a Boblo tradition for first-time visitors.

I tell her I'll take a rain check, and she gives me a second Diet Coke on the house instead. It's the off-season and the bar doesn't serve food, but Susie offers to make something. The only thing available here before "boat day" later in the week is a frozen hamburger, which I gratefully order without the bun, and a side of dill pickles.

No one asks me where I'm from or what I'm doing on the island. I think this is politeness, but it turns out that they have all known about me since I got off the ferry. They believe I am there to write about their island; I believe it myself at that point.

I love the feeling of camaraderie, the ordinary conversation that goes on around me, the talk of gardens that got frosted and trees that came down in the wind and a deer that got lost on the ice the winter before.

They tell me I should see Victor Babcock, the man whose great-grandparents settled the island. They look for the phone book so I can call him, but then, not finding it, it turns out everyone there knows Victor Babcock's phone number by heart anyway. Someone dials for me and before I know it I have plans to see the Babcocks at eight o'clock that night.

There were forty people on the island the winter before, they tell me. Then they dispute that. Maybe it was thirty-seven. Maybe it was forty-two. Someone has found the phone book while this conversation is going on: there is a scant one and one-third pages devoted to Bois Blanc Island.

They go through the list, naming people who left for a while and came back, taking the count all over again. They are like expatriates in Paris in the 1920s, except that they are here on a Michigan island in the early autumn of 1991. They are fixed-income retirees, laid-off auto workers, woodcutters, artists, young people with no attachments, modern-day expatriates, the kind one finds in every outpost of America and maybe the globe, waiting out the storm in more ways than one.

Some now work, on and off the island, in construction. One man says he has a friend on the island who just got back from working a big construction job in Saipan. Susie White and some of the younger people with no savings, pension, or other income will go downstate for the winter and work.

No one here has children in the school, although clearly there are at least four children on the island. These people have raised their children, if they had any. They talk about how hard it was to raise children in cities. They talk about the crime and violence: the woman they know whose child was kidnapped from her front yard, the man who was mugged in the parking lot of Farmer Jack's and was never able to walk again. Many were working two and three jobs when they lived in the Detroit area, commuting long distances; they say they hardly ever saw their spouses or children because working and commuting took up all of their time. Many are now divorced. A few remarried shortly before or after coming to the island.

In the winter, they tell me, there are potlucks at the tavern fairly often. They put a big piece of plywood over the shuffleboard game and thus convert it to a long table, and everyone brings a dish to pass. In January the bar closes, and people get together for breakfast potlucks at each other's houses Sunday mornings.

"There's compassion for your neighbor," Scott Galbraith says.

"We fight and feud," Greg Smith says, "but if you broke your leg, your worst enemy would be over there the next morning cuttin' your wood for the winter."

"You got to," someone down the bar says. "You couldn't live with yourself if you didn't."

An older blond lady with a deep Mae West voice says, "There'll come a time when you might need someone to help you, so that's in your mind when you go to help someone else."

Someone looks out at the stormy waters and says something about "the witch of November," making reference to the Gordon Lightfoot song about the sinking of the *Edmund Fitzgerald* with all the men on board in Lake Superior and the line, "'twas the witch of November come stealing."

Someone says the ferry has stopped running and might now run in the morning. Someone says there's a tree down in the road.

Sheriff Edgar Arnett comes in, the island's sole law-enforcement officer, and someone asks him about the tree. He says he cut it up and moved it. Someone else says they heard on their scanner the wind is blowing fifty-two miles per hour. Someone else says they rode that afternoon in a private boat across from Cheboygan in six-foot seas. The speaker is a large, burly man. Someone asks him how it was, and he says, "It was different."

The ferryboat owner comes in, looks at me, and laughs and says, "You plan on leavin' in the mornin'?"

Clyde Bishop comes in and looks at me, and says, "What's *she* doin' here?"

Someone tells him I'm there to see how many people on the island are in the witness-protection program.

Clyde tells me there are bald eagles on the island, as well as bobcat, deer, otter, and fox. Apparently there are no skunks, porcupine, or bear on the island, but no one seems to know why; perhaps these animals, which could theoretically cross on the ice as well as any others, are hibernating at that time.

Clyde says there are Michigan rattlesnakes on the island, as well as the garter snakes I saw at the school earlier in the day. "Oh, them rattlers are good eatin'," someone from the end of the bar says. I turn to Janie and Scott Galbraith, who are sitting next to me. "Do people eat the snakes?"

"Yeah, some of 'em do," Scott says. "I've never participated in them myself."

I leave the Bois Blanc Tavern and go back to my motel to take a shower and rest and read. I turn the heat up as high as it will go. I am still freezing. I get into the motel bed with its polyester coverlet and then I get up again and put on half the clothes I have brought with me. I can't seem to get warm. I get out my books.

On the ferry I had started reading *Gilgamesh*, and now get it out again. Gilgamesh is grieving for his friend Enkidu, whom he enticed into battle and who got killed. "No one grieves this much," the barmaid Siduri, who lives in a cottage at the edge of the sea, tells Gilgamesh. "Forget your friend. He is dead."

I find I am crying. I am wet with salty tears. Big waves of grief sweep through me like the contractions of child labor. I am grieving, like Gilgamesh, but I don't know for what. Gilgamesh is sleeping in the river god's house on the floor while the river god and his shuffling old wife go about their daily affairs. I fall asleep finally, too, a deep but troubled sleep.

When I awake, I am sweating profusely and have kicked all the covers off. I am having trouble breathing. I don't recognize where I am and don't know if I am alive or dead, male or female. I feel someone is sitting on me, and only slowly do I realize I have been having a dream of the river god's wife on my chest, her long gray hair sweeping to and fro over me.

As if rising from beneath an undertow, I stand to turn the heat down. Out behind the motel, there is a dark green rectangle of lawn in front of a rectangular dwelling. I lie back down for a while in gray, post nightmare.

I get up and get dressed. I want to call home. I walk across the road to the restaurant but the pay phone seems to be out of order. I feel more disappointed than the broken phone warrants and force myself to recognize that every day some waitress, some traveling salesman, and four hundred others suffer the same or similar problem. Back outside I am fascinated by the way the storm light seems to create strangely falsified contours in the woods. Even my car looks eerily outlined, as if it has a fine fluorescent border around it.

Night is coming. The storm seems to have subsided. I walk back to my room up the gravel trail, and then put my raincoat and notebook in the car to go back to the Babcocks's on the other side of the island.

The moon is rising as I drive down the shore road toward the Babcocks's. Mine is the only car on the road. The island seems to be in for the night.

I follow the directions Mr. Babcock gave me when I talked to him over the phone from the tavern. In behind the one-room school, down the two-track, to the brown house. His wife, 'Berta, invites me in through the back, apologizing for not having me in through the front door, explaining that the back way is drier.

We go through the kitchen. A black frying pan with a picture of their house hangs on the wall. An artist somewhere did it for them, she says. She takes me in to where her husband, Victor Babcock, a man in his late fifties, is sitting in the living room, a room with overstuffed chairs and afghans.

Victor has never lived anywhere except on Bois Blanc, he says. 'Berta tells me she has been here since she married Victor thirty-five years ago. He has just retired from the Mackinac County road crew, where he was the county's sole island employee. The couple has two grown sons who do not live on the island. These sons went to the one-room school on the island through eighth grade, at which time they then went to school in Cheboygan, boarding with friends or relatives through the school year and coming home only for holidays.

"It's awful hard on the kids to go," Victor says of that period of time when his sons left the island for school on the mainland. "Awful hard on the folks here, too, having them away. So many things can happen to a child. You want to be there with them."

The older son graduated from Michigan State University and the younger son from Northwestern Michigan College. The older son is in the field of social work, and the younger one reads blueprints for a company that does steel construction work for shopping centers. Neither live on the island, nor could they and have the careers they have or earn the living they do.

The Babcocks found a way to live comfortably on Bois Blanc, but they couldn't find ways for their children to do the same. A simple life, a safe existence are not so easy to achieve beyond a generation or two, even in a place as uncomplicated as Boblo.

I ask them about the tree line and the snowmobile accident. They tell me what the people at the tavern have told me. That there had been some heavy drinking, and the man driving the snowmobile, who was not from the island, did not realize the danger of not sticking to the tree line.

Later, Roberta Babcock will write to me and describe in detail the annual ritual of putting up the tree line. "When the island men decide to check the ice for thickness," she writes, "some of them walk across it. They keep checking the thickness of the ice. Some come behind on snowmobiles, if the ice is thick enough—usually six inches thick. Then they cut small pine trees to plant in holes they drill in the ice. One man has a gasoline power machine with a large drill bit that drills the holes in the ice. The men bring small trees on trailers behind their snowmobiles, or Hondas, to put in the holes. The trees are put in the ice for safe crossing as you could get lost on the ice in a snow storm or in the fog. The ice can get up to twelve inches or more in thickness."

"My dad made his money moonshinin' and cuttin' wood for Mackinac Island," Victor says that evening. "They had hollow-bottom boats. I guess they'd put the moonshine in the bottom and the wood on the top." He said islanders also made their living providing services to the resorters, doing plumbing, carpentry. "You name it, we did it," he says. "Still do."

He tells me about going to another one-room school on the island, and how the school teacher would cook their lunch on the wood stove while the children were studying their lessons. They sometimes had potato soup and cornmeal mush for lunch. "The children would bring raw, cut-up potatoes and onions, and canned milk for the potato soup," his wife says.

Victor says he wouldn't know how to live anywhere but Boblo. "This way if I want to walk out in the woods, I just walk out my front door." They have a one-hundred-year-old lighthouse on the island, and until 1947 there was a man who lived there and tended it. There are many spots deep in the island that only islanders know about, Babcock says, one where there is virgin hemlock and another where there is a virgin stand of pine.

"There's another spot on the island," he says. "We think it happened thousands of years ago—it's just *perfectly round*—where maybe a meteorite hit. Now that's a thing a person oughta see if they has a chance to."

The Babcocks entertain me well into the evening with Bois Blanc Island lore, inviting me back in the spring to see where the meteorite hit. They are like people I knew when I was growing up on the Leelanau Peninsula in the 1950s.

As I drive down the white gravel road, I shut my lights off and just drive.

It is almost midnight in pale moonlight: night's noon. I think back to the way the Babcocks walked me out to the car, the way they shook my hand two or three times before I left.

What is it about the Babcocks, I ask myself, that makes them resemble the people I grew up with? They are trusting, I decide. We've lost that, in a world of strangers. People come to Bois Blanc to find that ability to trust again that they once knew in themselves and their fellow humans.

I drive down this empty gravel road on a small island in northern Michigan where all forty of the residents have gone to bed for the night, thinking that we have all been pushing too hard, ourselves, our world.

Pilots call it "pushing the envelope," a way of taking the corner too fast. We all need to find those islands in ourselves, those islands in our world, where things are basically simple and we know our neighbors and have compassion for them.

The next morning, I am back on the ferry. All my fears from the night before seem as remote as if they'd never existed. The sky is the white, misty sky of early morning, promising a mild day; no dragons plow the mist. It is cold this morning and so I move inside the cabin with the other passengers. They are talking about someone they know who has moved away.

"He's downstate now. Fell *in love* with a woman named Flavia."

"Flavia?"

"Yeah, Flavia. Can you imagine bein' in bed and callin' out her name in the night? 'Oh, Flav. Oh, Flavia.'"

The talk turns to the storm the night before.

"I was out here once in ten-foot seas, with water comin' in over the deck and freezin' and the cars rollin'. I'll tell ya, I didn't know whether it was worse to be on the boat or in the water."

"It got pretty roiled up last night."

"The radio said fifty-five miles an hour."

"Who won at cards last night? It was card night for Lani White and them."

Susie White, the bartender from the tavern the night before, says she's going to Cheboygan for the day to see the dentist.

There's an old man in a life vest sitting kitty-corner from her.

"I see you got your life vest on," she says.

"Yep. I never took no chances with no boats."

The old woman next to him says, "He's wore that life vest ever since the dinghy sank."

The old man says, "It was September, late, like about it is now. The water was warmer than the air. We went down, just like that. Sank our groceries, everything. I stayed in that water two hours 'fore they come to fetch me out." He smiles, shakes his head. "But I was a lot younger then."

Susie White laughs. The whole cabin laughs with her.

"I figure if I go down now," the old man taps his life-vest-covered chest, "I'll pop right back up again."

When the ferry docks in Cheboygan, I get in my car and drive off. It seems suddenly calmer and quieter, as if the wind had been blowing and now it isn't. Even the ground underfoot seems more solid.

I feel a slight pang of separation. I understand what Susie White was saying moments before, about not wanting to leave for the winter, not wanting to leave even for a day. Their whole lives are encapsulated there, like *Days of Our Lives* for real, and there's no newspaper that will give a running account of the days they miss so they can catch up. So that's why they stay. They have made lives for themselves—the McCoys and the Babcocks and the people at the tavern—in which they are real because their neighbors know them. They do not need to be images of themselves for each other. They are who they are without ever saying who they are, and it is this that makes me want to go back to their island and live there, too, that makes me feel as I drive away that the island ceases to exist a little with each mile and each hour. I think it is this quality of illusoriness, of immateriality, of elusiveness, that is the essence of what both draws me to islands and sends me away from them, simultaneously and endlessly.

A Mother Reaches Satori on the Tenth Anniversary of Her Son's Drowning in Lake Michigan

RASMA HAIDRI

oday the water is still. This is what they call mirror water, glass water, quiet-face-of-the-sky water. If you could have waited ten years, my son, my daring boy, the water off the break wall would have been this water: calm, cradle-safe for even a baby, my baby, you, my rumble-tumble boy.

But no, today you would have been twenty-eight, too old, too safe, too cautious to be my boy: my lost-youth boy; my just-man, just-barely-grown boy; my climbing see-me-jump-Ma! see-how-high-I-am boy.

It was a colder October, a dark-sky October, a wind-lifting October when the lake rose, the great lake heaved and sighed, and the hum of its turning sounded like song to your ears. The waves sung your name like love on the tongue, a song your soul was also singing, a song your ears heard as waves and wind breaking over the wall, and like the boy you were, you ran out over the narrow line of stones.

Thrilled by the thrill of your daring, you thought you were just this: boy body bone muscle dancing feet and open arms. And voice. "Come! Come on! Oh God, this is great!" you called over the waves to your friends as your legs ran, your arms swung, your heart raced, and you laughed out loud in the joy of your daring, thinking this was you, thinking this boy body you carried out to the waves was all of you.

You turned to run back to the shore, but even as you ran your soul was rising, your body dissolving, merging soul and being, and in that moment you saw your true self: body outside of body, the fluid world where wind, waves, rock, and all that you thought you were merged into one pulse beating, one heart song, one whisper in the mouth of God: no end no begin no birth no drown. Just you, just you tumbling in pure joy at the sound of your own name calling you home.

Lake Huron's Tide

RACHAEL PERRY

I already know what I'm going to do when I get there.

I will drive, windows rolled down, along a two-lane road that ribbons through fields of beans and corn. I will bring my grandmother and grandfather with me, two close family friends, my uncle if he wants to come, because we are all in this together and they can help me remember the way. We will choose the back roads out of Imlay City, a series of norths and easts that zigzag us past Decker and Argyle and Ubly, lonely roadside cemeteries and whitewashed Amish homes and cows. The wind will be sweet, fresh; we might stop at an ice-cream parlor to stretch our legs and slurp root-beer floats.

I will feel the lake before I see it. The air cools and smells faintly of fish, the bloated half-carcasses of smallmouth bass picked over by gulls. It's possible that we'll nearly miss Kinch Road: a gravel lane, unsigned and camouflaged by wild grasses and a forest of pine and birch.

Then there is Lake Huron at the end of Kinch, a blue so comfortable it must come from my dreams, or the womb.

◆ ◆ ◆

My first swell of real homesickness for home as a *place* and not a *person* or *my family* came months after my husband and I moved to Düsseldorf. I had proudly mastered the language skills necessary to ask for water without gas and express my approval of meals, the weather, and the state of my health with *super!* and *beautiful!* and *fantastic!* It was early spring, and the winter in northwestern Germany had been dark and long, not super and not beautiful. My mother mentioned Lake Huron. That was all. She said the family would open the cottage for the summer, as if it were a natural thing for them to do while I lived a million miles away. She said a whole lot of nice things, too, like "We wish you could be here," and "It won't be the same without you," and, although I'd scribbled the same hurried messages on postcards from Rome and Berlin and Prague, I felt left out.

Our family has owned the place for years, since my grandparents bought it in 1957 from a rum runner who was once arrested for flying his airplane underneath the Ambassador Bridge. I've been in love with this cottage perched on a sandy hill for as long as I can remember: a warm kitchen with appliances reminiscent of a '57 Chevy; an old toilet you need to flush with a bucket of rusty water; yellowed posters that lay down such rules as THERE IS A SIX-PERSON LIMIT PER BED, and A MAN CAN'T LIVE ON BREAD ALONE, HE NEEDS A TOMATO ONCE IN A WHILE; a wall of windows on the front porch that stare unblinking into Lake Huron.

In Germany, I ached for the lake, and almost didn't care that I was being a child about it. Couldn't I drink hot chocolate and huddle over my notebook in Heinrich Heine's birth house whenever I wanted? Wasn't I able to hop in the car or on a train and be in the Netherlands, Belgium, or France in less time than it would take my family back home to make it to Bad Axe?

I tried to turn to the Rhine for comfort. River of mythology: Siegfried's cursed red gold and the luring songs of the Lorelei. The Rhine is swift and strong and brown, especially in the spring when it overwhelms its banks and spills over acres of meadows and trees. It is spellbinding, ancient, unsafe. Over time, I began to think perhaps the sailors who had thrown their ships against the cliffs near Koblenz had done it not out of desperate love for something unattainable, but out of a desperate loneliness, so far from home.

I'm not sure what the lake will make of me after all this time, but I will gather all my ghosts, close my eyes, plug my nose, and plunge in.

◆ ◆ ◆

I am at the lip of the lake; cool water and slick skipping stones lick my toes. Of all that I've considered, I haven't given this part much thought. I can't make a running start and splash my way in, open my arms, grab the lake, and hold it, because the beach is overgrown with a wild-root shrubbery I've never seen before. I'm not sure I want to hang around the moist, muddy beach, either; there is a foam to the last wave that rolls in, muck and watery weeds.

I'm nervous, like before a high-school reunion, but I don't want to be shy about this or overly formal. The September sun is warm on my bare shoulders; the water shimmers. I take one step, another—slowly at first, then, when I'm up to my knees and the lake begins to reclaim me, as quickly as I can.

My sister joins me. So do my husband, my brothers, and the dog, who is sticky and smelly and proud of himself. We half swim, half walk to a sandbar and cover ourselves with mud. Although the water ripples on and on toward Canada, I don't see land on the other side, and I can't imagine it. When I close my eyes, Lake Huron wraps itself around the world, something that the Atlantic or Pacific might do. An enormous freshwater ocean, but nicer—and not mysterious.

I swim and I splash and I float and I soak until there are goose bumps all over my body. I don't think about pollution or mercury levels or the safety of eating freshwater fish or subdivisions that used to be farmland or gas-guzzling rust buckets. I don't think about how foreign home feels to me. The lake clings to my hair, is absorbed by my skin; my blood, my water, must know that this is where it comes from.

I am reluctant to leave. The lake carries me to shore, where I step out and dry. When I open the screen door and shuffle in, my mother asks, "Well, how was it?" and I don't really know what to say.

◆ ◆ ◆

A few months later, someone breaks into the cottage. My mother repeats the story: the gas man was on a routine check and he noticed a missing window. He called my mother. She called the police, the neighbors.

"Who would do such a thing?" she asks.

We can't make the drive to check for ourselves, so the facts of the case come to us slowly: the window isn't broken, it is simply unscrewed, placed on the ground outside. "You can unscrew a window?" My mother assures me it's possible. Nothing is missing or ruined or stolen, not even a chair askew or out of place. The Monopoly game my brothers started still sits on the wooden table, rainbow money sorted and stuffed under the board. The police, the neighbors, my mother are baffled.

"Who would do such a thing?" she wonders.

To me, this polite breaking and entering is a marvel. I envy the ability, the trickery. I imagine a thin woman who wears thin clothes—probably some thin windbreaker or thin cotton shirt, thinning at the elbows. She visits the lake often, at the public beach about a half-mile down the road, and knows not everyone lives here year-round. She considers it, maybe even battles a few qualms—"There could be trouble," she thinks—but the lake tempts her with such whispers, such golden sunsets. All she has is a single-wide mobile home in town, so she figures, just this once, she will break and enter into someone else's life.

The technique she culls from a hardware freebie, some pamphlet about insulation updates for homeowners. She stuffs three different kinds of screwdrivers into a brown bag: a flashlight, a scarf, some bread and cheese, a couple of beers. She rides her bike from Port Austin and arrives at the cottage about an hour before the sun goes down. The ground is hard with frost but there isn't much snow, so she doesn't leave any tracks. It is cold outside—she needs to take off her mittens to feel for screws around the windowpane—but the sounds of the lake are exhilarating, an invitation; the sounds envelop her as if she is already under water.

It is easier than she thought it would be. She unhinges the screen, lays it on the ground with care, pushes the glass in, and checks to make sure there are no cracks. Tugging herself inside is a bit more challenging—she drags a plastic chair over from the deck to give her more height. Once indoors, she treads quietly around each tiny room, runs her fingers along a dresser or a counter or a mirror. She thinks about starting a fire in the stone fireplace, then decides against it. Instead, she grabs a few blankets from the linen closet, wraps herself tightly, settles into a wicker daybed on the front porch, and gazes at the lake.

I imagine Lake Huron through this thin woman's melancholy eyes. I can hear her breathe deeper; her heartbeat slows. She nibbles her cheese sandwich, sips from her beer. The sun hauls itself down slowly, in strokes of oranges and pinks. The colors, she thinks, of hope. And the lake mesmerizes, hypnotizes; it swells and stretches out to an infinite horizon; it promises her the life that she wants. Her hands and feet are freezing, but she does not have any trouble falling asleep.

In the morning she leaves. It must be quick because she doesn't take time to replace the window—the telltale sign. It is simple, her polite breaking and entering. It is simple and easy and quiet. I wonder, if I had the chance, whether I might break in too, when nobody's looking, and reenter my old life. It could be seamless, unobtrusive. I could do it without getting caught, without disrupting chairs or Monopoly games. Only the lake would share my secret. And after we'd exchanged our stories under the cloak of darkness, on a night when a slim slice of light shivered across calm waters, I would know my secret is safe.

Uptake and Down

Slowly, as we walked and foraged for mint, the cloud of mayflies grew, spreading above us like a canopy of a great tree. The closest were near our heads, dropping suddenly, and then bouncing up, erratically, puppet-like. Gulls flew openmouthed through the top of the swarm, gorging, wild-eyed and squawking. Mayflies are relics from another time, having outlived, as a species, their contemporaries and dodged extinction. How have they managed, food as they are for so many fish and birds? For a year they prepare for their brief emergence, when they molt to wings and fly. In a day, or a few, the males swarm to attract females. They do not eat or sleep. Some are eaten, some mate, some lay eggs, all die. Sometimes, the swarms are so large they blanket the ground, inches deep, dying. I didn't know all of this as we sat watching them. I was mesmerized by their dance, the randomness of it, its breathtaking beauty, and all the while watching them die in the mouths of gulls. We share with the mayflies an origin in water, a short life, the randomness of fate, a chance at mating and offspring, the certainty of death.

—*Tracey Easthope*

From inside the cottage, a freighter passing meant all the windows were filled with the steel-hulled bulk of the thing. Up close, and moving slowly, a ship that size is remarkably quiet. If your back is turned, you won't hear the low vibration until it is very close. My siblings and I would play on a tree swing that we'd ride over the seawall to drop in the St. Clair River. When a ship came through, almost every hour, some force in the water would pull you toward it. It wasn't a current so much as a magnetic force created by so much bulk. The water level would quickly drop several feet, sometimes more, and then slowly refill as the boat passed.

—*Tracey Easthope*

The next day we motor carefully through the Amygdaloid Channel, a narrow strait lined with rocky outcroppings, summer home to cormorants and ring-billed gulls. Rough and pitted, age-old lava fingers point north, the direction we're headed to round the tip of the island. We drift through pockets of dense fog, grateful for radar and the GPS. Blips on the screen warn us in time of fishermen blurring in and out as they troll the coast. We wonder if they see us. We wonder what they catch.

—*Michele Bergstrom*

People sometimes ask how it was living on a "dead lake," as Lake Erie came to be known in the 1960s. The truth is, back then we didn't realize how bad it really was. I thought the masses of algae and dead fish that washed up on the beach were just part of the Great Lakes experience. We used the fish for fertilizer and we all swam in the water whenever the weather was hot.

—*Nancy Dunham with Bonnie Jo Campbell*

The Kettle

ALISON SWAN

The brew pub was dark and cheerful, the air redolent of fresh beer. Next to my husband and me, a huge aquarium full of freshwater fish glowed brown-green. I was appreciating the nod to locality when a young woman poured a plastic bag of water and minnows into the tank. I watched the tiny silver fish dart or hang among the stones and weeds. Most were eaten immediately. One managed to evade capture for several long moments. I silently rooted for it. I am not a lighthearted person; when a bass gobbled it up, my stomach lurched.

"So I'm really going to do it. We're not just going to talk about it. I'm going to go up there and get that kettle." I was cheering myself on.

Dave sipped his pint and nodded. "And whatever else you want."

We'd driven to Kalamazoo's warehouse district through gray January countryside from our new house in Saugatuck, a small town near the Lake Michigan mouth of the Kalamazoo River. Half a dozen Great Lakes fish digested their meal behind glass. Outside, cold winter rain melted the snow cover to slush. And I thought about the little cabins in the woods five hundred miles away near the frozen Lake Superior shore. It was my thirty-sixth birthday, and I was conspiring to smash a window or jimmy the door at somebody else's summer place.

Somebody else's summer place. It makes me cringe now to describe it that way. Fifty years ago, on land owned by his father-in-law on Lake Independence near

Big Bay, Michigan, my grandfather converted the cinder-block garage of an old hunting camp into a three-room cabin, a rustic second home where he, my grandmother, my mother, and her four sisters spent summers and some weekends. They lived the rest of the year in Marquette, a small Victorian city perched on the cliffs above Lake Superior. The cabin was just an hour's drive along the coast from home, but it was a world away.

Established by a logging company around 1902, when almost everything or everyone arrived or departed via the notoriously unpredictable waters of Superior, Big Bay never prospered, at least not for more than a few families. It is too remote or buggy or cold, depending upon which local you ask and what the most recent challenge has been. Everyone complains about the isolation, mosquitoes, and weather, but no one who sticks around really doubts that those three things keep the town exactly how they want it: peaceful and plain.

By the early 1970s, when I was a schoolgirl spending summer vacations with my family and grandparents in their cabin, Big Bay had a few paved roads but was absent from state road maps. "We go here," I'd tell curious friends from my downstate home, pointing at an irregular blue pentagon, Lake Independence, the large inland lake that, on a map, looked to be a stone's throw from Superior, at the literal end of the road. There were a few decades around the turn of the last century when transient lumberjacks swelled Big Bay's population to a thousand. Since then, no more than a few hundred hardy—or hiding—individuals have lived there year-round. Even summer visitors are relatively few: there are just several tiny motels and one small campground. Summer cottages are scattered along the lakeshores, but there are no condominium complexes. Indeed, only a few buildings are taller than one-and-a-half stories.

Spring was a couple of months old, the morning hazy and still, when I packed the car for the trip north to retrieve the kettle. I tried to think like a thief, choosing our less conspicuous car and loading it with what I imagined to be breaking-and-entering supplies: flashlight, screwdrivers (Phillips and flathead), mallet, wrench, crowbar, tote bags, small stepladder, and hand drill. Camps—as second-home cabins are called in Michigan's Upper Peninsula—all around the lake are mostly deserted in May, and I expected the new Tennessean owners wouldn't leave their mild spring weather for Big Bay's rainy season. I was probably going to be able to be as loud and slow as I wanted. Something would give; a window or a door would have been left unlocked. When I was a very small girl, local custom was to leave unoccupied cabins not only unlocked but stocked with emergency supplies once the weather turned snowy, something which regularly happened in October. Someone, a hunter most likely, might seek shelter when a storm pounded down from Canada. Winters were that harsh and unpredictable. Twenty-five years ago, if I had timed things carefully, I could have walked right in.

Frivolous supplies went into a couple of canvas totes. I packed a spade, plastic pails (to transport wildflowers back for our garden), even packing paper (for old juice glasses, a couple of coffee mugs, the idea of which did make me smile), and my old manual camera with the excellent lens. The whole process would have been hilarious if it wasn't so sad.

◆　◆　◆

Here is the loss I was inventorying as I packed: three hundred feet of Lake Independence frontage, two rustic cabins with all furnishings—including the kettle, once our source of hot water—two well-tended outhouses, one wooden footbridge over a gully of sweet William, a dock that doubled as swim platform and sundeck, two aluminum skiffs with oars and outboard motors, and a meticulously maintained though oft-repaired ski boat and boat hoist, both of which seemed as old as my parents. All of this was priceless to me still—because of who once lived there, but also because of who I was there. In the cabins, and in the forest, hills, and water that surround them, I was a child rather than a girl, and it was in those wild places that I came to know the rich complexity of the natural world. I could give myself over completely to my imagination. I wandered almost as freely as the French explorers who came before me, giving names to all my special places: Secret Garden, Sand Dune, the Stump.

For my grandmother, Big Bay was a second home, with little of the glamour that appellation now implies. In 1916, she was an infant when her father moved from their uptown Marquette home to backwoods Big Bay to take the post of station agent. Local legend has my great-grandfather bragging that, thereafter, he never spent a night away from the hamlet nestled between Lake Independence and Lake Superior. Family legend has it that my grandmother grew up in a house with hired help. Even during the Depression, my mother has said, the family "never went without."

My grandmother's recollections were less gilded. She spent many weekdays and nights living with an aunt and uncle so she could attend a proper school "in town"—Marquette. She'd ride the train between that north-woods college town and Big Bay, past clear-cuts and hardscrabble farms, which only sounds romantic. She often arrived in Big Bay cold, tired, hungry, and torn between wanting to be with her parents and back with her friends. She was thirteen when my fifteen-year-old grandfather—poor, but smart and gentlemanly—entered her life through a mutual friend. Photographs of the two teenagers when they were still courting reveal not just giddy love but deep contentment. They lean into one another comfortably, serene smiles on their faces, his fair head bent to her dark waves. I knew my grandpa as a quiet, strong, civic-minded man who adored his "Gracie," and my grandmother as a supremely organized housewife who adored her "Kennie."

Nonetheless, "I was a woman's libber before anyone knew the words," Grandma told me on a number of occasions. "Everyone thinks your Grandpa is so . . ." My grandmother's voice would trail off as if she was unwilling to speak ill of him. "He's as much of a male chauvinist as your dad." But her eyes would twinkle in a way that suggested she loved him just as he was.

Grandpa never showed me his sexist stripes. I watched as he ducked his head to his plate of eggs and bacon while Grandma instructed the rest of us sharply: "Sit down. Eat. Take more." Around their house and cottage, clearly, she was in charge. On other occasions, she'd tell me about their lunch hours together once the girls were all in school. "Your grandpa came home for lunch every day" from Getz's clothing store, where he was the manager six days a week. "I had some of my best times with my hair up in curlers." Her voice winked if she didn't.

She was the only grown woman, indeed the only adult in my family who talked with me that way—and it seems I was one of the only grandchildren she gave so much of herself to—so it was only natural that when she and my grandpa put our camp on the real-estate market, I would be the one to try to find out why, and exactly how serious she was.

She was absolutely serious. It was their daughters' inheritance, she said. It was too much work to keep up. I heard the same explanations over and over again from aunts, uncles, and cousins. The proffered reasons for selling sounded convincing. My mother and her sisters all lived hundreds of miles away. Three of them rarely visited the cabins at all. But to me the explanations rang false.

"They intend to pass it down to their two boys," Grandmother told me once, about the buyers, in one of the few lengthy long-distance phone calls she and I had in thirty years. We both much preferred in-person to over-the-wires.

Our discomfort with talking on the phone certainly hampered our attempt to understand each other in that loaded moment, but her apparent oblivion took my breath away.

I couldn't help it. I snarled, "How nice for them."

"You don't want to own those cabins, Alison. They need so much work. You have no idea." It wasn't long before I was crying.

I stared out at our little urban backyard—bounded by neighbors' garages and fences—at our smudged French doors and book-strewn dining-room table, and raged silently. My grandmother was fastidious in a way I hadn't yet connected with the reality of living in a small house crowded with children. No, you are the one who is clueless, I wanted to tell her. You don't have to rake every day, sweep after every meal—hell, you don't even have to clean weekly, especially not when you're living in the woods.

"Please just give us a week to figure out a way to buy them," I begged her. She never did answer.

My grandparents raised six girls on a clothing-store manager's salary in a three-bedroom house with one bathroom and one car. Not only was my grandmother tidy, clean, and organized in a way that intimidated most people, she was practical and unsentimental to an extreme. Each of her grandbabies arrived without a visit from faraway Grandma. By the time I was old enough to read, gone were my mother's treasured books. There had been unkindnesses, if not outright fights when my grandmother's own father had died and the Lake Independence property passed down to her and her siblings. She and my grandfather ended up buying out her own brothers and sisters, something I think she may have always felt as a slight. A couple of her brothers were wealthy by then, and perhaps more significantly to my grandmother, she'd been the primary caregiver to their father and to many of his aunts and uncles. She was forever heading somewhere with dinner for an old person.

My grandparents probably wanted to spare their daughters the divisiveness that can come with shared ownership of something impossible to divide. And despite four of us grandchildren wanting to buy the cottages and a portion of the land, our grandparents refused to subdivide the property. They knew that none of us could afford to buy all of it, individually or together. I'm finally considering that they may have thought they were sparing their grandchildren, too. It seems impossible that camp was as sacred to my grandmother as it is to me.

. . .

As I packed the last items into our car before heading north for the kettle—and whatever else I could filch—a red-bellied woodpecker churred invisibly from the massive oaks and maples on our street. The tropical sound recalls for me southern Florida, where I first connected the bird song with its singer, and where I worked my first real job, as a high-school teacher. My life has been a chain of relocations: six different homes before second grade, twelve more in the years since I graduated from high school. I thought of our Lake Independence camp as my one solid place in the world. By the time the For Sale sign went up at the end of the dirt two-track driveway, it had become a touchstone.

The woods and fields along Michigan's interstates were studded with For Sale signs. Somewhere mid-state, posted in front of a mature coniferous forest that reminded me of the forested hills across Lake Independence from our cabins, I saw one sign the size of a small billboard which read simply "Vacant Land," and gave a phone number. I snorted, then frowned. Vacant, huh? The homes of how many wild creatures? Whose touchstones? Whose stories? Places hold stories, often with a tenacity humans can rarely muster. When I lived away from the Great Lakes—though always by big water, it was never fresh and it was never home—I found myself bereft of my stories, fumbling for a sense of connectedness. Now, back home where my stories are countless, I struggle mightily with the transformation of the landscape into a paved and built place I scarcely recognize.

I spent the whole trip glancing at the passing scenery or staring into the backs of cars, entertaining myself by making up stories about their occupants. One old sedan traveled along a full twenty miles per hour below the speed limit and stayed (stubbornly? obliviously?) in the passing lane. It held two silver-haired couples. The men sat chatting in front, the women in back. I could see their animated silhouettes as they turned toward one another. I envied the leisure of their drive. Were they long-time marrieds or second-time-arounders? Were they part-time locals, full-time locals, or road trippers from somewhere south of here? If I could have pulled them over and talked to them, what would they have told me about the changes they have seen? Do they have grown children like me who resent, ever so slightly, the senior citizens who have bought up and built up Michigan's open space as part of their retirement plan?

Just before I crossed over the Straits of Mackinac, I caught a radio report about lake sturgeon. Like salmon, they leave open water and swim upriver to spawn. Like many living creatures whose life cycle requires specific habitats, the sturgeon has had a rather rough time of it since the Industrial Revolution. Lake sturgeon are nearly nonexistent now in the Great Lakes, an especially poignant situation because *Acipenser fulvescens* has remained essentially unchanged since the age of dinosaurs. Individuals can grow to be three hundred pounds and live as long as one hundred years. In Wisconsin, the report explained, sturgeon were being transported by pickup truck past dams to their upstream spawning grounds. Their fingerlings were then transported, again via pickup trucks, back to Lake Winnebago. Of course, I thought wryly, settling into my own speedy little vehicle for a trip to a place that felt (and still feels) as essential to me as oxygen.

◆　◆　◆

I was nine when my father and I were drift fishing in the weed bed offshore from the Lake Independence cottage his parents had rented when he was a boy. No doubt he'd been telling me one of his "stories from the mouth," made-up stories that, when told in a fishing boat, usually involved sea monsters and great underwater adventures, when I caught the biggest northern pike anyone in our family had ever caught. It fought me with a force that nearly pulled my slight frame over the edge of the open boat. Pike are like that. They don't land easily, and with their mouths full of sharp teeth, demand a careful reeling in. They can easily razor the line or slice a grasping hand. Later, we took a photograph of me, in baggy jeans, sweatshirt, and light blue fishing hat, the pike hanging from the stringer I clutched at my chest with two hands. The iridescent brown-green fish hung down to my knees. A few minutes later, I cut off the fish's head myself. Through all of it, my father cheered and beamed like I was the greatest thing on earth, and for the rest of the evening I felt like I was.

This was not my usual place in the family. I am the oldest girl in a family of boys, and my grandmother may have been a feminist, but my mother was not. I learned to clean bathrooms, do laundry, wash dishes, and look after babies, and I got plenty of practice. I never cleaned the dog's kennel or washed the cars. I don't think I ever even shoveled snow, though I do remember distinctly how thrilled I was to be allowed to drive the riding lawn mower. I received all the dance, piano, drawing, and tennis lessons that I wanted. My mother shopped tirelessly with me for clothes and struggled patiently with my thick, unruly hair—and with me, a tomboy who was not always appreciative of her efforts. But what I recall most vividly is the proud pleasure with which both of my parents met my quiet obedience. "She is such a good helper!" I heard often. And I was. From my earliest memories, it is clear, I was being prepared for traditional motherhood. The only problem was, this didn't match my dreams for myself, which had more to do with pulling that big fish into the boat, out on open water, under a big sky.

◆ ◆ ◆

At the north end of the Mackinac Bridge, the southern reaches of the Upper Peninsula, the scenery turns rugged. Even now, it takes just a few minutes to leave the stretch of small old hotels, gift shops, and smoked-fish shacks, and shiny new chain restaurants, gas stations, and convenience stores behind. Although I had another two hundred miles or so to go before I reached our old camp on Lake Independence, I was "Up North," where as a teenager I believed I might one day make a living in the wilderness, and where I hardly thought at all of the boyfriends I caught but couldn't seem to hold.

Instead of feeling lighter, I felt the weight of gathering fear. Surely the cabin had a caretaker now. Surely any number of people would note my passage through town. It was a quiet time of year, perhaps the quietest, and the town of Big Bay is literally not on the way to anything. My thoughts became pep talks that went something like this: "Once I get there, I am going to break in, and not only am I going to break in, I'm going to take anything I want." This, of course, would not include anything that wasn't in the cabin when my grandparents owned it—nothing of any real value, actually, except perhaps the antique fireplace tools. I considered the pros and cons of leaving some money on the table, a note even.

I rehearsed what I might say to anyone who caught me. "This little cabin has been in my family for half a century. I have slept in every room. At this dining-room table, I have learned how a woman might stand up to a man, and that a lady can drink beer. At this fireplace, I've learned that oak burns hot and long, and that a nearly extinguished fire makes for the best marshmallow roasting. In these woods, I learned paper birch and balsam fir, starflower and lady's slipper; in that lake, northern pike and walleyed pike, to shuffle my feet around freshwater clams the size of my mother's hands, and to catch minnows for bait. My Marquette mother met my Detroit father fishing, right out there." Legally irrelevant as the arguments were, they steadied me.

Mature second-growth forest crowds the edges of Big Bay now, and when I finally rolled into town around dinnertime, I was struck by how the views from the edge of town out to Lake Independence have changed since my childhood. What was once open meadow was now a tangle of small houses, driveways, and the trees and shrubs their owners have planted—or let grow.

"That's where they milled the side panels for the first Country Squires," my parents would tell us as we rolled along Big Bay's main drag in our 1970 Country Squire sporting fake wood siding. "They used to be made from real wood." I don't know what I pictured, but I do know that the thought of putting real wood on a car struck me as hopelessly old-fashioned. I hated our station wagon anyway, and dreamed of the baby blue Gran Torino I'd buy myself one day. I'd look down the grassy hill at the crumbling brick lumber mill looming seven stories above the meadows on the Lake Independence shore. Modernized by the Ford Motor Company in 1943, it was superfluous to Ford Motor Company's operations and closed several years later. A modern ruin, it captivated me, as did the abandoned train depot where a few decades earlier, Henry Ford had sat right down in my great-grandfather's chair, propped his shiny leather shoes on the desk, and engaged the ambitious man in conversation.

"I climbed that smokestack as a girl," my mother would tell my younger brothers and me, leaving out the rest of the details we never thought to ask for. Our graceful, gracious mother was once a tomboy! This seemed impossible. "In high school, probably," she tells me when I ask her about it now, adding that she remembers nothing at all about the climb, except that she's sure she wasn't alone. She is, I know now, terrified of heights, and even as kids who saw our parents as indomitable, I'd look with doubt at the iron ladder bolted the length of the 190-foot stack. Certainly one had a view of Lake Superior from that tower. "Could we—"

"Oh I'm sure it's much too deteriorated by now."

．　．　．

I drove through town, past my great-uncle's old store, the small white church where I'd sat next to my grandmother for many Saturday-evening masses, and the tavern where my grandparents used to pop in for a nightcap once in a while, and then back out of the Lake Superior side of town. I glanced down the turnoff for Squaw Beach, where the big lake is relatively quieted in one of its few natural bays, and where we had a bonfire each August. "Later," I thought. Ditches of "swamp marigolds," as my grandfather calls the brilliant yellow flowers the books name "marsh marigolds," made me wish my purpose was more playful.

Certain the neighbors wouldn't be there—they almost never were, even in summer—I pulled into their driveway, a dirt two-track nearly identical to ours, closing the space between me and my goal to a hundred feet of birch, spruce, fir, and oak; ferns, wild lily-of-the-valley, *Clintonia* lilies; and windswept late-afternoon light. The roaring south wind swept all the down-state relatives into my mind, even as I tried to put them out of it. Most of them wouldn't approve of my errand, except for David of course, who would have driven straight up the driveway and knocked on the door. I liked to think my brothers would have cheered me on, perhaps even my mom and dad. I almost wished I'd brought some reinforcements with me. For better or worse, I was left to my own devices.

I can be a bold person, especially in conversation, but when a time for risky action is at hand, I hold back. I sat in the front seat, breathing the stale air of the car and listening to the wind. Had decades really passed since I'd taken my Barbies on wilderness expeditions in those woods? Since I'd rushed out to the outhouse and back during nights so black everything beyond the glow of the cabin's windows disappeared?

Once upon a time, arrivals here went like this:

I'd jump from the book-cluttered nest I made in the back seat, not quite out of reach of my noisy restless brothers, who tumbled out the back, board games and comic books sliding out with them. The trees would close over my head as I raced up the short slope to the Lake Independence bluff top. My sneakered feet would kick up moss and acorns, then thunk down the wooden staircase and out to the end of the dock. There I'd gulp the lake air and scan the distant shores—the scatter of cabins looked like toys—for signs of change that came so gradually they were nearly invisible.

The wooden screen doors would have begun slamming, and in moments I'd be back collecting hugs and kisses from my grandparents. We called the converted cinder-block cabin the "little cottage," to distinguish it from the white cabin on the bluff. Dinner would be waiting in the little cottage, the kettle full of water pumped by hand and warmed on the stove for dishwashing. The sound of that hand pump rattling, and of the large old kettle clunking against the burner punctuated all of the days and nights of those summer weeks when I felt freer than anywhere. We bathed a couple of times in the lake. We let our clothes get dirty, and put them on again the next day anyway. My grandmother braided my hair into neat French braids that stayed out of my way all day. And she was a tireless and uncomplaining housekeeper and cook. All of which gave me—and my mother too, I hope—a break from pretty much any drudgery whatsoever. And woe betide the unlucky little boy who tried to push our grandmother's buttons the way they pushed our mother's. We were all a little afraid of her, I think; but for me it was a relief to have my advocate in charge.

♦ ♦ ♦

I pushed the car door open and fresh north-woods air, warmed by the southern wind, rushed in. It took me several trips to pile all my supplies under the ferns behind the little cottage. I approached the kitchen door first: locked. Hunched in the blasting wind, I pressed my forehead against the window, drew deep breaths, and tried to subdue jitters. The kettle, large as an old-fashioned milk bucket and bearing the same sort of wire and wood handle, was exactly where I'd expected it to be, directly across from the door on the old white stove, back left burner. I pictured my mother, asking carefully, as she and her sisters helped their mother clean up the cabin one last time, "May I take the kettle? I've brought one to replace it." My grandmother wouldn't hear of it. The cabins were listed as for sale *with all furnishings except a few valuable antiques.* The kettle would stay with the cabin. I noticed that the sideboard which I coveted, and which would in fact end up in my dining room, had already been moved, probably to my grandparents' basement in Marquette. There was an arbitrariness to this giving and keeping that made me confused and sad. My eyes wandered over to the old iron hand pump with its faded red paint, silenced at the edge of the white ceramic sink. I could see my grandmother at fifty—dark-haired, tiny, and powerful—vigorously pumping: one, two, three heaves to fill the kettle, for dishes and washing up before bed.

Under my feet lay the worn rag rug I'd watched her shake a hundred times. She'd pause and call to me as I raced from the lake to the outhouse, "You'd better go before you find you've already went." It wasn't until I entered the front door's screened porch and encountered my grandfather's work gloves, the curves of his fingers preserved in the worn gray canvas, that I was almost knocked to my knees by grief. From atop the heap of kindling he'd left for the new owners in the old willow basket, I picked one glove up, then set it back.

But the front door was locked. My grandfather's weathered wooden ladder, propped on its side along the outside of the cottage, reminded me that the loft window had never been lockable. I propped the ladder against the wall and climbed—giddy with triumph—to the loft window. It wouldn't budge. Someone had screwed a thin piece of wood between the lock and the sash, perhaps my grandfather, suspecting exactly the sort of stunt I was trying to pull now.

All the windows were locked tightly. I peered into each with a sinking heart. Seeing the care with which my grandparents had closed things up filled me with tenderness and yearning. But they'd left our belongings! Coasters, crocheted long ago by church ladies, awaited the hot coffees and cold beers of strangers. Our old rotary phone would ring for new ears. Our fireplace tools would poke other people's fires, and of course our kettle would warm gallon after gallon of water for somebody else's cleanups.

Around back, I rooted through my supplies, tossing around break-in ideas and feeling pretty much out of my league. The first-floor windows seemed to be the best bet. I chose one around back, above the narrow bed with the painted iron foot and headboards that I'd slept in once I'd grown too adolescent to share the loft with my brothers. I examined the window lock—such a simple gizmo, really. All I had to do was figure out a way to rotate it out of its catch. I decided to drill a biggish hole through the sash and insert a curved hanger. I'd be able to maneuver the lock that way. I watched with mild horror as a little stream of paint chips and wood dust dropped onto the bed.

I pictured my grandparents, not an hour away, whom I hadn't seen in half a year. I missed them terribly, and now that I'd damaged the window, I wouldn't be able to stop and visit. I fought off a wave of guilt and anguish, held the drill steady till I'd made a hole, then began poking around with the hanger.

Dusk was falling. I was hungry and cold, and worried about what I couldn't hear because of the wind, which continued to roar. I thought of my car parked brazenly in the neighbor's yard. I thought of my parents, my brothers. I thought of Dave. They all felt much too far away. I couldn't angle the hanger the way I needed to. I considered breaking a window, but the thought made me queasy and sad. Perhaps I didn't want the kettle nearly as much as I thought I did.

I wandered the yard, cutting a roll of beautiful white birch bark from a tree on the bluff and tucking it into my pocket. For a while, I sat at the base of the old wooden staircase to the water, letting the cold waves soak my shoes. Lake Independence was whipped into a white-capped frenzy. Steady wind across open water can be one of the most agitating natural forces, literally bone-chilling. The futility of my errand was becoming unavoidable. It wasn't that I didn't want the gloves, or the kettle, or the fireplace tools; it was that I wanted everything and everyone back the way they were, back the way they could not be again. I knew as I sat there, in a way that I could not know from five hundred miles away, that the cottages were lost, that anything I took would be diminished by the act of separating it from this place.

To assure myself I'd left nothing that would incriminate me—and to put off leaving just a while longer—I walked the grounds one more time. Even in the golden twilight, the place looked much more worn out that I'd ever have described it from memory. I blew a parting kiss and slipped back through the woods to the car. The wind had not let up for a moment; perhaps it was a message to me: the time wasn't right. I like to think I will return and try again.

I turned off at Squaw Beach, stopping in a turnaround at the edge of Lake Superior to dig a clump of the forget-me-nots I'd promised Dave from the forest behind the beach. It was much quieter there than it had been on Independence—Superior dark blue and heaving, but relatively calm near shore, the northern sky darkening to a dusky lavender. As I pushed aside a soggy clump of last year's leaves and plunged the spade into loamy black soil that probably hadn't been disturbed in half a century or more, I took deep breaths of air fragrant with cedar and rot. The plant bloomed for the season in our sandy yard, then self-seeded for a few more. This year we found no forget-me-nots in our yard at all, but the roll of birch paper rests on my desktop, no longer bright white, but still beautiful, a reminder that I am a child of the north woods, Gracie and Kennie Goldsworthy's firstborn granddaughter.

Reflections from
a Concrete Shore

Donna Seaman

I sat and cried in the glare of the black-and-white television, frightened
and confused by hectic images of helmeted Chicago police viciously
beating and dragging away antiwar demonstrators. As a girl growing up in
Poughkeepsie, New York, that violence, abuse of power, and display of hatred
were all that I knew of Chicago, and it was enough to convince me that it was
a place to avoid. Yet a decade later, after attending art school elsewhere in the
Midwest, I loaded up a rental truck with my modest belongings and, accompanied by a big black and white cat, drove into that mean town, that checker-
board city, determined to make it my new home.

By some strange chance, I first visited Chicago on December 20, 1976, the
very day Mayor Richard J. Daley, the despot responsible for the bloody con-
frontations during the 1968 Democratic Convention, died. I caught my first
glimpse of Lake Michigan from the car as we blustered our way through heavy
traffic in the fast-falling winter twilight. The tall, hard-edged buildings of the
Loop stood like ranks of robotic volcanoes, spewing out great billowing,
wind-twisted exhalations, and the lake looked like the surface of a distant
planet, Neptune perhaps, its metallic skin heaving as viscous vapors seethed
into the splinteringly cold air. It was a harsh and menacing sight, brittle and
spiky, possibly toxic. But it was eerily beautiful, too, an enigmatic and provoca-
tive face-off between the human-made and the wild.

I returned for better or worse two years later in October, a far more hospitable month overseen by enameled blue skies and festooned with golden leaves. My boyfriend and I found a decent apartment in Lakeview, then a scruffy neighborhood well off the gentrification radar, now an upscale enclave. I have a terrible sense of direction and a propensity for getting lost, but even I learned that everything in Chicago is oriented toward the east because that's where the great Lake Michigan lives and breathes, the glorious protector of the horizon, the sparkling barrier to sprawl, its urban shore a place for contemplation. Find the lake and you find your way.

Our modest three-flat with its contorted front-yard apple tree stood less than twenty blocks from Belmont Harbor, an inlet where boat owners dock their cabin cruisers, speedboats, and yachts during the all-too-brief ice-free seasons. The marina is set within the city's precious greenway, Lincoln Park, a slender and much used strip of open land that stretches all the way from Grand Avenue—a half-dozen blocks north of the Chicago River and not far from Madison Street, Chicago's Mason-Dixon line—on to Bryn Mawr Avenue, where the city gathers itself up for one last dash north before the smug suburbs lay claim to the shiny lake.

These nearly seven miles of heavily used lakeshore are embellished with bicycle and running paths, playgrounds, parking lots, ball fields, a golf course, a yacht club, a U.S. military reservation, a conservatory, a zoo, a zoo farm, two ponds, sandy beaches, picnic tables, two spiral jetties, and at the northern end, until very recently, huge stone blocks creating a giant-step staircase reaching down into the swirling water. Over the years, the battering lake rounded and pitted, tilted and gapped the great quarried stones until the old revetment, or protective barrier, no longer performed its task of corralling the lake. It was dismantled and removed, and in its place stand acres of concrete in the form of hard-edged, sterile, gargantuan, futuristically Romanesque steps. The stark new revetment turns the lakefront into an arena, with step sitters forming a complacent audience critically observing every passerby. And yet quiet spots can still be found, and the shore remains a cherished site for sitting and staring out at the great inland sea. A place to put things into perspective, to turn your back on the clamoring city and try to imagine the hushed, swaying deep of the cold, clear lake, and the time before man and machine ringed the noble body of water with fire, iron, steel, concrete, brick, and glass.

Chicago's now prized and protected lakefront is utterly man-made, and a bit of a miracle given its neglected state just over a century ago. Late nineteenth-century photographs of the city's shore record an atrociously cluttered industrial wasteland, an endless scrap heap lapped by filthy water. Fortunately, the more visionary of the rude city's citizenry recognized this as an abomination and took action by rallying behind the Chicago Plan of 1909, which called for a massive cleanup and ambitious reconstruction. Landfill was trucked in and installed at a steady pace between the two world wars, while the Lakefront Ordinance of 1919 ensured that Chicago's shoreline would remain free of commercial and industrial sites, and accessible to everyone. This remarkable urban refuge remains the city's saving grace.

Within weeks of becoming a Chicagoan, I acquired the sanity-saving habit of lakeshore walking. During the colder, cloudier months, the lakefront is blissfully empty, visited only by the most fit and the most melancholy. But whenever the sun is out and the temperature is safely above freezing, streams of joggers, bicyclists, dog and baby walkers, and roaming groups of flashing-eyed young men and preening young women promenade. Everyone checks out everyone else, and my impulse to walk briskly and deflect intrusive stares, or meet them with my own, conflicts with my desire to linger and gaze out over the water, absorbing its shimmer and swell, dazzle and gleam, moodiness and mystery.

Lake Michigan's palette extends from the dullest of grays to the most radiant of jades, the deepest royal blues, and the most resplendent turquoises. Its surface can lie like beaten lead, glimmer and swell like molten silver, or ruffle and puff, crease and crinkle like the silk of a fallen parachute. The winds can lift delicate, winking whitecaps, or storms can induce the ordinarily placid lake to churn and heave, throwing itself furiously against stone, cement, and sand in fully cresting electric-green waves. When the lake is wild it mocks its containment, reminding city dwellers of its colossal size and might, its ability to smash, flood, and devour; then, when the winds die down and gravity reasserts its insistent influence, the chastened lake turns gray and sullen, sloshing disconsolately in its stone-rimmed bowl, peevish and perturbed until the sun once again rekindles its countless gold-spangled dimples, or the full moon paints an iridescent path from the solid shore to the dreamy horizon.

I go to the lake seeking solitude and communion with lake and sky. And I'm often moved to scribble descriptions of the scene in small notebooks. But humans, like all animals, are compelled to enact courtship rituals, and the urban lakefront, like any seashore strutted upon by assorted birds, or pressed beneath the bulk of sea otters or seals, is the scene of compulsive spring and summer mating displays. Males and females alike flock to the lake when temperatures rise, and remove as much clothing as is legally permissible. Some perform athletic feats; others choose a more subtle approach, stretching out on the sun-warmed stone to be admired in carefully arranged angles of repose. Not in the market for a mate, I practice various subterfuges to thwart unwanted advances. I pretend to be deaf, or not to speak English, or to be a bit crazy; or, weary of playing defense, I lie elaborately when asked my name and other particulars, and then become intrigued by the odd life of my fictional alter ego.

I was lucky to find work just north of the Loop in the neighborhood that pays tribute to the Great Lakes with streets and avenues named Ontario, Erie, Michigan, Huron, and Superior, and I soon established the practice of taking lunchtime lake walks. For years my beat has been the shore between Oak Street Beach and Ohio Street Beach, which lies just over a mile to the south. Oak Street Beach is the city's most glamorous, with its backdrop of aristocratic Gold Coast high-rises. Here the rich and cosmetically correct come out to play, although their turf is infiltrated by headphone-wearing, Rollerblading college students, nannies and their chubby little charges, addled tourists, and office escapees.

While others sunbathe, romp, chat with friends, or eat, I walk and stare out into the distance, casting my print-weary, office-constricted gaze as far as it can reach. I soak up sunlight, the caress of breeze or pull of wind, the mineral smell of the water mixing with that of the warm sand and asphalt and the taint of exhaust, as the surging and snatched-away sounds of traffic, music, talk, shouts, and the thrum of bicycle and skate wheels coalesce into a jittery soundtrack.

I enjoy the curve and slight rise and fall of the shore just south of Oak Street Beach, a rare stretch of sensual terrain in an otherwise relentlessly flat, right-angled place. Here the shore has a notched edge, worn cement encased in thick rusted steel that presses like a dull saw blade into the clear water. I lean over to look at the sandy, stone-strewn bottom, hoping to see fish and not garbage, and see neither. I decide to sit at the edge and choose a spot from which I can see the breakwater, one of two long and narrow angled slabs that interrupt and scatter the march of waves before they reach the susceptible shore and the water-filtration plant at Ohio Street. This breakwater, the closer and smaller of the two, points to one of seven water-intake cribs that asterisk the coast like floating brick mansions. On the outside or the north face of the breakwater, the lake curls and foams and dashes itself repeatedly against the cement bulwark, feral and insistent. Within the rigid arm's embrace, however, the calm water gleams like glass, mirroring the sky. I relish the contrast, seeing it as emblematic of the division between the tumult of thought and feeling, and a cool and collected demeanor.

LAKE NOTES

July 12, 2001

It's a perfect summer day, cooling down slowly in the lengthening afternoon shadows like a freshly baked pie on a windowsill. The great lake is relaxed and resplendent, deeply turquoise, silky, gently breathing, rippling and dimpling, somehow sweet and expectant. The horizon is drawn with startling precision—a straight edge, an exact division between sky and water absolutely certain in its designation.

The well-off are frolicking in sailboats, and a motorboat pulls a water skier. People on more prosaic errands race their cars in close proximity on congested and sinuous Lake Shore Drive. To the west, all is hard and gritty, brick and metal, hustle and hurry. To the east, the wind teases the sashaying lake, lifting bits of white like lace from its coy surface.

July 26, 2001

Today, large clumps of lakeweed float near the concrete and iron shoreline, plants torn up from the lake floor by violent storms. Mother ducks have brought their sleek little ducklings to feast on the slimy bounty. One has five plump babies; another has ten tiny ones swimming anxiously behind her, bobbing nervously on little choppy waves. Can they all be hers, or is she baby-sitting? A daycare duck? There's trash mixed in with the lakeweed—paper, plastic, foil. Further on, a lone female duck feeds and floats in contented solitude. Has she convinced her sister to watch her children so that she can enjoy some time to herself? Or is she a rogue female, childless like me?

The wind nicks the choppy waves, leaving gouges of white. People are swimming further out than before; the water must be warming up. A posse of trim cops-on-bikes confer, suited up in regulation blue shirts, shorts, and helmets. I'm walking north after crossing beneath the Drive at Chicago Avenue, and when I reach the beach, the sound of the surf swells and my heart lifts. The teasing summer winds have taunted and riled the usually lulled and meditative lake, turning it loud and marauding, and it churns in a frenzy of crisscrossing collisions of incoming and outgoing waves. I'm reminded of a magical day on the spiral jetty near Montrose Harbor. It was autumn, and cold with a rampaging north wind, and the lake was rushing the jetty like a herd of galloping horses, their white manes streaming behind them, their proud chests and heads and pounding legs surging along the cement curve, snorting and sending up great plumes of spray. I stood in the mist and roar, my own heart pounding, and thought of Neptune riding high on a chariot pulled by great broad-chested horses of the sea.

Back to the present, where the muscled and fashionable are stripped down and arranged on the cement as languidly as though they were lounging on upholstery. Others are not so relaxed, and they sit fully clothed in the hot sun, stiff, hunched, preoccupied, some with headsets fuzzing out the call of the lake, others with eyes cast down, denying themselves the radiance of the scene. I think about video monitors mounted in SUVs, conduits for pop culture that yank the attention of children away from the great outdoors, away from nature. Are these devices preparing them for a future when there really won't be anything worth looking at outside a vehicle's windows?

It's already like that in the city's dreary outback. There, mile after mile of farmland has been transformed into franchised suburbs where retail and fast-food chains—and chains they are, shackling us to the corporate imperative—line the automobile-dense, stoplight-studded, multilane streets. One town blends into the next, with only the names painted on humongous water towers offering any sign of former discrete settlements. If we continue to cut down forests and pave farmlands and wetlands, meadows and foothills, driving myriad plant and animal species into extinction, nature too will become chained and dull. What appalling loss looms before us? Human beings are persistently optimistic and adaptable creatures, and no doubt future generations will find beauty in their world, however contrived and limited it may be. Yet, unbridled optimism is what gets us into trouble.

Four bullet-like planes fly over the lake in tight formation, their pilots practicing for the annual air show, the annual display of military might. Each summer, good citizens mass along the lakeshore by the hundreds of thousands, standing beneath the broiling sun and craning their necks to look up at flying, spying, and killing machines that cost far more than most states spend on educating and caring for people, and burn massive amounts of fossil fuels, filling the air with tyrannical noise.

August 3, 2001

Today the lake is breathing quietly beneath a fog that hazes the sun, blurs clouds. The horizon is smudged. A cool breeze stirs the still clinging dampness and carries a potpourri of smells both northern and tropical. The haze is like a sluggish state of mind, those impenetrable hours when you can't think, know nothing, and don't care. Hungry, tired, and blue, I'm sitting in the wrought-iron-fenced playground that dots the exclamation point of the straight-shot park that connects the Museum of Contemporary Art and Lake Shore Drive. Old skyscrapers I can no longer picture have been torn down across Pearson Street, and now huge dinosaur-like robots forage in the pit, their jaws crammed with debris. There's grinding and clanking and drilling and thunking as water is pumped onto the scene in a feeble attempt to keep the dust down. The traffic is heavy, the cacophony dunning. The sun is behind me, and so shadows dance before me—shimmying leaves and quivering branches— and my hair, sticky from the lake's moist exhalation, twirls and whips snakelike across my lap, hands, the page. The news is biblical this season, full of floods and huge forest fires and a plague of bark beetles devouring pine trees. I feel abraded, choked, obliterated.

September 10, 2001

It's a perfect day, sunny and clear, yet this curve of city lakefront is all but empty. It's a week after Labor Day, the summer's last hurrah, and suddenly everyone's serious again, back inside at desk and counter. Even the ducks and gulls seem to have gone back to work and school. Even the wind is elsewhere occupied. The party is over, but I'm still here, watching. The surface of the water is mesh-like today, a cellular membrane. It looks conscious, respiratory.

September 12, 2001. The day after.

A police boat rushes over to intercept a small pleasure craft, and, I assume, guide it away from the water-filtration plant. The Coast Guard is out too, monitoring the shore; the air force is patrolling the sky. Shaken and teary-eyed,

I stare at Chicago's great towers, John Hancock, Sears, with trepidation. Suddenly everything seems so precious, so vulnerable and fragile.

October 18, 2001

Has it really been over a month since I sat here last, since I last visited this great lake? The leaves on the trees are gold, the sun low down even at noon, the wind long-traveling and insistent, bringing news of the cold to come. Earlier, before the wind grew strong, jet trails angled sharply in the sky, forming a pair of protractors taking celestial measurements. Now, clouds and lake are roughed up, uneasy. The traffic is extremely loud, aggressive, devouring. Very few people are out on foot. A ladybug is fastened to a broken bit of pavement, weathering the wind in the sun. Rebar is exposed in the crumbling cement step on which I perch. A fringe of fluorescent green crabgrass waves from a crack between the step and the flat asphalt.

No boats of any kind are in sight. White gulls are flying so high they look dark against the clouds. A plane swims past like a barracuda. I walk to the beach and see that it is rimmed like a dirty tub with dark green mulchy weeds. Small transparent waves smash into the iron and cement wall. The sand further north is wet and pocked. The light refracted within the neat, orderly inland waves is iridescent against the startling white of carelessly discarded Styrofoam cups. Gulls stride about, plucking food from the wrack; some ride on the water, bobbing gently. A white man, tanned nut brown by a summer in the sun and wearing brief black swimming trunks, walks in the shallow, edge water, windmilling his arms as though he were swimming. His hair as white as the gull's feathers. Ladybugs are bristly when they fly, spiked and seed-like. Hillocks of sand newly delivered to combat the brutal beach-consuming winds and waves of winter stand like miniature mountain ranges, a shrunken Afghanistan landscape.

November 6, 2001

I wish the clarity of today's sky was reflected in my head, where the weather is far more turbulent and overcast. The light is pristine, stained-glass-window bright and redeeming. I've walked south today along the ruler edge of the cement shelf. The lake is very low. I walk along the small sandy beach tucked between the shore and the jut of the peninsula on which the water-filtration plant stands. I continue on to the little park which memorializes the great Chicago humanitarian and social-reform activist, Jane Addams, who was awarded the Nobel Peace Prize in 1931, the first American woman to be so honored. The earth has been scooped out to form a nest, a bowl-like sanctuary brimming with grasses and rose bushes, on which tiny red blossoms still cling. The grasses are tasseled, silken, mauve, gold, white, green, glistening and rustling. The reeds are still supple and elegant.

The gentle, grassy declivity holds a set of sculptures by another remarkable woman, Louise Bourgeois. Six rough-surfaced, gently carved, charcoal-dark stone pedestals, modest in height, stand among the grasses. One displays a child's hand, another the hand of a young woman, another supports two strong clasped hands; on another, four mighty hands are gripped together, the forearms forming an "X." Each sculpture is beautifully modeled and gleaming black. This is "Helping Hands," and a plaque offers a quote from Jane Addams that elucidates Bourgeois's vision: "Perhaps nothing is so fraught with significance as the human hand." The instrument of love and cruelty.

The Jane Addams Memorial Park and sculpture garden is one of Chicago's most refined spots, a respectful, sheltering, and peaceful place. A sanctuary in honor of a founder and president of the Women's Peace Party. But we are at war, as is much of the world.

And when I stroll back to the beach to admire the lake, which is veined with ripples, gilded with sun, a fine gold net floating in satiny deep blue, the serenity of the scene is abruptly shattered by the darting arrival of an ugly red helicopter. It hovers, slashing the air and growling. Directly beneath it, a self-indulgent, angry man demands attention by ripping the water's delicate meshed surface with a monstrous red Jet Ski, a shrieking, nasty, gas-guzzling, poison-spewing toy. As this decadent man in his clinging wetsuit spins and lurches about like a hyperactive boy playing cowboy, his bucking machine looks like a huge cock, his frenzy both masturbatory and rape-like. I stand and stare, rocked by my boiling blood, until I finally force myself to walk unsteadily away, unexpressed anger painting spots before my hardened eyes.

November 19, 2001

It's been deliriously and inappropriately warm for the season. Morning fog burns off by ten A.M. to reveal a blooming blue sky, but the sun is so low, the shadows of the buildings block out great dark blue rectangles of the breeze-frilled lake. The air is vapory, the horizon soft, blurry, and to the north the skyline is rendered in powdery pastels. The only creatures I see are humans on wheels. The scant and determined trees are bare and heartbreakingly beautiful in their arabesque arcings. Calligraphic, they cast the graceful script of a lost language against the muted sky.

◆　◆　◆

I will keep walking east to the lake, seeking the radiance of nature and being confronted with the handiwork of humanity. There's no separating the two. Linked to its four great sisters to form the largest fresh surface-water system on Earth, Lake Michigan, the glorious, life-sustaining creation of glaciers a mere seven to nine thousand years ago, is vital and evolving. Chicago—brash, bristling, and greedy—is also young and in perpetual flux, and utterly depend-ent on the majestic, patient, shining, living sea along which it percolates. Fresh water, essential to life, has become a rare and contested commodity on a pol-luted and crowded planet. Lake Michigan, like all watery realms, nourishes us body and soul, and by doing so, becomes vulnerable to our abuse. Life is a process of give and take, a grand and complicated balancing act; but our will-ful and perverse, creative and destructive species disregards this dynamic, feel-ing free to indulge its mysterious and potentially catastrophic fascination with risk, upset, and extremes. Shore walkers and lake watchers must be vigilant, protective, and appreciative to counterbalance those who see the Great Lakes as dumps or playgrounds, rather than as entities that are as close to divine as human beings are ever likely to experience.

The Least Thing

STEPHANIE MILLS

ne summer day, as I mounted my bicycle after a swim at the nearby lake, I asked a little boy who was seining for minnows if he would put them back, thinking that he might just be catching them to get a closer look. "No," he replied brightly, "we use them for fishing bait." I said nothing but pedaled off, fantasizing some uninvited taboo-tossing pedagogy, starting with "Only take as many as you need. If there aren't enough little fish left in the lake to grow up, then in a year or so there won't be any big fish to catch and eat." Then a pathetic fallacy: "Try to imagine that those little fish—the fishes' kids—have feelings just like yours." Further research, however, disclosed that minnows aren't juveniles but are small grownups. Even if, despite being a deep-ecological spinster, I am nonetheless a member of the village that it takes to raise a child, it was just as well that I spared that child my misinformed sermonette. Besides, fishers can be natural historians and waterside contemplatives par excellence.

My salvific vision is that if everyone could experience some joyous, muscle-powered liberty of the body and fascinating fraternity with nature, then faster, noisier, fossil-fueled modes of engaging the world would fall away. This is perilously close to saying, "What a grand world it would be if everyone could just be like me"—not the everyday real me, of course, but the idealized me-projection. The moment I needed something practical, like the services of a good mechanic or a week's groceries, and came to find out that everyone who had hitherto been doing their jobs within the getting and spending paradigm had seen the light and wandered off to muse on the butterflies and the minnows, the flaw in my nature-epiphany fantasy would materialize.

As I bicycled home through the short, dim tunnel of broad-leaved trees that shades the dirt road, one red-spotted purple butterfly caught my eye, fanning its wings as it rested on the damp, packed earth. Then another butterfly, dancing in the brighter space where the lake road meets the pavement, delighted me too. I felt more affiliation with these insects, and with whatever warbler was singing up in the green canopy, felt happier to be in their company, than I ever feel about sharing the lakeside with a gaggle of humanity—local moms, dads, and little boys seining minnows, all of us refreshing ourselves in our various ways at the water's edge.

The reader may have noted a tinge of misanthropy to this epicurean. Unless those humans happen to be field biologists, modern novelists, or organic farmers, it's creatures other than her fellow humans that enjoy her highest regard. In my pagan philosophy, nature is not the problem; culture is the problem. A culture that would understand and disavow humanity's imperialism in nature could be quite an improvement for all concerned.

Just as Epicurus could not conceive of a good that excluded the pleasures afforded by the senses, I can't conceive of a good that does not include some engagement with wild beings in free nature. Wonder is our erotic affiliation with all of life. If we develop this, enjoy it, and follow its promptings, our wants will be fewer and needs plainer. "Those who contemplate the beauty of earth," said Rachel Carson, "will find reserves of strength that will endure as long as life lasts."

For human beings to "live unknown," or not more known than the thrashers and monarchs and hylae might be a workable search image. The creativity of Malcolm Wells—whose underground architecture envisions handsome, contemporary settlements designed so that the soil isn't buried under our shelters, but shelters us and can still host green life—comes to mind, as does John Todd's invention of solar-powered water-purification systems that bring together novel but native aquatic ecosystems—the "Living Machines" of Ocean Arks International—to treat municipal sewage or to restore degraded water bodies biologically rather than chemically. These individuals and hundreds of other ecological designers and "bioneers" are sensitive apprentices to the magic maker and don't seek to be Faustian magi.

Because they are tangles of interacting forces, all the scenarios are shifting fast. Climate change ramifies throughout systems; so does the introduction of exotic species and of hormone-disrupting chemicals. Biologists speak of "cascades" of extinctions, for no species is an island. Even running over a squirrel in Anytown, U.S.A., means there's one less tree planter at work. Now that these big, systemic derangements are becoming more evident, I discover that I, too, have been in denial; I hadn't anticipated immersion in the big system-crashing consequences—not here, not yet. But in the summer of 1999, for the first time, there were wads of algae rocking under Lake Michigan's waves on the rippled, sandy bottom of Whaleback Bay.

Lake Michigan is oligotrophic—big, young, and cold, without much aquatic plant life. Ordinarily, there's no conspicuous lake weed. By the mid-twentieth century, the lake's ecosystem had been revolutionized by the invasion of parasitic sea lampreys, which led to the virtual demise of the lake trout, thus eliminating the predator that might have kept the eruptions of another oceanic invader, a little fish called the alewife, in check. Now alewives, ill-adapted to freshwater life, proliferate wildly in the lake, but die en masse, littering the beaches by decomposing millions.

That beach at Whaleback Bay was one of the stops on the whirlwind tour of the splendors of the county (my friend) Phil conducted in honor of my initial visit in the summer of 1984. How novel to me and lovely it was to drive to a beach through a hardwood forest. There were groves of white cedars along the creek that flows into the bay, as well as oaks, maples, birches, and beeches. Thick by the edge of the dirt road were wild roses, grapes, and alders. Willow thickets make a portal to the foredunes, with their blowing fringes of beach grass. All this opened out to miles of pale, sandy beach and clear water. Coming from California, from the Pacific Rim, I hadn't realized that Lake Michigan is a freshwater sea. I certainly couldn't believe that such a beautiful beach could exist and not be completely aswarm with beachgoers.

It became my birthday custom to visit Whaleback Bay for a ceremonial swim. In mid-September 1995, it was a loner's day at the beach. There were only two other people in the whole expanse—a brilliant blue sky, turquoise waters deepening to ultramarine, a clean beach, the constant sound of waves, sunlight and warmth, and high, fine moiré clouds. I walked a long way south on the beach for the sheer, dumb pleasure of feeling myself walk.

Eventually, I stopped walking and went for a swim. The water was cold, but not heart-stopping. As I swam, I savored the lake's transparency and the clean, tawny color of the sandy bottom, looked through the water, seeing shapes, and looked landward to the long, sweeping curve of the beach, the pale, windswept whips of beach grass, the brooding, raw silhouettes of the white pines, and the lush hardwood foliage on the headlands.

By the 1980s, Lake Michigan's waters had received enough pesticides, including atrazine gone airborne and carried north from farmlands in the Mississippi River Valley, and enough chlorinated hydrocarbons, polychlorinated biphenyls (PCBs), dioxin, and other hormone-mimicking compounds to cause fish-eating waterfowl, such as cormorants and gulls, to produce deformed offspring or exhibit hermaphrodism. Fish-eating humans were being advised to limit their intake of Great Lakes fish.

The lake I met for the first time in 1984 was far from pristine, but for years after that, having swum in Lake Michigan, I could catch a whiff of the mineral freshness of clear water rather than of rotten alewives in my wet hair. This recent algae bloom was attributable to the siphoning activity of billions of zebra mussels. These invasive, exotic mollusks had arrived in the Great Lakes via some oceangoing freighter's Baltic bilge water only in 1987. The zebra-mussel plague cleans the water too much, reducing the lake's turbidity so dramatically that more sunlight penetrates, fostering certain kinds of algal growth.

The degradation of this inland sea has progressed from alewife infestation to bioaccumulation of toxic chemicals to pond slime in only a few years. Those clouds of algae in Whaleback Bay made blatant that there's no place to run, no place to hide, no "away" to get to. There's no natural feature too large to ruin.

Privately, quite a few of my fellow ecocentrics believe that the fight for the wild, for the health of the biosphere, is lost. The degradation of the land, oceans, and atmosphere is so widespread and acute that its momentum, they say, is unstoppable. What is interesting is the fact that we mostly believe that it behooves us to belie our gut sense of futility when we aren't talking only among ourselves. None of us plan to give up trying to accomplish our valiant ecological aims, to stop the extinction cascades, to save the wild, and to restore and reinhabit our life places. If we can get past the staggering practical, moral, and aesthetic implications of extinction's finality, then perhaps we can get on with the business of doing something Ecozoic with what remains. But the weeping is unavoidable.

In *The Heat Is On*, his book about global warming, Ross Gelbspan relates the following story:

> In January 1995, a vast section of ice the size of Rhode Island broke off the Larsen ice shelf in Antarctica.
>
> Dr. Rodolfo Del Valle, an Argentine scientist who witnessed the disintegration of the ice shelves [while] flying 6000 feet overhead in a light plane . . . saw that the ice shelf, up to 1000 feet thick in places, was beginning to break up into smaller icebergs . . . [Del Valle said.] "The first thing I did was cry."

The paradox is that even though I cannot realistically foresee a future that doesn't appall me, the present still abounds in simple pleasures. However dismal the outlook, how could one fail to enjoy such once-ordinary, now-scarce phenomena as sweet, crisp air, soaking summer rains, and fireflies blinking in the swamp? For the past four billion years, this planet has been churning out the wonders: bacteria, nucleated cells, diatoms, jellyfish, slime molds, ruby-throated hummingbirds, goldfish, tiger moths, shield-shaped beetles sporting the colors of an okra blossom, tamaracks, sturgeons, and thirteen-lined ground squirrels. Natural phenomena, with their implicit beauty, their grandeur, and their proportion, could, by any measure meaningful to us ephemera, be regarded as infinite.

Some of this sense of nature's infinitude lies within the beholder. Ronald Reagan infamously declared that if you'd seen one redwood, you'd seen them all. Visionary urbanite William Blake, on the other hand, suggested: "To see a world in a grain of sand / And a heaven in a wild flower, / Hold infinity in the palm of your hand / and eternity in an hour."

Although there is an ethical imperative for humanity to desist from any further destruction of nature, my concern for the earth's ecology is epicurean also, motivated by a pleasure that is not so small and slender. Some days, that curiosity about life as it manifests in the five kingdoms of biology is the Eros keeping me alive.

Thanatos and Eros have some relevance here: The death wish of civilization, its all-too-successful antipathy to wild nature, is producing circumstances—ecological breakdown—that would seem to justify a personal wish not to live on into a prosthetic future in which nature is weedy, domesticated, manipulated, and monotonous, and artifacts dominate existence. There's an awful tension between the desire to witness and understand as much as I can of what philosopher David Abram felicitously terms "more-than-human nature" and the horror of the daily earth rape perpetrated by bulldozers, chain saws, pesticides, and all the vast armament of progress.

Despair is not a particularly respectable condition, yet despair and delight alternate like systole and diastole in my heart. Throughout my life, there have been moments when depression or despair have laid me so low that I've contemplated taking my own life, as my neighbor finally did. I've been helped to decide to continue living by friends, therapists, fellowships, and pharmacy. Were it not for my existential alliance with the larger life, none of this help would have availed.

Sometimes in the murk of a dark night of the soul, when I am desperate for a glimmer of a reason for being, I catechize myself: What if you could never hear another crow or never watch another caterpillar? What if you were never to see another snowfall or eat another apple? Would you want an end to those experiences?

One July morning a few years ago, I got out of bed and took a mug of tea onto the back deck to sit and sip in the full sun. I watched a scruffy, voluble chickadee busy itself in one of the cherry trees. A female hummingbird visited the feeder, making a big noise coming and going. On the beat-up locust shrub that has volunteered right next to the porch, I noticed half a dozen different kinds of insects, among them a lovely little black wasp with a dash of vermilion on her abdomen, some coral-colored aphid-like critters, and a lime green katydid-like animal casting a sharp, linear shadow. As ever, I felt a sense of community with all these remarkable beings. Their insides are real. They are individuals with real lives and important business in this world. Some of them pair off. A lot of them look after their young. Surely they, too, feel a sense of release when the sun returns to warm things up and dry things out after a few days of slashing rainstorms.

I took off my nightshirt and sat there palely naked as the next animal. With the sunlight on my skin and the good air to enfold us, I felt that I was in the body of my Mother, very much a part of the earth's living tissue.

There is a sense in which it matters not what may come. A life alert to simple pleasures, with perception cultivated and attuned to beauty, and a large capacity for friendship can serve us well come what may, be it Ecotopia, corporate fascism, or Armageddon. Whatever befalls, it behooves us to honor the moment by savoring what there is: light and shadow, bitter and sweet, harsh and tender, fragrant and foul, lyric and discord.

· If we cultivate our delight in and gratitude for the least thing—a drink of water, a night's rest, the sight of a blue jay—we cultivate the life strong within us and enliven possibility itself. Although I fancy being a nun in a contemplative order with a membership of one, I sense that learning the limits of having, remembering the nature of true pleasure, and becoming the change I wish in the world involve finding a way to talk with that kid catching minnows, and, more important, to listen to him.

Amphibians, Reptiles, and Boats: Excerpts from a Naturalist's Lake Huron Journals

Aleta Karstad

15 September 1983

My husband Fred, our daughter Elsa, and I had lunch on Doctor Island off the northern tip of the Bruce Peninsula after he gathered a little more negative information about there being any reptiles or amphibians at all on the island. It may perhaps have been logged for steamship fuel in the 1930s, which would have dried up the earthworm population. No worms for salamanders to eat, and no worms or salamanders for snakes to eat. Fred did hear one *Hyla crucifer* peeping.

I heard a Pileated Woodpecker, a Red-breasted Nuthatch, and a Peeper while I was drawing the pitted limestone shoreline of Griffin Cove on Russell Island, the island on the far side of Doctor Island from Tobermory. Elsa discovered echoes with her voice and dabbled in the water beside the canoe while Fred explored the lowland around the north side of the cove, finding one young Water Snake and a number of medium-sized Green Frogs. I helped to record their measurements, and Elsa helped to release them before we left. As we paddled out of the cove, Elsa recognized which island was Bears Rump, having had it pointed out to her the other day. We stopped once on the broad north side of Russell, and Fred walked through the woods to the wetland interior. By the time I had regained my equilibrium enough to feel like painting one of the lovely miniature crater gardens in the rocky shore, Fred was back with one Green Frog and no *Plethodon* (salamander) sighting. (He had found one *Plethodon* on the island in July.) We scraped the aluminum canoe through the shallows by the little island off the northwest corner and into a bay on the west side. The swells were quite impressive, and the waves seemed to push us in, although the water was not choppy at all.

Elsa was getting quite tired by then, and so I laid her down on the floater jackets in the canoe and went into the woods to look for salamanders; but instead of falling asleep, Elsa bumped her head while chasing a fly and called me back out. I brought two kinds of small droppings—Rabbit, and young Porcupine or fawn—and a small sample of the lovely pale, almost bluish-green moss that grows in tight, rounded clumps, perhaps associated with wood or bark. The *Potentilla* leaves were also very silvery-haired and silky. Their stolons were long on the rocks by the water.

We paddled leisurely home to Tobermory with a slight breeze at our backs, into a nearly glassy Little Tug Harbour. We passed close to the ferry *Chi-Cheemaun*, "big canoe" in Ojibwa, where it was docked for the night. Its big flat hull was like the wall of a tall building. There was some water pouring from its side above the waterline, and Elsa said that it was making this water deeper and deeper. It keeps an engine running and lights on all night and its hooked beak of a bow lifted open, to fit at the dock. It is said to be the fastest boat on the Great Lakes. A double-masted schooner was in harbor too, and we paddled down to see it—a black hull with red and white stripes along it, and plenty of natural wood and polished brass above deck. It looked like a real museum piece. The people on board were talking about peeling potatoes and pitching wash water over the side—just like us in our Behemoth at a campsite.

We slipped quietly back to our dock, over one of the wrecks that countless divers come many miles and use great wealth of equipment to see. Our friend John says they're engaged in "diver macho," and he calls them "Knights of Neptune." In this clear water, the old deck timbers and hull ribs were as clear to see as through a glass-bottomed boat. John was at the dock to call us in for supper—cheese and cauliflower soufflé, and cobs of corn. John and I have made up a verse to Stan Rogers's tune "Make and Break Harbour":

CHORUS:
In Little Tug Harbour the boats are so few,
So many have gone back to Toronto.
Now it's September,

The shops are all closed.
There's nobody left to spend money.
VERSE:
The thermocline's down
Past the wrecks in the bay,
The divers are swarming like mudpout.
We steer round the buoys, the floats and the flags,
Where they kick up their flukes in the harbour.

19 SEPTEMBER 1983

We're using John's boat now, as he has given Fred instructions and a trial run. Fred, Elsa, and I went out in it for the first time yesterday. It is a fourteen-foot aluminum "Springbok," a plane-bottomed boat with a small outboard motor. We towed the canoe part of the way to Cove Island and then had to bring it close alongside because it was swinging dangerously from side to side and beginning to tip and fill with water. The wind was crossing the direction of the swells, so the waves seemed to come from all directions. Fred counted some *Plethodon* in LaRonde Harbour, and a Canada Parks boat came up and asked us how we were doing. I asked them if the water would likely get worse, and they radioed in to ask, and answered, yes, would we like them to accompany us back right away? which was done. It was quite exciting. The swells were so high that at times the Parks boat disappeared from view. Not unusual water for these parts, or very dangerous for most of the craft here, but for a small open aluminum boat, "sporting"—as John terms it.

So, having seen Fred handle the boat quite well in water that he will do his best to avoid, I felt perfectly confident about his trip out alone today to Cove, Williscroft, and Harbour Islands, using the canoe for poking about while there.

Elsa and I locked the dogs in the Behemoth and walked to town, finding some sunny Herb Robert to paint, growing from the rock face along the dock, and then went to get something to eat. We took my bird heads (watercolors of White-throated Sparrow, Downy Woodpecker, and Brown Thrasher) to Ben at Circle Arts to see what he would think of them. Wanda had lent him her copy of my book, and he had ideas of promoting me, not just as some artist who was "passing through," but as "artist-author." He liked the bird heads. When I first dropped in on him a couple of days ago, to show him the Herb Robert painting and my journal, I found a very fine gallery full of beautifully crafted pottery and dyed and woven goods, and the work of only two painters—pretty exclusive, and Ben gave me to understand it as such. He did not want to show and sell an artist who would be here today and gone tomorrow. So I was very pleased to return today to find that he had been thinking of me, and how I could fit into his way of doing things. I had mentioned before that if Fred were to get a summer-long contract to study the fauna of the Bruce Peninsula for Parks next summer, we would locate in Tobermory, and I thought that I would be able to afford to be quite productive. Ben mentioned today that the office of the Bruce Trail Association was just upstairs from the gallery, and the nature buffs who often pass through his shop would be pleased to find a local nature artist of good quality. I responded, after only a little thought, that if it were to be that lucrative it would be well worth my while to spend a month or more of each summer painting on "The Bruce." It's an open market, as there seems to be no one else here who does birds, wildflowers, and suchlike.

So I had that to think about, and Elsa to tell me stories from her imagination as we perched on the rocks and I drew and began to paint my second miniature of Herb Robert, until Fred chugged by to moor the boat after a productive afternoon "out."

20 SEPTEMBER 1983

Cepaea nemoralis snails all over the place here, except on the Tobermory Islands. Walking back to the truck from the docks this warm, rainy evening, we found them, like carelessly hidden yellow-striped Easter eggs, in the woody areas beside the road.

It has been windy today, and Fred did not go out in the boat. Elsa and I went back to my current Herb Robert painting site and found that after last night's rain, the rocky overhang was dripping water all over our perching area. Elsa stayed in the sunshine on the dock, and I found a way to protect myself from the drips. The limestone background was wet anyway, and had changed from light and speckled, with delicate shadows in the pits, to dark and shiny. We watched a man set up a sailboard and then be blown about the harbor on it.

On our way back to camp, we found another painting subject. On the rocky slope near the cement stairway from the dock to the road, I noticed a *Cepaea* snail high up in a dry flower head of Tansy. It was sleeping—not fully retracted, but sealed in "snailaphane," with a pinprick of a hole in the clear, stretched shield marking where the pneumostome was. The leaves of the Tansy were curled and nearly dry, but still greenish, the whole thing a study in browns and thin curved lines: the rigid, slight curves of the plant's stem and flower "branches," and the snail's thin, spiraled stripes. I cut the stem and took it back to the van to paint in safety from weather in a controlled environment.

By late afternoon, the sky was just right for a watercolor sketch that I would like to do of a boat that is being welded together out of sheets of rusty steel at the icehouse dock on this side of the mouth of the harbor. Just around the dull red wooden corner of the building there, this rust-tinged shell of a boat sits on its keel, blocked and chained against a grey lake and sky. All its lines are so lovely and curved, even those of the wheelhouse, which has just recently had window holes cut in it. It will be a diving and salvage boat. I'd like every boat to be a fishing boat, but that's not all of what goes on around here. The busiest of the few fishing boats here are "Turtlebacks"—strange, closed-in, at first unlovely-looking shapes. They are nearly bullet-shaped with closed-in foredecks, only the windows of the wheelhouse breaking the profile of the top shell. John explains that the fishing boats of the Great Lakes do not need a high, curved bow like oceangoing boats. Here, sailors have developed a protection from the rare but devastating fifteen-foot waves caused when two trains of swells come up each side of the peninsula then collide, or some such phenomenon. This is the shape of the *Dyker Lass*, the biggest boat in the harbor. We watched it come in and unload its catch of whitefish yesterday, the crew of three in a jubilant mood.

22 SEPTEMBER 1983

On the night of 20 September, we found snakes on the road instead of all the salamanders of a few nights before. The air was colder, and there were few frogs, a very few salamanders and efts. There must have been a lot of snake movement during the day, however, as Fred, walking along in the lights of the creeping Behemoth, picked up a milk snake, two DeKay Snakes, an Eastern Garter Snake, an Eastern Smooth Green snake, and a Massassauga Rattlesnake, all dead on the road.

I spent most of yesterday doing a quick colored-ink sketch of a snake that has turned out to be a painting. It was a small *Sistrurus* (rattlesnake)—hard to see all the scales. I had a couple of hours left to work on the *Cepaea* painting before dark, and got many little flower heads done as well. Fred spent another day *not* exploring the Tobermory Islands, due to wind and rough water, but kept busy preserving his road-hunting specimens and measuring salamanders from Cove Island.

Last night, during sporadically driving rain and cold wind, Fred walked about Tobermory looking for amphibian activity on the roads—too cold. He did come back with more *Agaricus* mushrooms. He and Elsa have been finding them at the interface of pavement and sand at the edges of roads. Fred cooked some of them with eggs for breakfast this morning, then packed to go to Cove Island. Rain had been gusting at the front of the cabin all night, but the sky and water seemed much calmer before he left. Elsa and I, sitting on the little deck in front of John's place, watched Fred pull out of the harbor. The sky was clearing, the wind picking up and blowing the tops of the waves to whitecaps. I tried to attract Fred's attention before he picked up speed past the ferry dock, to discuss the risk of the trip, but he opened throttle. The nose of the boat went way up against the wind, and off he went toward Cove Island.

We walked up to the Parks Canada Office to ask them about the weather and water, and whether they would be sending a boat out today. It began to blow hard and hail while we were in the office. They suggested that I phone the Coast Guard, who would better know the water conditions. They were concerned that Fred was in a small aluminum boat, and were further alarmed that he did not have any visible orange with him, or a radio—and he is diabetic. So the Coast Guard decided to take a cruise out to Cove Island. John could have warned Fred not to go out, as he had been up and listening to the weather before Fred left, but he figured that we wouldn't consider it, and we hadn't thought to see whether he was up and ask!

John and I watched the Coast Guard vessel through binoculars and saw them put out a raft, which we later learned they used to go into the Gut on Williscroft Island, where they found Fred sitting in the boat and measuring salamanders—a first for Spotted Salamanders on Williscroft. The Coast Guard was quite cheerful about it all and happy to notify me by phone that Fred had arrived safely. And he arrived back at 5:30 P.M. safely, too, with the wind at his back, after a cold and windy day on Cove, where he had even used a single paddle to sail and steer in the air.

Hunting and Fishing

MARY BLOCKSMA

*E*xtensive wetlands at the west side of Lake Erie block me from the shore. At last I have discovered some Lake Erie wilds—thousands of acres of wetlands smack on the track of migratory flyways, alive with wings, singing, snakes, flowers, and water-loving plants.

Along the road to Crane Creek State Park, an area flanked on one side by Magee Marsh Wildlife Area (hunting in season) and on the other by the Ottawa National Wildlife Refuge (no hunting), I observe egrets, herons, and flocks of ducks, and brake for families of Canadian geese crossing the puddle road. Inside a lovely beam-and-glass building, I discover nine huge glass cases crammed with beautifully mounted birds, from an astonishing assortment of tiny warblers and songbirds to hawks, owls, eagles, ducks, and other water birds.

"This area is one of the richest places in the Midwest for birds," a ranger tells me. "We've had over three hundred species sighted here—as many as a hundred in one day! Ducks come in from the middle to the end of March, songbirds in May—our biggest day is Mother's Day weekend, when all the Audubon people come here." I mention that Audubon shot many of his subjects so they would hold still for him, but the ranger assures me that these birds were all found dead or injured beyond recovery.

It was probably the decoy display and gun collection that inspired that comment. I suddenly realize that western Lake Erie is not just a great place to sight water birds, it's also a great place to shoot them. Hunters and fishermen are

Mary Blocksma

among the eccentric few who have not in the past treated wetlands as wastelands and can probably be thanked for the small percentage that have not been drained and filled. It's the destruction and pollution of habitat, not hunting, that accounts for the decline in waterfowl populations, hunters often insist. Many acres of these remaining wetlands were once owned and kept at considerable effort and expense by hunters' clubs, for the purpose of raising, attracting, and killing ".game" fish, "game" birds, and "game" animals. The "gaming" priority is still a big one—clear from the name of this building, which, although housing the Crane Creek Wildlife Experiment Station ("Ohio's center for the study of wetland wildlife"), is called the Sportsmen Migratory Bird Center.

Hunters, whose donations and license fees finance the rehabilitation of many waterfowl-attracting areas, often have no time for "bleeding hearts," who are in turn appalled at those who take pleasure from taking life. So it seems odd to me that such a place caters to bird watchers, even providing for them a beautiful beachside boardwalk over the wetlands, which, during a brief respite from the rain, I explore, feeling as if I were walking through treetops. Tiny wings flit everywhere, dripping and bedraggled—flycatchers, warblers, sparrows. When the rain resumes, I dash for the van, parked overlooking the mile-long beach where sometimes twenty thousand people play. Today I see only two, a girl and a boy, swimming and kissing in the rain.

◆   ◆   ◆

In contrast to the rich wildlife areas, the nearby Maumee State Park camping area resembles a suburban-mall parking lot—flat out in the open, no sheltering trees, no view of the lake. The campground is just the beginning, the ranger assures me, showing me a map that makes the place look like a plush resort. There are big plans for a major recreational area.

"End of April, beginning of May, when the walleyes spawn on the Maumee River, thousands of fishermen come here," he tells me. "You can't believe—these guys line the river, in all kinds of weather. Sometimes they fight when their lines get tangled up, or they get picked up by a ranger—you aren't allowed to snag a fish [hook its body with an unbaited hook], you can only catch him by the mouth. If you snag one, they can take your car and take you to jail and all kinds of things, so it's kind of a unique place. People come all the way from Texas to go fishing here."

"Do you fish?"

◆ 220

"Not really. I don't have time, and Lake Erie is a dangerous lake. Storms blow up real fast. You get these big rolling waves, twenty, thirty feet high. Or ten-footers close together. Guys go out in these little boats and some of them die out there. I had a friend got caught in a storm and never made it back." Speaking of storms, he tells me, there's a tornado warning out tonight—about twenty funnels have been sighted in Illinois and Indiana, and the storm is heading this way.

The sky looks okay now, so I drive through a lot of country to a lakeshore restaurant he recommends called Sonny's Bay Shore Supper Club, where Sonny Berry himself tends bar, treating me to a sidecar, then a brandy Alexander made with ice cream, claiming, "There's very little alcohol in that one—it's for a short person." Then, as he washes glasses, he says, "This area was a swamp years ago. Wasn't really that much to it. Then they drained the swamp and they cut down the trees and stuff."

"Was that an improvement?"

"Not really. But it is what they call progress. Civilization. It had to happen. No way could we live like they did a hundred years ago. We got two atomic energy plants now—one right across the lake at Monroe, another up the road. Some people come back, they'd never recognize the area."

The restaurant is very crowded, although it seems to me located a healthy drive from any town. Sonny talks while he works. "This place used to be a dance hall. During Prohibition, when the mob ran booze across the lake from Canada, that"—he points a dish towel at a table against the wall—"is where all the gangsters sat. If we took our paneling down, you could see bullet holes."

Back at the park, amid scattered RVs, I watch the storm, my view unblocked by anything taller than a trailer. Lightning, horizontal and vertical, shatters the sky; thunder crashes; rain drums on the roof; the wind tears through the park like a train come alive, screaming and rocking the van. My battery-run radio reports damage here, damage there. I move the van to a site next to the concrete washrooms, the only available shelter, then sit in the back, upright, tense as a cat in a boat, listening to storm warnings and terrible music until three o'clock in the morning.

◆ ◆ ◆

I turn north into Michigan, where more wetlands block the shore. Then, at Sterling State Park, Michigan's only Lake Erie state park, I park near a narrow gravel beach flanked by a coal-burning power plant on one side and a nuclear power plant on the other. The view is so uninspiring that I eat my lunch in the driver's seat, not bothering to get out, until two things change my mind: first, a guidebook propped on the steering wheel informs me that this nearly thousand-acre park has an excellent wetlands trail, and second, I see two killdeer mating at the edge of the parking lot. Wow!

I set off in a cloud of gnats, clutching a trail map, binoculars around my neck, bird book in my back pocket. Soon I encounter an educational display, which declares that "a wetland is not just a wetland." I learn about five kinds of wetlands and some things I didn't know about the American lotus, the adopted symbol of Lake Erie wetlands revitalization: it has seeds that can take ten years to germinate, leaves that grow three feet, and flowers, served up at summer's end, as big as dinner plates.

Along the two-mile-or-more trail, I am entertained by a Baltimore oriole's liquid song, a woodchuck dashing across my path, a muskrat slipping into the lagoon. I am dive-bombed by a blackbird. Cotton from cottonwood trees drifts through the air. It's just turning into a nice little hike when I pass under sizzling power lines coming from the power plant. I climb a wildlife observation tower and find myself directly under fourteen power lines, slung between a series of towers straight out of *Star Wars.* Electricity crackles and spits, buzzing deep in my guts. Surely, I think, an observer, standing at some distance, can see my bones. Below me, all manner of birds flit, spawning carp slap the lagoon, pale lavender fleabane blooms, and a bluebird shares a tree with a yellow warbler.

Back on the trail, I cut through woods along a dirty-looking channel under arching branches. Mosquitoes whine, dine on the softest part of my neck. Birds sing against a far-off hum of factories, jets, power lines, and trains. A chipping sparrow, chestnut head nodding, hops importantly in front of me. I observe a blue heron, an egret, a long-haired young man aiming an arrow into the lagoon. *Zing!* He pulls in a huge carp, yanks out the arrow, slings the carp into the grass, aims again with a powerful-looking weapon strung with lines and pulleys.

"What do you do with the fish?" I ask him.

"Throw 'em over there."

"Do you come here often?"

"Two, three times a day." The carp, bleeding from large holes on either side, wriggles back into the water. The boy shrugs. "Won't live long," he says.

Back at the office, I'm told that shooting carp with a power bow is perfectly legal. Some towns, like Caseville on Lake Huron, even celebrate it with an annual festival.

Note: I became confused about wetlands—everything I read seemed to type them differently. One source divided wetlands into wet meadows (mushy, but without much standing water), wooded wetlands (waterlogged only during certain seasons), coastal marshes (with aquatic plant communities surviving various water depths and conditions), shrub wetlands/marshes (with a few inches to a few feet of water), and bogs (depressions filled with decayed vegetation and standing water). Another source, pointing out that coastal wetlands are affected by wave action and changing water levels, divided them into "zones" similar to the first descriptions but not quite the same. A poster from the Michigan Department of Natural Resources admits that its categories— marsh (flooded grassland), swamp (flooded woodland), and bog (depression filled with decayed vegetation, acidic soil, and standing water)—are vastly oversimplified. I also encountered other descriptive words like "swale," "fen," "strand," "wet meadow," "seasonal wetland," "permanent wetland," "aquatic wetland," "riverine," "delta," "unrestricted bay," "shallow sloping," "pond wetlands," "sedge meadow."

Much of the confusion is due to the fact that until recently, few of us even knew the term "wetland." Those who did tended to be sports persons, or naturalists who described the different areas in terms of their specialties—plants, freshwater ecology, soil, and so on. Then, about twenty-five years ago, the sharp decrease in many bird populations and the polluted condition of the Great Lakes began to alarm everyone. Even the government realized that without wetlands, the Great Lakes couldn't be saved. Wetlands probably produce more wildlife than any other Great Lakes habitat and are also necessary to help clean pollutants from streams and rivers before the water enters the lakes.

Unfortunately, two-thirds of the original Great Lakes wetlands and three-quarters of Michigan's have vanished, most of them drained, filled, and "civilized." Saving wetlands has become a big issue. During the 1970s and 1980s, both federal and state laws were passed protecting our few remaining wetlands. It suddenly became very important to a wide variety of ordinary folks to know exactly what defines a wetland. Could a retiring auto worker build a retirement home on that sometimes soggy piece of real estate bought twenty years ago? Could a farmer sow winter wheat in a dry depression that became a pond in spring? The sport and scientific terms were not clear enough. Legal definitions and very particular descriptions of various wetlands were needed. Today, it's politics that influences those definitions most.

◆　◆　◆

At the Point Mouillée State Game Area, I discover an unusual attempt to actually build a wetland. "This marsh wouldn't exist without the dikes here," Rex Ainslee, game area manager, tells me. "We're restoring the marsh as best we can." Working with over half of the area's four thousand acres, the U.S. Army Corps of Engineers and the Michigan Department of Natural Resources are cooperating to manipulate water levels and provide vegetation to attract waterfowl, "which is our main objective." Let us not forget, Rex Ainslee reminds me, that this project is paid for by hunters, who are taxed for licenses, guns, ammunition, and other sports equipment.

Outside, I find two men on a tractor on their way to plant corn, millet, and buckwheat for the birds. One of them guesses that this might be the largest project of its kind in the world. "First, they're building a dike here"—he points to a place on a map. "Second, they're putting a dam and a pumping station across Mouillée Creek. Then they're going to divert the water to come back out at the lake down here."

"Woodchucks dig holes through the dikes," observes the second man dryly.

Well, no one said it'd be easy. Building a marsh must be like replacing a rain forest—close to impossible.

Down the Drain

Janet Kauffman

*T*he stream on my farm, St. Joseph Creek, meanders through rich flood-plains with cardinal flower, joe-pye weed, stands of old beeches, and understory colonies of pawpaws, leafed for the tropics. Pawpaws bear a custardy fruit, the Michigan banana, in early October. The fruits hang singly or in pairs high up in the trees. They're not easy to see, with skin that's leaf-green and smooth as your own skin. But when you spot a few up there, picking's a party. In that tangle of prickly ash and wild grapevines, you designate somebody as spotter, then shake the slender pawpaw trunks. If the fruits are ripe, they fall with a *thub, thub*, and the spotter nabs them.

The flesh is so soft, we carry spoons to the woods, slice open the pawpaws, and scoop the bright yellow mush right there. It tastes dreamy—aromatic and floral, musk at the edges—as if it had dropped somehow from a jungle canopy or cloud forest, a taste of Trinidad.

But this is Michigan, and the St. Joseph Creek flows east to join Bean Creek, which heads south to Ohio, into the Maumee River for the last wide stretch to Lake Erie.

• • •

They say in Michigan you're never more than six miles from a lake or stream. Where I live in southern Michigan, you're also never more than six miles from a Confined Animal Feeding Operation—a livestock factory. We've got a dozen of these factory operations—some with hogs, but most of them here are dairies, with thousands of cows confined year-round.

Ten thousand cows—you can picture it—produce a huge waste stream. And it's *literally* a stream. The animal waste is liquefied with clean groundwater and pumped to lagoons, holding pits the size of small lakes.

Here, I'm never more than six miles from a manure lagoon.

Milk production at livestock factories may be high-tech, but the tail-end system is as low-tech and old-fashioned as it gets. The waste is so liquid, it's often pumped through irrigation systems and sprayed onto crops. Or it's hauled in tankers to fields and sprayed on the ground.

In open farmland, that's country life these days: particulate emissions, earthmovers, dredging equipment, sand mining (for cow stalls), fly infestations, twenty-four-hour lights and noise. Industrial livestock operations are hard-core agricultural sprawl.

◆ ◆ ◆

Not far upstream from my farm, about five miles away, a slope in the woods is the drainage divide that shapes the headwaters of the St. Joseph Creek. Several springs contribute clear water along the way. The creek winds through woods, falls through cobble and gravel runs, cuts a wider swath through acres of marshland, and then drops and takes S-turns through the beech woods of my farm, before opening into flatter farmland downstream.

Nobody's built a livestock factory upstream from my farm, or dumped liquid manure on fields there—yet. Just downstream, though, it's another story.

◆ ◆ ◆

Since the first livestock factory was constructed here in 1997, the operations have had pollution problems. The pit-and-pump system contaminates water coming and going, from the barns to the pits, and that's just the beginning of it. To see the worst, when liquid manure is sprayed on fields, you have to get down in the ditches. You have to know what's happening underground.

Buried under farm fields throughout the Great Lakes basin is a complex network, estimated at *millions of miles*, of drainage pipes called "tiles." Agricultural tiles drain away rainwater; that's their purpose. But they also carry farmland pollution direct to streams. Out of sight, subsurface drainage is agriculture's dirty secret.

Here in southern Michigan, nineteenth-century settlers found forest and swamp. To stake their homestead claims, these settlers did two things: they cleared the trees, and they drained the water. You can't farm in forest. And you sure can't farm in mud, wet peat, black muck, bog, cattails, and hit-and-miss mire. Some parcels, like mine, had drier upland ground, glacial moraines, and gravel heaps, but every slope had a downside, a sidehill seep, a bottomland wetland.

The land was drained by dredging streams, trenching ditches, and burying the water. Pipes were laid in long narrow trenches, creating underground tributaries. The word *tiles* comes from the early use of foot-long clay sections of pipe, manufactured in the brickworks of many small towns. Tiles were hauled by the millions into fields. The clay tile pipes were laid end to end, with a slight space between them, in trenches below the plow line. These days, farmers use perforated plastic tile, laid in grids, laser-sighted downslope. Water percolates through the soil, down to the gaps between the tiles or through its perforations.

• • •

St. Joseph Creek is a natural stream. In Michigan that means you can't legally dredge it, and you can't bury it. But many streams flowing through flatter land—the ancient lakebeds of Michigan and Ohio, the Black Swamp south of here—were designated as "drains" in the late 1800s, giving farmers the right to channelize them and to dredge them. Field tiles jut out into these ditches at regular intervals, every thirty feet or every sixty feet, pouring the field-drained water into the drains. Drains which are streams. Tributaries of the Great Lakes.

• • •

Every few weeks for the last two years, I've been out in the ditches, monitoring the water. I drop the probe of a dissolved-oxygen meter into the stream for a digital readout; Kathy in her babushka, or another volunteer, extends a long-handled grabber with a sterile bottle attached and scoops out a water sample for bacterial testing.

Like many others, I got into watershed watch-dogging after a massive manure "spill" in March 2000. Millions of gallons of polluted water flowed into Lake Hudson, a nearby state park. I joined a grass-roots organization in Hudson: Environmentally Concerned Citizens of South Central Michigan (ECCSCM), a group that advocates for responsible agriculture. We set up a monitoring project, and for two years sent our test results to the Michigan Department of Environmental Quality, to county health departments, and to any legislator who'd listen.

Many politicians would rather not hear about pollution from farms, from factory farms. Industrial agriculture proclaims its conservation ethic; livestock producers say, "Heavens, we wouldn't pollute our own land, our own livelihood." And off the farm, who wants to give up that dream of green pastures and grazing animals for a nightmare vision of confinement buildings and manure pits?

But if farmers don't pollute, the liquid waste sure does. It rains black on fields from tanker haulers. It seeps through soils to tiles and to streams.

Look in the ditches. Look below the surface. When liquid waste is sprayed on fields, it flows over the surface of the land and into the streams and ditches that feed the Great Lakes.

People around here keep an eye on the ditches and call up Lynn, another ECCSCM volunteer, when they smell foul water or see discoloration in the streams. Lynn drives her pickup around the livestock facilities several times a week, checking drains and streams. She takes photos of brown water, green water, black water—we've seen it all. When pollution flows, we try to get bacteria samples before everything's gone downstream.

◆ ◆ ◆

In April, the American brook lampreys, like small silvery eels, spawn in the rippling place where I set a bench, for listening to the best stream sounds. Out of the gravel substrate, the lampreys surface after four to seven years in larval form. Living just a few days as adults, they spawn in these stretches of cold water, twining in clusters and twisting as their bodies exert tremendous effort, latching onto pebbles with their sucker mouths, moving the stones to make a nest.

Slippershell, fatmucket, ellipse, squawfoot, rainbow, pocketbook, fingernail, spike, giant floater, elephant ear—at least ten species of freshwater mussels live in the sandy holes and cobble runs of St. Joseph Creek. I find empty shells on the shore where raccoons have feasted. If I put on my rubber boots and walk up the stream, I can see the live ones, with shells slightly open, siphoning and filtering water.

Mussels, native freshwater lampreys, mottled sculpin, darters, water pennies, stoneflies—they all need cool, clear, and unpolluted water to survive. The mussels cannot relocate if the water is fouled. The American brook lampreys live where they hatch, only those graveled and rippling neighborhoods.

♦ ♦ ♦

In cities, storm water usually drains underground through one set of pipes, and human waste flows through a separate sewer system to treatment plants. "Combined" sewers have been a serious municipal problem in the past, causing flooding and overflows contaminated with human waste.

But agriculture has largely ignored its own combined—and continuous— sewer contributions to waterways.

Most fields in this part of Michigan, about 80 percent of them, are drained with subsurface tiles. The first thing the big dairies did here was bring in equipment to retile the fields where liquid manure would be sprayed. These new grids drain water and wastes even more quickly, more completely, than the old tiles.

The Michigan Department of Environmental Quality recently found *E. coli* bacteria counts in a drain downstream from a livestock facility at 7,600,000 per 100 ml—that's 7,600 times the acceptable level.

The DEQ confirmed 120 water-quality violations between the years 2000 and 2005 from the livestock factories in this area, including the Bean Creek Watershed. Almost every citation notes the illegal discharge of animal wastes through tiles to streams.

Some manure haulers plug tile outlets with inflatable devices to halt the flow; but sooner or later, it rains or thaws, and they have to pull the plugs. The pollutants flow. Neighbors call it "plug-and-play."

♦ ♦ ♦

Toad Creek is a stream through farmland, like St. Joseph Creek, another tributary of the Bean. It's in flatter territory, a designated drain, and the official drain map calls it Blanchard Joint County Drain. When I first saw Toad Creek three years ago, it was a clear stream, with plenty of toads, fish, and mussel shells strewn on the sandbars. Shrubs along the banks gave some shade and shelter for wildlife. Since then, two big dairy operations have been spraying liquid manure in the vicinity. Drain work was done, removing the vegetation—"cleaning" the drain. And in March of this year, thousands of gallons of liquid manure were sprayed on a field, on frozen ground. Within hours, the contaminated waste ran off the field, down a drain inlet, and reached Toad Creek through the underground plumbing. The liquid manure poured out a pipe onto the ice of snow-dusted, frozen Toad Creek. It flowed on the ice for days, a black stream.

Through May and June, Toad Creek was often grayish, with scum floating along the banks. The dissolved-oxygen levels registered well below Michigan's water-quality standard of 5 mg/L, which means aquatic life is at risk, especially the mussels with their one-foot grip of the streambed, unable to swim away or seek out new habitat. I haven't seen a mussel in the stream, or a shell on the stream bank, all summer.

•   •   •

Across the country, agriculture now contributes more pollution to lakes and streams than any other industry.

No wonder. The problem is overwhelming. Here in the Midwest, the web of unmapped tiles delivers contaminated liquids to streams and to rivers. Some field tile systems are new, some a hundred years old, with fixes from every generation along the way. Tile outlets to streams may be far off a farmer's property.

In many soils, wormholes—more than you'd think—and macropores, large cracks in glacial soils, are direct pathways, like straws, to subsurface tiles. Liquids can move from the surface to tile pipelines at incredible speed, sometimes in just a few minutes.

•   •   •

In the 1960s, Lake Erie was declared dead; the Cuyahoga River caught fire. Lake Erie is the shallowest Great Lake, and especially vulnerable to pollution. With the Clean Water Act of 1972, Lake Erie was brought back to life, with actions to stop industrial pollution. Agricultural practices were also improved, and new tillage practices like "no-till" cut back on surface runoff of fertilizers.

But *subsurface* drainage, and the pollution pouring through tiles, was not addressed.

Now in Lake Erie, where our streams flow, a new dead zone is forming. Areas of low dissolved oxygen—like the widely reported dead zone in the Gulf of Mexico—are one consequence of pollutants from liquid manure and fertilizer nutrients, which spur algal growth. Decaying organic materials, consumed by bacteria, deplete the dissolved oxygen that aquatic species need to survive.

The systemic pollution from livestock factories and the dead zone in Lake Erie have raised loud alarms—finally—about tile drainage. Knowing what we know, it's time to phase out liquid/lagoon systems. Instead of trying to stop liquid animal waste from flowing, with stop-gap measures in the field, livestock production must change the system and dry up. Like other industries, livestock factories should be required to treat their waste. There are plenty of industrial models for dry systems of waste-handling: liquid/solid separation with screens or screw presses, and wastewater treatment. It's not a huge leap; agriculture doesn't have to reinvent the wheel.

Better yet, livestock operations could downsize to farm size. Get lean and green. Taxpayer subsidies still help build multimillion-gallon lagoons and help purchase liquid-manure sprayers. We're paying up front for pollution of our streams. And we'll pay for a long time, cleaning them up. It can't happen soon enough—the end of agricultural welfare as we know it. It makes sense to support community-based agricultural systems that enrich rural areas, protect the water, and restore soils. Rotational grazing, with winter composting, brings benefits to agricultural communities, instead of the harms and health risks that have come with livestock factories. It makes sense to return cows to pasture, where dry manure decays and enriches soil.

. . .

In the shade of sycamores, beeches, maples, nannyberry, witch hazel, ironwood, and buttonbush, the St. Joseph Creek stays cool. The roots of the trees hold the soil. The leaves fall in the water, and caddisfly larvae attach there, or they stick scraps of leaf on their bodies and crawl the streambed in camouflage. Stoneflies and dragonfly larvae congregate under rocks, part of the complex web of living and dying and feasting.

When I'm in the water, that's what I think—I'm in the water. I'm by and of and for the water. It's my democracy.

Homeland and habitat, every watershed is worth protecting. Water's in our blood, it's our lifeline, and it binds us. To stoneflies and stones, to rotting leaves and cooking cake.

Every spring, we have a party at the stream when the brook lampreys spawn. We celebrate what they have, while they have it.

Littoral Drift

MARY BLOCKSMA

*L*ast night I pulled into a private campground after dark, slept to the banjo banter of bullfrogs, and pulled out early in pouring rain. A long drive down gravel roads through dripping tunnels of green ends in Conneaut, just over the Ohio line, where I find myself in a magically lovely town park. A creek meanders through undulating lawns canopied by spreading trees and scattered with picnic tables, a pavilion, a playground, mossy nooks. It's large, too, for such a small town, but no one else is here; the sudden appearance of a gnome or a flying cat wouldn't really surprise me. There's even a spacious, if gravelly, beach. Something's drawing me to Conneaut—the lushness, perhaps. It feels different from anywhere else I have been.

I drive along the lakeshore, dense with houses, looking for overnight quarters, but find no motels, no bed-and-breakfast places, only a little cottage declaring itself FOR RENT. I inquire next door and seconds later I am sipping coffee at a kitchen table, admiring the lake view and talking with Margaret "Bunny" Thayer, who fills me in on Township Park.

"When my children were young, we went there every single summer day and stayed for four or five hours," Thayer says. "It's got a mile of beach and it's still free. This town has always given away everything—every time we have any kind of tax levy for Township Park, it passes. On weekends, we get people from Pittsburgh and all over the place. I've suggested we charge a dollar a car, because they sometimes crowd out the townspeople. We are economically depressed, but everything we have that's good here we've always given away."

Maybe that's what I've felt about this place. There's something large-spirited here. I ask, "Do you like living on the lakeshore?"

"I'm addicted to it. My father was in real estate before me, and he used to say, 'Okay, Bunny, if you got to sell a place on the lake, all you got to say is, *Here's your million-dollar view, a panorama that changes every day.*' He was right. I can just sit and stare at the lake all day. People laugh when I say that my favorite time of year is winter. When I lived uptown, I never came down to the lake in winter, but here, I'm in love with the drama. Sometimes the water even freezes in mid-wave. When the lake is frozen, there's no sound; I feel like I'm on the edge of outer space."

I'm sold. I ask if there's an inexpensive house for sale on the lakeshore. Soon we are on our way, in a massive four-wheel-drive vehicle that makes my van feel like a toy, to inspect a charming $39,000 house one foot from a crumbling embankment. Looking down the precipice, I can see where brush and logs have been thrown and small trees planted to try to hold things, but the slender beach at the bottom looks to me a mere snack for a Lake Erie storm: waves will gnaw at the bottom and, well, the rest is gravity. I'm reminded of other narrow Lake Erie beaches I've been seeing, some resembling a war zone, armored with discarded tires, sandbags, riprap, logs, concrete in many shapes and arrangements, railroad ties, and other unattractive attempts to keep the eroding shore from gobbling up homes, industry, recreational facilities, and other structures built disrespectfully close to Mother Nature.

Why the expensive, frustrating effort to poke, prod, and girdle Mother? To developers, she threatens erosion, caused—in addition to effects of wind, water levels, unstable shore materials, human stupidity and greed—by waves. When a wave hits the shore at even a slight angle—waves rarely hit straight on—sand particles are pushed in one direction, resulting in littoral drift, or a river of sand along the shore, and a constantly shifting shoreline. If there is no beach to buffer the waves, or if the waves are particularly large and forceful, they may begin undercutting the bluff, which, particularly if it consists of sand or clay, is likely to fall (collapse), slump (huge chunks of the bank slide downward), or flow with debris (plants, rocks, and other material slip downward), most or all of which eventually ends up on somebody else's beach.

This capricious property shift can drive landowners crazy, but it's meddling that got us into this mess. Early in the 1800s, jetties were built perpendicular to the shore at the mouth of inland shipping routes to keep sand from clogging the entrance, or even to force the river to change course, wreaking even more havoc. As lakeshore property became valued, jetties were followed by a profusion of seawalls [called "piers" when they extend out into the lakes] (built of lumber, stone, or concrete, and often backfilled with anything available—logs, tires, riprap, even old cars), groins (structures of wood, stone, or concrete built, like mini-jetties, perpendicular to the shore), and breakwaters. By 1973, there were 3,600 of these battlements on Ohio's Lake Erie shore alone.

Unfortunately, most of these structures interfere with the littoral drift, and even the experts have not understood the full implications of what even one such interference can do to a neighboring shoreline. A jetty blocks the river of sand, which collects on one side to make a great big beach while the beach on the other side, where the littoral drift begins again but without the normal replenishment, may quickly disappear. Groins may stabilize one family's beach while effectively destroying the neighbor's. Interrupting the natural flow of sand, then, causes more erosion, which brings me to the ludicrous but logical and scientifically supported conclusion that the main cause of erosion on the Great Lakes today is not the natural fury of the lake, but the battle to control it.

"Thanks," I tell Bunny, "but no thanks."

The Forest Pasture

Jane Urquhart

*S*ince the year I was born, I have spent at least some of each summer at a beach on the shores of Lake Ontario between the villages of Brighton and Colborne. In the 1940s, early in their respective marriages, my parents and my aunt and uncle had teamed up to purchase an old two-story cottage at this spot, wanting as young professionals to spend at least part of the year close to parents and siblings who had remained on various farms in Northumberland County. This was not the traditional Ontario cottage with docks, jack pines, and rocks; it had been built at the turn of the century, along with five others of varying design, on lots that had been severed from the acreage of a century farm. The farm, owned by Leslie Rice and his sister Yvonne, was still in good working order by the time I came along.

As children, my cousins and I spent a portion of each summer day swimming in the lake, or when it was calm, floating in rowboats or canoes along its surface. But even more tempting and mysterious than these pleasures were our frequent excursions into the territory at the end of the lane known to us as "Mr. Rice's pasture." Most minds will conjure an image of a large field or meadow when presented with the word pasture, but Mr. Rice's irregularly shaped, rail-fenced grazing area was not like that at all. Open to the sky only at its entrance and exit, it was really a mixed forested area, made easily accessible to children simply because the presence of chewing cattle kept down the underbrush. A vast number of wonderful trees flourished there: maples, oaks, poplars, beech, and rows of dark cedars. Out of the soft, spongy earth grew hundreds of bright green ferns that brushed our bare legs, incredibly sweet raspberries in one or two spots, and the odd surprising, mysterious plant such as jack-in-the-pulpit. And through all this glided the large, serene shapes of beautifully patterned black and white Holsteins.

We made every conceivable kind of fort there: tree forts, ground forts, girls' forts, boys' forts (the latter being regularly raided by the opposite gender). As the summer progressed we became more and more domestic, making furniture from fallen logs or from the old boards and orange crates we removed from my uncle's storeroom. Rusty cutlery and cracked dishes were pressed into service for picnics and parties; treasures were buried and elaborate maps were drawn. Sometimes we invented a mystery, and complicated narratives unfolded when we pretended to be the Hardy Boys or Nancy Drew intent on solving the case.

It was in Mr. Rice's pasture that I learned almost everything I know about how a breeze sounds as it travels through a plethora of summer branches, or how the patterned shadows of leaves move in the company of sunlight on a forest floor. And it is into this pasture that I go in my imagination whenever my characters come across a forest in one of my books.

It is only in my imagination that I can return to the forest pasture now, for although I still spend part of each summer at the same beach, which has remained remarkably unchanged, Mr. Rice's pasture and the hundreds of acres of farmland that surrounded it have literally vanished from the earth, removed as "overburden" by a huge multinational cement company eager to get to the limestone beneath. And so, like far too much of southern Ontario's farmland, my favorite place has become an inner landscape, a terrain that can be visited only in the memory and in the heart.

Notes on the Contributors

Loraine Anderson is photo manager of the *Traverse City Record-Eagle*, where she has worked since 1978, the first six years as a reporter. She sits on the newspaper's editorial board and writes a column for the paper. "The Salmon" appeared there first in a slightly different form and under a different title. Anderson is a 1972 graduate of James Madison College at Michigan State University.

Judith Arcana's poetry and prose are published widely in journals and anthologies. Her books include *Grace Paley's Life Stories, A Literary Biography*, and most recently, a collection of poems and monologues called *What if your mother*. A native of the Great Lakes region, Arcana now lives in the Pacific Northwest.

Rachel Azima is a Ph.D. candidate in English at the University of Wisconsin–Madison, where she studies nature writing. She has received the John Lehman Poetry Award from the Wisconsin Academy of Sciences, Arts and Letters, and her work has appeared in the *Wisconsin Academy Review* and Vassar College's *Asian Quilt*. A Michigander by birth, she currently lives in Madison with her husband, Douglas Beal.

Jackie Bartley's poems have appeared in a number of journals, including *Crab Orchard Review, Gulf Coast*, and *Image*. Her most recent chapbook is "Women

Fresh from Water." *Bloodroot*, a full-length collection, appeared in 2002. She lives just five miles from the Holland beach on Michigan's west coast.

Michele Bergstrom's essay "Superior Sanctuary," from which the passages included here are excerpted, won the Wisconsin Regional Writers Association's 2004 Jade Ring. Her recent article in *PassageMaker Magazine* describes the 3,000-mile journey she undertook with her husband to bring their 35-foot trawler, *Ka-Ching*, home to Wisconsin from Florida via the Atlantic and the Great Lakes. She's retired from restaurant management.

Mary Blocksma has traveled the U.S. shores of all the Great Lakes, where she's become an amateur naturalist prowling their habitats, and learned to paint. Her many books include *The Fourth Coast, Great Lakes Nature, Lake Lover's Year*, and *What's on the Beach?* Two posters of her paintings present Great Lakes magic at a glance. Her websites are www.beaverislandarts.com and www.maryblocksma.com.

Gayle Boss writes, and with her husband is rearing two young sons, in Grand Rapids, Michigan. Her essays and poems have appeared in a variety of publications, including the *Mars Hill Journal* and *Weavings: A Journal of Christian Spirituality*.

Gayle Brandeis is the author of *Fruitflesh: Seeds of Inspiration for Women Who Write* and *The Book of Dead Birds: A Novel*, which won Barbara Kingsolver's Bellwether Prize for Fiction in Support of a Literature of Social Change. Her second novel, *Self Storage*, will be published by Ballantine in 2007. She lives in Riverside, California, with her husband and two children.

Amber Briggs is working towards a master's degree in public administration at Oakland University in Rochester, Michigan. This is her first publication.

Bonnie Jo Campbell is the author of the novel *Q Road*, and the award-winning collection *Women and Other Animals*. Her work explores the lives of women and girls in rural Michigan. She has won the AWP Award for Short Fiction and a Pushcart Prize, and she was named a Barnes & Noble Great New Writer. She writes and trains donkeys in Kalamazoo, Michigan.

Sharon Dilworth is the author of two collections of short stories, *The Long White* and *Woman Drinking Benedictine.* She is an associate professor of English at Carnegie Mellon University, where she also serves as the fiction editor at the Carnegie Mellon University Press. She has recently completed a new novel, *The Cousin in the Backyard,* which examines the intersection of family life and lawn care.

Nancy Dunham is a retired schoolteacher and a freelance writer, editor, and artist. She is currently working with the Ottawa County [Ohio] Historical Society on an oral-history documentary supported by the Ohio Humanities Council. She has lived with her husband on Lake Erie since 1955.

Tracey Easthope is the environmental health director of the Ecology Center, based in Ann Arbor. She has written for many environmental publications.

Beth Ann Fennelly received a 2003 National Endowment for the Arts Award. She's written two books of poetry: *Open House,* winner of the 2001 Kenyon Review Prize for a First Book and the GLCA New Writers Award, and *Tender Hooks.* She has a new collection of essays, *Great With Child.* She is an assistant professor at the University of Mississippi and lives in Oxford, Mississippi.

Susan Firer's fourth book, *The Laugh We Make When We Fall,* won the 2001 Backwaters Prize. Her third, *The Lives of Saints and Everything,* won the Cleveland State University Prize and the Posner Award. Recent work appears in two new anthologies, *Revisiting Frost* and *Sweeping Beauty.*

Linda Nemec Foster is the author of six collections of poetry, including *Living in the Fire Nest* (finalist for the Poets' Prize) and *Amber Necklace From Gdansk* (finalist for the 2003 Ohio Book Award). *Listen to the Landscape,* a collaboration with artist Dianne Carroll Burdick, is forthcoming. Foster lives in Grand Rapids, Michigan, where she is a program coordinator for the Contemporary Writers Series at Aquinas College.

Nancy Garrity, of Chicago, has owned and raced many sailboats in a sport traditionally dominated by men. She is one of a handful of women, among about three hundred captains, who have skippered boats in the annual 330-mile Chicago–Mackinac Island sailboat race.

Gail Griffin was born in Detroit. Her earliest memories involve fresh waters in and around Michigan. She has taught English, creative writing, and women's studies at Kalamazoo College for twenty-eight years. She has written two collections of essays, *Calling* and *Season of the Witch: Border Lines, Marginal Notes*, and her essays, poems, and short nonfiction have appeared in anthologies and journals.

Rasma Haidri's poetry and prose have appeared in many journals, including *Nimrod* and *Prairie Schooner*, and anthologies, most recently *Waking Up American: First Generation Women Reflect on Identity*. She makes her home on the Norwegian Arctic seacoast.

Aleta Karstad was born and grew up in Guelph, Ontario, but lived as a girl in Wisconsin and Georgia as her father studied wildlife pathology. Her formal art training was at Central Technical School, Toronto. Karstad's four books, most recently *A Place to Walk*, are drawn from her illustrated natural-history journals. Since 1995 she has been teaching others to make archival-quality journals.

Laura Kasischke is a lifelong resident of Michigan. She is the author of three novels, most recently, *The Life Before Her Eyes*, and six collections of poetry. Her work has been recognized with numerous honors, including the Pushcart Prize, the Elmer Holmes Bobst Award for Emerging Writers, and fellowships from the Ragdale Foundation, the MacDowell Colony, and the National Endowment for the Arts.

Janet Kauffman lives in Hudson, Michigan, where she has restored wetlands on her farm and works for watershed protection with Environmentally Concerned Citizens of South Central Michigan. Her most recent books include a novella, *Rot*, and a collection of prose poems, *Five on Fiction*.

Jacqueline Kolosov has published poems, nonfiction, and fiction in journals including *Shenandoah* and *Poetry*. A full-length collection of poems, *VAGO*, is forthcoming, and she has published four chapbooks of poetry—including *Souvenir, Modigliani*, winner of Winnow Press's 2004 Award—and a young adult novel. She teaches creative writing at Texas Tech University and lives with her husband William Wenthe and two Welsh corgis in Buddy Holly's hometown.

Belinda Kremer teaches literature, composition, and creative writing, and is an administrator of the writing program at the CW Post Campus of Long Island University. While working on her MFA at the University of Michigan, she fell in love with the Sleeping Bear Dunes area of Lake Michigan. The passage included here is excerpted from "Lake Diary," a long poem about Michigan's big and small waters.

Margo LaGattuta, 2005 winner of the Mark Twain Award from the Society for the Study of Midwestern Literature for her "distinguished contribution to Midwestern literature," has her MFA from Vermont College and four collections of poetry. In 2002/2003, she received a Michigan Creative Artist's Grant to complete her newest poetry collection, *Bears Are Taught to Use Cameras*.

Susan Laidlaw writes from the eastern shore of Lake Michigan, where she lives with her husband and son. She is currently working on a collection of natural-history essays, with topics ranging from the peculiarities of insect life to the benefits of an unkempt yard.

Lisa Lenzo's stories have appeared in many literary journals and anthologies, including *Michigan Quarterly Review*, *Third Coast*, and most recently, *The Italian-American Reader*. One of her stories won a PEN/Syndicated Fiction Project Award, and her collection *Within the Lighted City* won the 1997 John Simmons Short Fiction Award. She recently completed a memoir and is working on a novel.

Ann Linnea is the author of *Deep Water Passage: A Spiritual Journey at Midlife*, a memoir of the dangerous 1,800-mile circumnavigation of Lake Superior she made by sea kayak, and of *A Journey through the Maxwelton Watershed*. She coauthored the award-winning *Teaching Kids to Love the Earth*. Linnea makes her home on an island near Seattle, where she codirects PeerSpirit, Inc., an educational company. The passage here is excerpted from new writing about her Superior journey.

Linda Loomis, in her position as director of journalism at State University of New York at Oswego, helps students develop skills in observing and reporting news about people in communities. She was named Writer of the Year by the

New York Press Association before joining the faculty at Oswego State. She enjoys sharing the beauty of Lake Ontario with her family, especially her grandchildren.

Josephine Mandamin, a member of the Anishinabe Nation, lives in Thunder Bay, Ontario. She helped organize the First Annual Women's Walk in 2003. With a small group of men and women, she walked around Lake Superior (approximately 1,800 miles) to raise awareness about the importance of keeping our waters clean. She is a great-grandmother.

Anna Mills has written essays and poems for *North Dakota Quarterly, Under the Sun, SoMa Literary Review, Banyan Review, Lodestar Quarterly*, and *Three Candles* She teaches English at City College of San Francisco and holds an MFA in nonfiction from Bennington College.

Stephanie Mills has been engaged in the ecology movement for more than thirty years, and in 1996 she was named by *Utne Reader* as one of the world's leading visionaries. Her books include *Epicurean Simplicity, In Service of the Wild*, and *Whatever Happened to Ecology?* A prolific writer and speaker on issues of ecology and social change, Mills lives in the Great Lakes bioregion in the Upper Midwest.

Judith Minty is the author of eight books of poetry, most recently *Walking With the Bear: Selected and New Poems*. Among her awards are the Villa Montalvo Award for Excellence in Poetry, and the Eunice Tietjens Award from *Poetry* magazine. She lives close to Lake Michigan with her yellow dog named River, and frequently retreats to her hermit cabin on the Yellow Dog River in Michigan's Upper Peninsula.

Thylias Moss is the author of seven volumes of poetry, including *Tokyo Butter.* Her *Last Chance for the Tarzan Holler* was a National Critics Book Circle Award finalist. A 1996 Fellow of the MacArthur Foundation and a recipient of a Whiting Writer's Award, she has received grants from, among others, the Guggenheim Foundation and the National Endowment for the Arts. Moss is professor of English at the University of Michigan.

Anne-Marie Oomen is author of *Pulling Down the Barn*, a 2005 Michigan Notable Book, and two chapbooks of poetry. She edited *Looking Over My Shoulder: Reflections on the Twentieth Century*, and she has written and produced several plays, including the award-winning *Northern Belles*. She serves as chair of creative writing at Interlochen Arts Academy, where she is faculty editor for the *Interlochen Review*.

Rachael Perry's first collection of stories, *How to Fly*, was published by Carnegie Mellon University Press in 2004. She lives and writes in South Lyon, Michigan.

Susan Power is an enrolled member of the Standing Rock Sioux tribe. She is a graduate of Harvard Law School and the Iowa Writer's Workshop, and the recipient of James Michener, Radcliffe Bunting Institute, and Princeton Hodder fellowships. Her first novel, *The Grass Dancer*, won the PEN/Hemingway Prize. Most recently, her prose collection *Roofwalker* won the Milkweed National Fiction Prize. She lives in St. Paul, Minnesota.

Virginia Sanderson is retired from Anoka-Ramsey Community College in Minnesota, where she taught French, English, and the humanities. She has also taught at Cornell University and Ithaca College. Her work in the film industry included a stint as Martin Scorsese's personal assistant. She is writing a biography of natural healer Ann Wigmore. Her essay "An Egg in Each Pocket," from which the passage here is excerpted, won an honorable mention in the 2003 New Millennium Writing Awards.

Donna Seaman lives in Chicago, where she is an associate editor at *Booklist* and a frequent reviewer and essayist for the *Chicago Tribune* and other venues. She created the fiction anthology, *In Our Nature: Stories of Wildness*. Seaman hosts the radio program *Open Books*, and her author interviews are collected in *Writers on the Air: Conversations about Books*.

Heather Sellers is the author of *Georgia Under Water*, a collection of short stories, as well as three volumes of poetry, including *Dating Men With Children*, forthcoming from New Issues Press. Winner of a National Endowment for the Arts fellowship, she teaches creative writing at Hope College. Her current project is a memoir. Her website is *www.heathersellers.com*.

Gail Louise Siegel's lyric essays and fiction can be found in such journals as *Post Road, Night Train, StoryQuarterly, Ascent,* the *North Dakota Quarterly, Salamander,* and in anthologies including *Lost on Purpose: Women in the City.* She lives in Evanston, Illinois, and has an MFA from the Bennington Writing Seminars.

Sue William Silverman's first memoir, *Because I Remember Terror, Father, I Remember You,* won an Associated Writing Programs Award. She has a second memoir, *Love Sick: One Woman's Journey Through Sexual Addiction,* and a poetry collection, *Hieroglyphics in Neon.* She is associate editor of *Fourth Genre* and teaches in the MFA in Writing Program at Vermont College. Her website is *www.suewilliamsilverman.com.*

Anita Skeen is the author of four volumes of poetry, *Each Hand A Map, Portraits, Outside the Fold, Outside the Frame,* and *The Resurrection of the Animals,* and her poetry, short fiction, and essays have appeared in numerous literary magazines and anthologies. She is currently professor of English at Michigan State University, where she also serves as the director of the Residential Option in the Arts and Letters Program.

Claudia Skutar is a poet born and raised in the Michigan landscape; its lakes, trees, and animals, as well as its cityscapes, often make their way into her work. She's currently completing her doctoral degree in contemporary American and British poetry and creative writing at the University of Cincinnati.

Annick Smith was born in Paris, grew up in Chicago, and summered during her childhood in the Michigan dunes near Warren Woods State Park. She has lived in western Montana since 1964, and was a producer of the films "Heartland" and "A River Runs Through It." Her books include *Homestead* and *In This We Are Native: Memoirs and Journeys.* "The Importance of Dunes" mingles two essays, one from each collection.

Leslie Stainton is the author of *Lorca: A Dream of Life.* She has published articles and essays in the *New York Times, Washington Post, Opera News,* and *American Theater.* She teaches writing at the University of Michigan Residential College.

Kathleen Stocking, author of *Lake Country* and *Letters From the Leelanau*, has received awards from the Michigan Council for Arts and Cultural Affairs, the Arts Foundation of Michigan, and the Lester and Anne Biederman Foundation, among others. In recent years she has taught writing in California, to prison inmates and homeless children; and school in El Salvador, to children of the elite, and in northern Michigan, to rural children.

Judith Strasser is the author of a memoir, *Black Eye: Escaping a Marriage, Writing a Life*, and a chapbook of poems about Lake Superior's Apostle Islands, *Sand Island Succession*. Her new poetry collection, *The Reason/Unreason Project*, won the Expedition Award from Lewis-Clark Press. She has lived in Madison, Wisconsin, for thirty years.

Alison Swan's prose and poems have appeared in many publications, including *Fourth Genre* and *Peninsula: Essays and Memoirs from Michigan*. Recipient of an MFA from the University of Michigan, she has taught writing and literature to college and high-school students. She is the award-winning cofounder of Concerned Citizens for Saugatuck Dunes State Park and the mother of a sixth-generation Great Lakes girl.

Elizabeth A. Trembley writes her passions, hikes the dunes, trains dogs, and promotes social justice, all within a stone's throw of Lake Michigan. Associate professor of English at Hope College, she is working on a mystery novel.

Jane Urquhart's novels have been bestsellers in Canada and published throughout the world. The place described here was the inspiration for Loughbreeze Beach in *Away*, which was shortlisted for the International IMPAC Dublin Literary Award. Among Urquhart's other awards are the Governor General's Award for *The Underpainter*. She has a new novel, *A Map of Glass*. Urquhart lives in Southwestern Ontario.

Diane Wakoski has published more than twenty collections of poetry, most recently *The Butcher's Apron* and *Emerald Ice*, a new edition of her selected poems. Among her many honors are a Fulbright Fellowship, a Michigan Arts Foundation Award, and grants from the Guggenheim Foundation and the National

Endowment for the Arts. For more than thirty years, she has been the Poet in Residence at Michigan State University.

Alinda Dickinson Wasner has won the Wittenberg Poetry Prize and the Tompkins Awards for Poetry, Fiction, and Essay. She grew up in Ohio, where her parents fished Lake Erie for food. At an early age, she learned to count by counting fish on a stringer or minnows in a bucket, and the first word she could spell was "fish." A librarian and teacher, she lives in Lansing, Michigan.

Leigh Allison Wilson is the author of two books of fiction. Her second book, *Wind*, was published in 1989 and nominated for a Pulitzer Prize that year. Her prose has appeared in *Harper's*, *Mademoiselle*, *Grand Street*, the *Georgia Review*, the *Southern Review*, the *Kenyon Review*, and the *Washington Post*.

Mary Ann Zink lives in the lower peninsula of Michigan with her husband and their two cats. A grandmother, she is retired from teaching English as a second language. She summered with her family at Mary Torsky's upper peninsula summer resort for more than twenty years.

Acknowledgments

*M*ore than a decade ago, a friend planted the seeds of inspiration that became this book as she hiked with me through the cold autumn woods for a so-we-can-say-we-did-it plunge into Lake Michigan. Brand new to the Great Lakes, she wondered aloud, "How big is this lake? Are we going to walk around it?"

Like all books, *Fresh Water* would not exist without the contributions of many people. I received hundreds of submissions, many of them from strangers. All contributors were exceptionally generous with their time and energy. Linda Loomis, Judith Minty, Lisa Lenzo, Michele Bergstrom, Sue Silverman, and Donna Seaman also offered enthusiastic support from the project's inception in 2001. Many others sent encouragement even when they could not send work.

Clay Harper, Keith Taylor, and Christopher Hebert offered thoughtful professional advice early on. Cheryl Lousley, Sue Ellen Campbell, Stephanie Mills, and Dave Dempsey connected me with contributors I might not otherwise have found. Jack Ridl, especially, spread the word far and wide, as did many others whose names I will never know.

Annick Smith, William Kittredge, and our workshop at Centrum offered invaluable comments on "The Kettle," as did my Chicago writers' group, especially Gail Louise Siegel and Miles Harvey, who both went beyond the call of duty. David Burdick, Sandra Harris, Ruth McDowell, Susan McIlwaine, Kate

McPolin, Teresa O'Brien, Michelle Shaw, and David Swan—lake lovers and avid readers—shared their ideas about the book's contents and structure. Martha Bates and everyone at Michigan State University Press worked their magic behind the scenes.

Annick Smith allowed me to integrate two of her essays about the Lake Michigan dunes. Susan Firer, Judith Strasser, and Alinda Dickinson Wasner allowed me to shape prose poems from their lineated poems. Mary Blocksma was exceptionaly generous with excerpts from *Great Lakes Solo*.

Great Lakes environmental activists, members of the Association for the Study of Literature and Environment, and Karl Pohrt and everyone at Shaman Drum Bookshop give me hope. All of my teachers, but especially Keith Taylor, Charles Baxter, Alice Fulton, Joy Williams, Dan Gerber, Mary Ruefle, David Scobey, June Howard, Richard Tillinghast, Diane Wakoski, Linda Wagner-Martin, and Albert Drake—through their words, both written and spoken—continue to influence me.

Roberta Casasanto, Julie Carten-Crandell, Jean DenHerder, many other friends, and especially David Swan helped me look after our home and our daughter.

And, dear reader, you have opened this book when there are so many others you could have chosen.

To all of you, thank you, thank you, thank you.

My mother and father, Nancy and Robert Zink, brought me to the shores of the Great Lakes over and over again and filled my childhood home with books. Thanks and love.

My husband David Swan, our daughter Sophia Grace Swan, and our golden retriever Keweenaw have been at my side the whole way. Thank you. I love you.

A NOTE ABOUT THE SECTION EPIGRAPHS

With a few exceptions, the section epigraphs are excerpted and shaped from unpublished longer works with the permission of their authors. I am very grateful.

Ann Linnea, Thylias Moss, and Mary Ann Zink have my special gratitude, as does Bonnie Jo Campbell, who conducted lengthy, often multiple, interviews with several lake women, making it possible to include the words of Josephine Mandamin, Nancy Garrity, and Nancy Dunham.

PERMISSIONS

Loraine Anderson: "The Salmon" originally appeared in the *Traverse City Record-Eagle* in a slightly different form under the title "Treasuring the Gift of Life." It is reprinted here with the permission of the publisher.

Mary Blocksma: "Aboard," "Hunting and Fishing," and "Littoral Drift" are excerpted from *The Fourth Coast* (Penguin Books, 1995) with the permission of the author. The book has been reissued by iUniverse under the title *Great Lakes Solo* (2001).

Beth Ann Fennelly: "Finding My Way Home" was originally published in the *Black Warrior Review.* It is reprinted with the permission of the author.

Janet Kauffman: A part of "Down the Drain" was published in an opinion piece, "A Dirty River Runs Beneath It," written for the Prairie Writers Circle (The Land Institute, Salinas, Kansas). It is reprinted with the permission of the author.

Constance Merritt: Lines from the poem "Ars Poetica," from *A Protocol for Touch* (University of North Texas Press, 2000) are reprinted here with the permission of Ronald Crisman, director of the press.

Stephanie Mills: "The Least Thing" is taken from the last pages of *Epicurean Simplicity* (Island Press/Shearwater Books, 2002) and is reprinted here with the permission of the publisher.

Thylias Moss: A portion of the poem "Lake Deirdre," from her forthcoming collection of poems, *Tokyo Butter*, appears courtesy of the author.

Susan Power: "Chicago Waters" is reprinted from *Roofwalker* (2002) with the permission of Milkweed Editions. The essay originally appeared, in a slightly different form, in *The Place Within* (W. W. Norton, 1997), edited by Jodi Daynard.

Donna Seaman: "Reflections from a Concrete Shore" originally appeared in *Triquarterly*, issue 118, in an extended form, and is reprinted with the permission of the editor.

Annick Smith: "The Importance of Dunes" combines two essays, "The Importance of Dunes" from *Homestead* (Milkweed Editions, 1995) and "Thanksgiving" from *In This We Are Native* (The Lyons Press, 2001). The new version of "The Importance of Dunes" appears here with the permission of the author.

Kathleen Stocking: "Storm Light on Bois Blanc Island" is reprinted from *Lake*

Country (University of Michigan Press, 1994) with the permission of the publisher.

Judith Strasser: "In the Apostle Islands" appears in a different form in *Sand Island Succession: Poems of the Apostles* (Parallel Press, 2002), and is reprinted with the permission of the Board of Regents of the University of Wisconsin System.

Jane Urquhart: "The Forest Pasture" originally appeared in the *Toronto Globe and Mail* and is reprinted here with the permission of the author.

BRADNER LIBRARY
SCHOOLCRAFT COLLEGE
18600 HAGGERTY ROAD
LIVONIA, MICHIGAN 48152